AF600604

JUSTICE BACK AND FORTH

Duties to the Past and Future

Justice Back and Forth

Duties to the Past and Future

RICHARD VERNON

UNIVERSITY OF TORONTO PRESS
Toronto Buffalo London

Toronto Buffalo London
www.utppublishing.com

ISBN 978-1-4875-0024-5

Library and Archives Canada Cataloguing in Publication

Vernon, Richard, 1945–, author
Justice back and forth : duties to the past and future / Richard Vernon.

Includes bibliographical references and index.
ISBN 978-1-4875-0024-5 (cloth)

1. Justice. 2. Reparations for historical injustices. 3. Intergenerational relations. I. Title.

JC578.V47 2016 320.01'1 C2016-903960-9

University of Toronto Press acknowledges the assistance of the J.B. Smallman Publication Fund, and the Faculty of Social Science, Western University.

University of Toronto Press acknowledges the financial assistance to its publishing program of the Canada Council for the Arts and the Ontario Arts Council, an agency of the Government of Ontario.

Canada Council for the Arts
Conseil des Arts du Canada

Funded by the Government of Canada
Financé par le gouvernement du Canada
Canada

Contents

JUSTICE BACK AND FORTH

Duties to the Past and Future

Introduction

This book discusses two topics that are not generally considered together: *historical redress*, or the question of what living generations owe on account of past generations' misdeeds, and what current generations owe to future ones, generally called *intergenerational justice*. What the two topics have in common is evident: they concern the obligations of people who are in a position to make decisions with respect to the lives of other people who – although for different reasons – cannot themselves make them. What requirements must they meet in deciding, and what restraints must they observe (if any)? I propose the term "temporal justice" for the set of concerns about what we owe to those who come before and after us in the stream of time. I draw on the resources of other domains of justice in offering my response to those concerns.

One very influential and long-standing approach to considering what one person owes to another is the contractualist view. Given that I expect you to submit to and play your part in supporting a set of common arrangements, what reason can I give you that, in fairness, you should accept? The idea of contract is emblematic of a basic moral idea that, in evaluating an arrangement, all parties equally have a stake and that, if what the arrangement requires of them cannot be justified from their own point of view, they have been wrongly denied the standing that they deserve; so that it is justified if, hypothetically, we can suppose them to endorse it.

The original and natural home of such a view is, for obvious reasons, in the political theory of shared citizenship, where the question just raised is an inevitable one. If political society is not to be taken as an arrangement whereby some people get to impose their way of doing things at others' expense, then clearly we need some device to help us sort out what is and is not justifiable to others. In recent years, however, one of the most striking developments in political theory extends the very same question to the global case and thus to relations among people who are not co-citizens. An issue that has engaged much attention is whether global arrangements are like (or sufficiently like) domestic political arrangements for the same idea of justice to apply. While some maintain that there is a structure of global relations that applies with coercive force, so that whatever sort of justice applies within the state must apply between states too, others insist that relations among co-citizens (or co-nationals) give rise to more intense obligations than global relations do. Do we owe more and, if so, how much to those who are close to us? Do distant people count at all, in fact?

This brings us to the topic of this book, for very similar questions apply to the case of relations between members of different generations, temporal distance replacing spatial distance in this case: do we owe more and, if so, how much to those who are close to us in time? Like global others, past and future people are not in a position, politically, to demand a justification from us; but from the point of view of justice, should their interests be taken account of? In acting with respect to them, do we have to consider – as we do in acting with respect to contemporary citizens' interests – whether what we do is something that fairness should incline them to accept? If anything, the question is even more pressing than in the case of global justice. For while global others can and do actually make their views known, and also resist, sometimes effectively, if we ignore or override their interests, distant temporal others can do neither of these things; and even close temporal others – our children – can resist only without access to the full political resources of citizenship. And while we enjoy some kind of reciprocity with global others – if less than we enjoy with our compatriots – the sense (if any) in which we enjoy reciprocity with temporal others is clearly going to be even more attenuated – a problem that, as we shall see, some people regard as fatal to the idea of justice among generations.

In political theory, at the time of writing, the field of temporal justice is – despite some strikingly valuable contributions – much less fully developed than the field of global justice. In part, this is because, as noted above, its past and future dimensions are rarely brought together. (A notable exception is the book by Janna Thompson [2009] on intergenerational justice, a work that, correctly but unusually, takes that term to have both a past and a future bearing.) Compounding this is the fact that the two dimensions have often been examined in different intellectual styles and with different preoccupations. Historical redress has been discussed predominantly in light of issues of memory, focusing on apology, reparations, and restorative justice. Justice for the future has been discussed in a more analytical style, focusing mainly on topics such as procreative ethics, "just savings" (following Rawls's influential contribution to the debate), and, of course, climate change. But in part, if we have less developed conclusions about temporal justice than we do about global justice, it may also be because the problems are even more intractable. Theories of global justice must indeed contend, at some point, with the fact that our control of outcomes is limited by the basic political and economic circumstances of the world as it is. But in the case of temporal justice, we have no control at all over past events, while our control of the future is, on the other hand, effectively absolute in that we can decide whether there will be one or not.

In both respects, then, we are very far from the approximate equality that is often taken (following David Hume's influential formulation) to be one of the "circumstances of justice," justice being understood as something that regulates the connections among people whose relations are mutually influential without there being natural (read: unavoidable) disparities among them. For different reasons, our moral relation to both past and future people escapes those circumstances – yet we may well feel reluctant to conclude that justice therefore altogether fails to apply, for exclusion from its scope amounts to the effective disenfranchisement of others and so is at the very least morally questionable.

This book is an attempt to bring together the backward-looking and the forward-looking dimensions of temporal justice – justice for the temporally disenfranchised, as we may call them. In considering how to approach the topic, I have opted for an approach that could be called inductive: rather than beginning with the premises of a favoured general theory and working out where they lead, the book makes its way through the topic by examining a series of known-to-be-controversial cases and attempting to bring out what we can conclude from them. The cases are varied, and each one raises its own distinctive issues, but common themes come into play. And one centrally important theme that emerges is that, at various points, we repeatedly face a choice between strong and weak views of continuity among successive generations.

Communitarian ideas begin by positing strong ties between present generations and their ancestors and descendants: they tend towards the view that societies carry with them liability for past generations' deeds, for example, or that they are connected in some basic way with their cultural products, that shared memory enters into their very constitution as societies, and that there is a duty to reproduce and transmit valued traditions. On the other hand, contractualism, mentioned briefly above, adopts a weaker idea of continuity: it is something to be established by advancing relevant considerations. Just as members of a political society are conditionally joined by obligations that meet the demands of justice, so too are relations between persons of different generations conditioned, not by a shared communal identity but, rather, by the moral demands that one person can justify to another. Obligations are, as it were, interpersonal rather than infra-communal. (The case of children, discussed in chapter 7, may make this distinction particularly vivid: are our children to be seen as part of the world that we create or as distinct persons to whom that world must be justified?)

Both views are, of course, well known to be controversial. On the one hand, contractualists can accuse communitarians of holding implausible metaphysical ideas about the connection between living persons and the past actions of their groups. Communitarians, in turn, can point to the limitations of any approach that is, at bottom, an individualist one – they could point to the much-discussed difficulties that are encountered by Rawlsians, for example, in explaining what we owe to future people. The conclusion eventually reached in this book is that the weaker of these two approaches is not only more defensible but also leads to much stronger conclusions than communitarian critics may fear. That conclusion draws on two general reasons. First, obligations of justice arise in relation to past events to the extent that their consequences impede just political relations in the present. Second, we have obligations to pass on to future people the conditions that make just political relations possible for them. These are demanding obligations that require us to look "back" and "forth," with an eye to dealing justly with those whose lives are shaped unilaterally by our decisions – not because there is a supra-personal communal entity, but because justice among persons demands it.

At first glance, opting for a contractualist approach may seem surprising given the importance it accords to the idea of reciprocity: contractualism is the clearest expression, in political philosophy, of the idea that what persons owe to each other is mutual, so that, for example, those who endorse political arrangements must be able to justify their demands to others who are subject to them. And it is exactly the lack of reciprocity, as was noted above, that makes intergenerational justice a problem for political philosophy. We are not in such a relationship of mutuality with past and future.

But I propose to view contractualism in a different light: as a response to basic facts about common human vulnerability. Kant, for one, put the emphasis here when he argued that the duty to form political society arose from our impact on one another, "living side by side," as we do (Kant 1996, 86), and from the moral necessity of bringing into order our frequent impact on other persons. Such impact, he reasoned, arose from the physical contiguity among persons that makes all their actions potentially other-regarding. But we can readily extend his point. Intergenerational impacts are certainly no less severe than those occurring in shared time and space; and perhaps they are potentially even more severe in that those whose acts they are may be even more invincibly ignorant about those whom they affect and those whom they affect are in no position to explain or resist. We are intensely vulnerable to what past generations have decided, and future generations are intensely vulnerable to us. So if the contractual idea is to track and mitigate vulnerability, it is especially important that we should consider its intergenerational reach, for if we do not, then its central ambition is defeated.

What can be done, though, with the inconvenient-seeming fact that contractual political philosophies require an idea of mutual agreement – something that non-overlapping generations cannot reach (and that may be problematic even for overlapping ones)? Here, once again, I believe, the case of global justice gives us a provisional model. Suppose we evaluate the requirements of distinct political societies in terms of a (fictional, hypothetical) contract: unless we grant each society an unconditional licence to do anything it wills to other societies, we must suppose that each distinct society's contract is in some way constrained by respect for other distinct political societies' capacity for self-determination. This may give us some guidance in thinking about the constraints on what members of each political society can justifiably do to members of other political societies. If so, then the analogy with the temporal case becomes promising. If we are thus constrained in our relations to those who are not "together" with us, then surely we are similarly constrained in our relations with those who are not "at the same time" as we are, to borrow two of Rawls's expressions.[1] We may term this general view "iterative contractualism" and define it as the view that the terms of social contracts have an external bearing that is limited by respect for the contracting powers of those others who are outside our own particular contractual arrangement. It is the view that, in exercising freedom of association, we may not knowingly obstruct the exercise of equivalent freedoms by others.

This is the view towards which this book works and that is developed in the Conclusion. It may initially seem unappealing that the emphasis should fall on the negative – that is, on restraining the damage that people may do to one another – rather than on the positive – that is, on the communitarian celebration of shared values and the continuity that they establish, often in very attractive ways. But, I shall argue, this is, after all, the right emphasis, given two important considerations. First, appealing to shared values is too optional as an approach, given not only the diversity of values but also the strikingly diverse interpretation and ranking of those values that we do actually share. Second, we need to think beyond the boundaries of political community in order to think about what we owe to future people, for the impact of what we do to them is both global and discouragingly diffuse, while community, in its motivating form, is both limited and affectively strong.

My hope is that along the way to the Conclusion, this book's chapters make its eventual case increasingly more persuasive. Each chapter, however, discusses a topic that is important in its own right, and I have tried to do justice to those topics on their merits, so that each chapter carries conviction even when read alone. In that sense, this is an inductive book: rather than taking a favoured general theory as a starting point, it discusses ten important selected issues of temporal justice and concludes by offering views about what we can draw from their discussion.

The chapters are gathered into two parts, each of which has its own overall theme. Part I looks back, discussing cases in which past events continue to have relevance in terms of present justice. It begins by considering the frequently made claim that historical redress involves a sort of moral anachronism: that it entails the mistake of applying the enlightened standards of our own day to the actions of people whose lives and cultures were moulded by very different ideas of right and wrong. Chapter 1 measures this claim against several historical cases that suggest, it is argued, that agents have significant freedom in relation to their moral environment, so that judgments of the past should not be seen as anachronistic, as they would be if successive generations occupied entirely different and self-enclosed moral worlds. What form should those judgments take, however? The remaining chapters of part I consider three modes of *judging*. Chapter 2, on retributive judgment, takes as its point of departure Karl Jaspers's seminal 1947 lecture on collective guilt, finding it unsatisfactory both in its formulation of the question and its proposed solution to it. Collective responsibility, the chapter argues, is best seen as a matter of liability arising from shared membership in political society rather than from common nationality.

Chapters 3 and 4, in different ways, take on the topic of restitution rather than retribution – that is, the topic of restoring what was lost by victims rather than the liability of aggressors to sanctions. Chapter 3 does so in a more general way, critically assessing the influential view that liability for making redress arises from the wrongful enjoyment of benefits, or possession of the goods that are owed to oppression or injustice, a view that leads us to an idea of redress as a matter of returning goods or an equivalent of them. Chapter 4 then considers the specific (and supposedly clear!) case of cultural artefacts that have been wrongly taken from their place of origin. Both chapters are sceptical of the idea that wrongness is defined by possession, and they advance the view that what matters from the point of view of justice is the current political relationship between the parties involved. Finally, chapter 5 takes the view that, in fact, it is neither retribution nor restitution, but, rather, memory that is at the heart of redress, and it offers some distinctions among kinds of memory, centred around what can be claimed for truth commissions. The chapter is sceptical about some of the (moral and political) weight that the theme of memory is made to bear.

Part II, like part I, begins with a radical challenge that, if successful, would make further discussion redundant: there should be no future generations at all, so that the issue of how to treat them justly does not arise in the first place. This far-reaching view, chapter 6 claims, is mistaken about the role that person-affecting principles can play in deciding whether persons should exist; it is also mistaken about some of the significant disadvantages on which its critique of human existence rests. But of course, even if it turns out not to be wrong to bring children into the world, their just treatment is problematic, and chapters 7 and 8 consider two different aspects of parental rights and duties, "micro" and "macro" aspects, as they might be called. Chapter 7 takes as its focus an important and much-discussed American constitutional case, *Yoder*, and tries to steer a path between the extremes of parental-libertarianism and child-libertarianism – between maximal and minimal views of what parents may justly do in terms of transmitting ways of life to their children. Chapter 8 introduces (what I take to be) the novel idea that, in addition to whatever parents owe their own children in terms of upbringing, they may also have political obligations that arise from their participation in demographic changes that profoundly affect the next generation's social and economic environment.

Chapter 9 moves to the issue of the political constraints that one generation is entitled to place on another. A generation imposes serious constraints by transmitting constitutions to them; can that be just, if one society should not impose its designs on another? The chapter suggests that what would be unjust in cases in which one has a choice to do nothing may not be unjust in cases in which one has no choice but to do something. Finally, chapter 10 discusses the topic of rights, a topic that has the potential to disarm the basic problem of non-reciprocity referred to above. Rights and duties may be non-reciprocal – i.e., you can have a right against me even though you have no duty towards me; so even though non-existent people can't be said to have duties towards us, could they not still be said to have rights against us? The chapter argues that here the cases of past and future people decisively come apart, for while there are good reasons for denying rights to past people, those reasons do not apply in the case of future people. This gives us a reason to avoid domination, even though we cannot attain reciprocity.

The book's Conclusion summarizes the chapters' arguments, then goes on to consider what can finally be drawn from them. The chapters in part I lead to the view that past oppression matters because its effects are still among us and demand a response. The chapters in part II argue that we become complicit in past oppression if we transmit its shadow to the future. So we should think of the present – this is the book's overall conclusion – as a remedial opportunity: a point at which our complicity in oppression can be discarded. In theorizing this conclusion, the book critically questions both of the principal available frameworks, the communitarian and contractualist views mentioned above: both views, it argues, face significant obstacles in moving backward from future rights or needs to present duties. As also noted above, the book proposes a solution in what is termed an *iterative* version of contractualism, a version that foregrounds the external effects of political association. The grounds on which we – living people – may constitute ourselves as a political association and entertain joint projects entail that distant people – spatially[2] or temporally distant ones – must have comparable opportunities, respect for which must limit our freedom. The way in which we construct and justify political arrangements among ourselves, as citizen-contemporaries, has strong implications for how we must take account of our impact on others.

PART I

Looking Back

Chapter 1

Should We Worry about Presentism?

If racism is the privileging of one's own race, and speciesism the privileging of one's own species, then we may take "presentism" to be applying the beliefs of one's own time in judging the historical past. "It is a commonplace of everyday moral reflection," Michele Moody-Adams writes (disapprovingly), "that it is 'only fair' to judge people by 'the standards of their own day'" (Moody-Adams 1994, 298). It is often taken to be an elementary error to do otherwise, a wrong equivalent to that of racism or speciesism. A well-known article on human rights, for example, uses moral judgments about the past as paradigm examples of moral obtuseness. "To criticize, say, Athenian slavery because it does not correspond to our understanding of human equality makes no sense because this understanding was not available to the Athenians. Any particular practice has to be contextualised" (Brown 1999, 113). This line of objection draws support from many sources – especially, perhaps, from a widespread and diffuse sense that "others" must be allowed to speak for themselves and cannot be subjugated by normative schemes imposed unilaterally by the powerful. Here Edward Said's *Orientalism* exercises a deservedly important influence. Moreover, in relation to making judgments about the past, those who currently live have untrammelled power over those who do not. In this case, the others cannot even offer intellectual or political resistance, as the orientalized subalterns in the world today can and often do.

Of course, the untrammelled nature of our judgmental power is nicely offset by our complete lack of power to do anything in the case of the long deceased, and so perhaps the power question is neutralized in that case and can be set aside. True, they can't resist, but then there is really nothing we can do to them, either (unless, as some propose, we regard their reputations as part of *them*, rather than as a retrospective construct). What is left, though, is the more important question of coherence. Does it make sense to evaluate societies or periods different from our own? Or does presentism rest on a mistake? I argue that it does not, discussing several examples. But there are two kinds of objection to presentism, only one of which relates to making moral evaluations of the past. The other is an objection, not to how we evaluate the past, but to our taking action to remediate past events or actions. Here I argue that if moral *standards*[1] change, it speaks, if anything, *for* remediation.

I

Slavery in the ancient world (see Brown's example above) may be the hardest case for the argument proposed here, for it seems to be generally agreed, among classical scholars, that contemporary advocates of its abolition are few and far between (Garnsey 1996, chaps. 4, 6). Even the unnamed critics whom Aristotle addresses, in defending slavery, are apparently hard to identify (Cambiano 1987). One may well ask, then, what sense it makes to condemn people for failing a moral test that they themselves were evidently so unconcerned to pass. We can, I think, at once set aside an objection based on practical futility. That objection starts from the true point that moral judgment is practical in the sense that, by its very nature, it bears on what should be done.[2] In this it is unlike, say, astronomy, whose truths do not point towards or away from any action whatsoever. It doesn't follow, however, that a moral judgment that cannot, as it happens, produce results is therefore meaningless. We may take the judgment to refer to what should be done in like cases even if, in a particular case, what should be done is blocked for one reason or another. So, for example, one can meaningfully judge that human rights abuses in a particular country are wrong, even if the judgment carries no (immediate) practical weight, and even if making the judgment obtrusively public could be counterproductive, or could lead to the Third World War, and so would be ruled out by prudence. So the fact that we can now do nothing about ancient slavery is a mere truism that is neither here nor there. Often we can now do nothing, even though, in the case of present injustices, we should if we could.

But what should we make of the fact that while the wrongness of slavery is – together with that of genocide – among the wrongnesses that are most clear to us, it was apparently far from clear two millennia ago? Its wrongness was, we may suppose, understood by many of its victims, and the frequency of slave revolts surely at least qualifies any belief that slavery was supported by the acquiescence of slaves, whose views surely count. But what we need to think about is not the partial acquiescence of slaves, which is readily explained by such things as fear, deference to their owners, or adaptive preferences, but the apparent imperviousness of the slave-owning classes to what we can now see as nothing less than an unconditional moral imperative – unconditional in the sense that its application is both atemporal and non-spatial.

Before we examine the profound difference between ancient views and our own, we should take account of two respects in which those views, while certainly differing from one another, are not exactly in stark conflict. First, while there is an available transtemporal definition of slavery in terms of human property, its actual historical instances are quite different, and we cannot simply suppose that approval of one instance carries over to approval of another (Finley 1998). Aristotle's own notably ambivalent account includes the claim that slaves have sufficient reason to be prepared for eventual freedom and also have a share in virtue; it also recognizes that there can be friendship between slave and owner (Mulgan 1977, 40–4). This, together with facts about the level of integration of (some) slaves in the life of Greek cities, makes it very much an open question whether Aristotle or his contemporaries would have approved of plantation slavery in the Americas two thousand or more years later.

Second, it will not do, plainly, to insist that different ages adopt different values while ignoring the different things that may be meant by "adopting" a value. It was part of Aristotle's project to make the best sense of *ta endoxa*, or what we may term the received opinions, of his time – of which, of course, the idea of slavery was one. One interpreter writes that, in Aristotle's view, a philosophical claim must "commend itself to our attention by showing its relationship to our lived experience of the world and giving evidence of its ability to organize and articulate features of that experience" (Nussbaum 1986, 262). Another interpreter finds that view to be somewhat overdrawn, but concludes all the same that, for Aristotle, "there is antecedent good reason to expect that some or all of what is reputably believed is true," for received beliefs are shaped by generations of beings endowed with intelligence, and human intelligence "orients us toward finding out how things objectively are" (Cooper 1999, 288–9).[3] So the claim that the ancient endorsement of slavery contradicts our own rejection of it can carry weight only if one also gives weight to the argumentative structure that supported it. That is, one cannot simply confine oneself to recording the obvious enough fact that conclusions differ; as a truly consistent anti-presentist, one would have to be prepared to accept that if they are answers to different questions, different conclusions may not actually contradict one another at all.[4]

That aside, however, Moody-Adams's powerful article proposes that we should discount defences of injustice when the injustice is clearly in the interest of those who defend it. It is a fair bet, surely, that most defences of injustice have been mounted by people who stood to gain from them, or were paid by people who stood to gain from them, so this view is one that has considerable reach. Moody-Adams writes (with nice understatement), "The support of ancient Greeks for the institution could well have embodied their choice to perpetuate an institution that benefited nonslaves in various ways" (Moody-Adams 1994, 296). Similarly, and with similar understatement, albeit in a different context, David Lyons notes that, in the eighteenth century, "European Americans traded with Native Americans. They gave African Americans sensitive tasks such as raising European American children. They held Americans of color accountable for their actions and punishable for their wrongs. European Americans' conduct shows that they failed to apply their own moral principles consistently – perhaps because they perceived the material costs of doing so" (Lyons 2013, 12).

This line of critique is tempting, but in terms of accusing people of (what amounts to) bad faith, it may set the bar too low. We may suppose that doing what is right may sometimes converge with an agent's own interest, sometimes not; that whether it is the former or the latter may depend on circumstances; and that, if this is so, then convergence doesn't necessarily tell us anything about the rightness of the act in question. An important current example is the case of humanitarian intervention. When terrible atrocities occur in other countries, there is a prima facie case, at least so some people think, for intervention by other states that have the capacity to stop them. But that prima facie case is often blocked by the consideration that the intervening states will rarely, if ever, have no interests of their own at stake, so that humanitarian claims serve as a cover for state interest. Empirical evidence of state interest is not hard to come by in such cases, even in those in which humanitarian considerations are most compelling. But state interest hardly gives us a knock-down argument against intervention. It would do so, of course, in cases in which the pursuit of state interest actually subverted humanitarian objectives, making things worse for the victim population, as may sometimes happen. But if state interest and humanitarian objectives complement each other, it becomes hard to see the objection (Wheeler 2000). In fact, it is sometimes argued, coincidence with state interest actually makes it more likely that an intervening state will see the process through, and so it should be seen as a good thing.

But the interest-based critique becomes more compelling if we add a second necessary condition. Suppose an agent has a strong interest in maintaining some state of affairs and also can offer no coherent defence of it? Then, despite the speculative nature of the connection, I think we would incline to the view that its defence should be seen merely as a cover for self-interest and so should be discounted. We need to move cautiously here, though, because what we see as an incoherence may not be so from the contemporaneous point of view. Here there is, above all, the issue of the perceived humanity of slaves. In an immensely careful and sympathetic study, Katerina Synodinou (1977) demonstrated that in the great dramas of Euripides, the humanity of slaves is clearly acknowledged. Although Euripides puts into the mouths of some of his characters the (presumably tritely popular) view that slaves are subhuman, he continually corrects that view by bringing the humanity of slaves to the fore, even introducing the thought that if slaves are degraded, it is a consequence, not a cause (or justification), of slavery – a striking anticipation of a point to be made, two millennia later, by Rousseau.[5]

On the basis of somewhat fragmentary evidence, it appears that the Stoic writer Chrysippus held strong views about the human status of slaves (Garnsey 1996, 129–30). But there is an incoherence between enslavement and humanity only if one already believes that, for some compelling reason, enjoying a human status counts for something. If what really counts is, for example, the distinction between Greek and barbarian, then shared humanity is beside the point, a bare fact from which nothing of a normative sort can be derived.

All the same, if that isn't the right way to define the incoherence, there does appear to be incoherence in antiquity's most famous account of slavery: in Aristotle's *Politics*. No interpreters find it satisfactory. Peter Garnsey writes, "His general strategy involves distracting our attention from the (thousands of) actual, unnatural slaves, and forcing us to focus on an imaginary, model slave, whose enslavement would seem uncontroversial" (Garnsey 1996, 105). Aristotle equivocates on the humanity issue, defining slaves as less than human to justify treating them as "living tools" or equivalent to domestic animals, while recognizing that a master may befriend a slave "as a man" and that slaves may have a share of human virtues. He rescues slavery from the category of tyranny only by ascribing natural deficiencies to slaves, while recognizing that slaves are actually acquired by conquest or sale. If his argument rests on the view that barbarians are non- or subhuman, it runs up against the problem that while most slaves were barbarians, many were Greeks. Here, according to one commentator, Aristotle abandons his usual view that some norm can be considered "natural" only if exceptions to it are rare (Cambiano 1987, 29–30).

One commentator reaches the conclusion that, for Aristotle, a world without slaves was "unthinkable" (Mulgan 1977, 44), and that word nicely points to the way in which the whole issue seems, for Aristotle, to have gone beyond the control of thought. Of course, as we have seen, he did not hold a view of ethics that called on him to expose all received ideas to radical questioning. He took the view that moral philosophy's task is to enable us to live well in the world, and slavery was undoubtedly both a feature of the world that he had and a means, for some, of living well in it. So perhaps what he offered was not exactly a justification of slavery of the sort that would have to be provided today, but something more like an account of what would have to be true, given that slavery is an important feature of a world that he took to be valuable.

II

One cannot find a better example of magnificent resistance to a thoroughly evil and engrained contemporary policy than Bartolomé de las Casas, the Spanish cleric who fought with such determination against the cruel treatment and enslavement of the indigenous peoples in the Caribbean and Central America. Defenders of their enslavement – generally for work in gold mines – relied, initially (Wagner 1967, 10), on a selective version of Aristotle's argument: those who cannot rule themselves must be ruled by another, and the backward condition of indigenous peoples, they argued, justified the forcible imposition of Spanish rule. Las Casas was no anti-imperialist – he actually hatched colonizing projects of his own design; but he argued for an alternative basis for imperial rule – that is, a duty to Christianize – a duty that did not confer a right to oppress and enslave.

Readers of his devastatingly graphic and passionate *Short Account of the Destruction of the Indies*, widely read in English translation, may perhaps not appreciate that Las Casas was by no means a lone voice. Others, especially members of the Dominican order, had already made the critical case (Wagner 1967, 8–9), a case that Las Casas initially resisted, in fact; and when he eventually took it up, he was not without allies in the Church and at the Spanish court. What makes him remarkable, apart from the fierceness and articulateness of his attack on his country's policies, is that he began his adult life as one of the oppressors, owning slaves and even participating in slave hunting. So he stands as an impressive example of the human capacity to recognize cruelty even when nothing in one's background, or one's interests, or one's own behaviour, provides a disposition or an incentive to recognize it. He became a forthright defender of the "Indians" whose mistreatment he had seen at first hand. For some time, his proposed remedies involved colonial projects that would substitute Negro for Indian slavery. But eventually he rejected that mode of enslavement too (ibid., 22–3), thus demonstrating not only openness to a particular injustice intimately known to him but also the capacity to generalize from it in ways that obviously did not seem easy or natural.

Las Casas's reforming efforts were resisted and obstructed at every turn by interested parties in the Indies and at the Spanish court, and the pro-slavery case was to find its ideologist in a theologian, Juan Ginés de Sepúlveda. In a celebrated exchange in 1551, Las Casas delivered a long refutation of Sepúlveda's case in a work translated into English as *In Defense of the Indians* (Las Casas 1974). To the modern reader, a striking feature of this work is its sustained and detailed appeal to authority. The notes are packed with references to a body of literature, classical and scriptural, familiar to Las Casas and his audience. This literature is, needless to say, emphatically Eurocentric. But Las Casas draws from it an immense volume of citations in support of his view that wars of enslavement against the Indians are unjust. Let us consider just one topic.

A hard case for Las Casas is the (supposed?) practice of human sacrifice in some Indian societies. The case for enslavement rests on the claim that Indians are so deeply barbarous that they must be compelled to submit to rule by others – based on the Augustinian principle that the more perfect must rule the less perfect, a principle that Las Casas sees as fundamental to the pro-slavery case (Las Casas, 12). He has a fairly easy time of it in showing that many prejudices about the Indians are unfounded – that they have well-developed artistic cultures, systems of government, and so on. But Sepúlveda and others advanced the view that people who practised human sacrifice were in violation of so basic a natural law that they could not be left to rule themselves. Las Casas devotes eight short chapters of the *Defense* (31–9) to undermining this justification for conquest.

Chapter 31 points out that only a few people are victims of human sacrifice, while many times more are victims of wars of conquest. The chapter concludes, "Since we ought not endanger a large number of innocent persons in order to free a few persons who also are innocent, it follows that neither the Church nor any ruler or any other member of the church ought to wage such a war" (ibid., 207). Along the way, Las Casas has cited Jephtha's sacrifice of his daughter (Judg.:30–9), Agamemnon's sacrifice of Iphigenia, Aquinas's *Summa* (eight references), and Gratian's *Decretum*. Chapter 32 describes the moral peril of killing the innocent in the course of punishing the guilty, drawing on the parable of the wheat and the tares (Mat. 13:28–30) and reinforcing it with citations of Chrysostom, Aquinas, St. Ambrose, Bartholus, and Gratian.

Chapter 33 adds a complex argument, to the effect that only those remedies that can reasonably be assumed to work can ever justifiably be applied, referring to Augustine's view that it is "sacrilegious, destructive, impious, and proud" to use force in clearly unproductive ways (ibid., 214); it also makes appeals to Aquinas, Gratian, Chrysostom, Aristotle, and a Bishop of Gerona. Chapter 34 raises the question of authority, in two ways: the Indians have no obligation to accept the Spaniards' word, and we must accept that practices supported by positive law and custom have a weight that we cannot simply sweep aside; Las Casas cites Aristotle, Eusebius, Clement, Plutarch, Herodotus, Strabo, and Polydore Vergil. Chapter 35, a particularly complex discussion, draws on Aristotle, Cicero, Augustine, Aquinas, and natural lawyers to make the case that while sacrifice of some kind is a universal rite, what is sacrificed is determined by local convention.

Chapter 36 appeals to the principle of the common good, depending mainly on Aquinas: that human sacrifice is required by the common good is, of course, a false belief, but not one that can be promptly removed. Chapter 37 invokes God's command to Abraham to sacrifice his son – "all things, even men, are owed to god" (240), and those who obey a "public law" that requires the "reverent and holy" to sacrifice men will be excused (243). Chapter 38, referring to almost all the sources previously mentioned, is a recapitulation. Chapter 39 assembles support from the Bible, the church fathers, Aquinas, and several popes for the view that attempts at forced conversion are counterproductive.

So there is not one word in all this to suggest that inherited intellectual authority is defective in any way. On the contrary, the insistently made point is that our inherited authorities forbid us to do what we have been doing to indigenous peoples, even in the face of the most damning item of evidence against them. It is hard to imagine that there could be a better counter-example to the common but anaesthetizing idea of subservience to paradigms. Perhaps that notion is illuminating in the case of disciplines in which a well-defined objective is adopted in advance and in which certain earlier achievements[6] are pre-selected as authoritative. Neither condition is remotely applicable to political decisions, which are typically justified with reference to choice among the desired objectives and among the authoritative achievements that are to be admired. Las Casas and Sepúlveda, despite the fact that they debated an issue at the very heart of what the modern world was to become, did not work within different paradigms. They worked within a shared complex tradition, drew different meanings from it, and foregrounded different kinds of evidence for their conclusions. The shared tradition that they drew from did not dictate practical conclusions, nor did it predetermine the kind of evidence that one should draw from in interpreting its practical implications. Traditions need interpretation, and interpreters are agents who bear responsibility for the interpretations that they arrive at and publicly defend.

III

Moody-Adams (1994) likewise contends that the strong culturalist thesis wrongly diminishes the role of agency, neglecting the fact that culture is not a thing-like entity that presses on people from the outside, but a set of beliefs and practices that people actively reproduce. Perhaps a culturalist could accept this, but reply, not at all implausibly, that there is a difference at least of degree between the agency that is contained in a simple unconstrained choice among readily available alternatives and the agency contained in reproducing a set of pervasively transmitted and powerfully sanctioned beliefs and practices. It is much more difficult, however, to come up with a culturalist reply to Moody-Adams's associated critique that nothing sustains the claim that people, as culturally situated beings, cannot act otherwise than they do: there is an obvious circularity in inferring what they had to do from what they actually did. Could people have acted differently? Moody-Adams is surely right to point out (ibid., 294) that this question hardly resolves into simple matters of fact, involving as it does views about the nature of selfhood: how much of me is essentially me? (Would I be me without the beliefs that I hold?) But empirical evidence, although not decisive with regard to such conceptual questions, can be highly suggestive.

One rich exemplary area of study would be the Salem witch trials and their aftermath. The culture in question, that of Puritan New England, could be taken as the model of a rigorously imposed and minutely pervasive cultural system, and so presumably the example is a favourable one for the strong determinist thesis – perhaps more favourable than that of an old country with complex traditions, such as sixteenth-century Spain, where disagreement is likely to be expected. But in that system of belief, individuals made very different judgments, prompted by such things as evidence, personal knowledge of others' characters, recent experiences, and what we might even call common sense. Samuel Sewall, who sat as a judge for the trials, is famous for the unusually frank and complete recantation that he later made (Francis 2005). Other judges, such as Cotton Mather – who even wrote an intellectually tortuous defence of the trials – never recanted; so here at once we have one difference, even among those whose decisions converged: the capacity or incapacity for self-reflection after the fact. (Remarkably, Mather was co-author of a sort of methodological critique of the trial's evidentiary procedures, but ignored the objections in practice. So he can hardly be said to have been *unaware* of the shortcomings of the process [ibid., 122–3].)

Sewall's biographer suggests that two immediate circumstances explain why he had entertained the charges of witchcraft: first, immediately beforehand, he had been rushed into what he saw as an imprudent act of clemency, and so he was anxious to display resolution (ibid., 131, 145); second, his own children's spiritual anxieties made him too sympathetic to the child witnesses who had made the initial accusations (120). As for his eventual change of mind, he became open to suspicions about the charges as the net of accusation began to entangle people whom he knew and trusted.

It is very unfortunate that Sewall's diary – as its editor points out (Thomas 1973, 1:289) – is so reticent about its author's change of heart: it simply records his (obviously contrite) recantation, without prelude or follow-up, and passes on. But Sewall's biography brings to light a whole range of responses to the trial among his contemporaries. It was possible to entertain the thought that even if there was such a thing as demonic possession, it was the witnesses, not the accused, who were possessed (Francis 2005, 160), and it was thought possible – on biblical authority, no less – that Satan could have incriminated the accused by impersonating them (105, 156). It was possible to believe that the child witnesses were playing "jug[g]ling tricks" (117). There was room for suspicion on various procedural grounds, such as the use of secular courts to decide spiritual matters (175), the prejudicial effect of allowing the accusers to collude, and the validity of "confessions" motivated by promises of mercy (146) – all of which cast doubt on the court's findings. There was the fact that those convicted refused to confess to save their lives (150). There was the patent fatuousness of the appeal to Descartes's authority to support the idea of "spectral" influence (159–60). All such things fed scepticism, even before we get to the emerging (crucial) idea that perhaps the explanations should be sought, after all, in human psychology (193), so that the entire premise of the trials was wrong.

The example of witchcraft bears on a particularly famous culturalist manifesto, a paper by Peter Winch on "Understanding a Primitive Society" (Winch 1964). Witchcraft is exactly the topic that Winch selects to make his argument that all beliefs are context-dependent and find their meaning only within a cultural framework. Belief in witches is meaningful (in the case that he discusses) in the culture of the Azande people; it is meaningless in a modern, secular Western culture. So we cannot ask the question, simply, "Are there such things as witches?" But as one acute critic points out, that was exactly the question that had to be asked at certain historical junctures – for example, in seventeenth-century Scotland (MacIntyre 1971, 228) or eighteenth-century New England. At certain points, people have to ask themselves, "Are there witches, really?" and it is plainly absurd that the answer to this question should depend on a fact about what the questioner happened to believe. For we don't, except in special circumstances, ask questions about what we believe; we ask questions about what is the case and what we can manage to figure out about it.

Winch's reasoning, supported by his close familiarity with Wittgenstein's work, is that "both the distinction between the real and the unreal and the concept of agreement with reality themselves belong to our language," and so anthropologists are mistaken if they believe that there is a reality against which a language may appraised; "this is not possible" (Winch 1964, 308). What anthropology can do, as Winch argues in his book *The Idea of a Social Science* (Winch 1958), is explore the internal connections among the beliefs that comprise a culture and the representations that it contains. It cannot stand outside. (So his view perhaps bears comparison with the more "coherentist" reading of Aristotle, mentioned above.)

This seems hard to square with the undisputed fact that members of cultures do actually engage in self-critique when, for one reason or another, they confront the inadequacy of their beliefs. That might be hard to explain if sets of beliefs were perfectly consistent and mutually reinforcing. But the apparent assumption that everything hangs together in this way may actually sit poorly with two famous Wittgensteinian metaphors, the family resemblance and the spun thread (Wittgenstein 1963, 32). Both metaphors tell us that all the members of a class may have no single thing in common, that they are connected contiguously with other members that are contiguously connected with another, and so on, there being no single unifying element. This is a brilliant way of making sense of otherwise inexplicable categories ("What is a game?" is the famous example), but of course, in relying on this view, one has to acknowledge that some element or piece of thread could have become connected in some different way, so that what now appears to us as a necessary unity appears so only as a result of a retrospective illusion. We can accept that the world doesn't have to be as our language contingently represents it, but then may it not be that the contingencies on which a language is based will open it to reflective critique?

It is for Wittgenstein scholars to decide between Winch's view and an alternative interpretation, offered in critique of Winch, that finds a very different meaning in Wittgenstein's work. On that interpretation, it is a mistake to suppose that one can see a form of life as a matter of rule-following without taking account of the fact that "the multiplicity of uses is too various, contested and creative to be governed by rules" (Tully 1995, 107). What we actually find is not a rule-*governed* activity but "a complicated network of similarities overlapping and criss-crossing: sometimes overall similarities, sometimes similarities of detail" (ibid.). Wittgenstein, on this interpretation, intended to persuade us of "the dialogical character of understanding," whereby – tennis-like – "we grasp a concept by serving, returning and rallying it back and forth with other players in conversations" (109).

This interpretation has been used to good effect in persuading us that communication among cultures calls for an open-minded back-and-forth. For the present purpose, however, one particularly interesting thing about the interpretation is its implicit but clear (although sometimes unacknowledged) tendency to undermine the notion that communication among cultures is qualitatively different from, rather than different in degree from, communication within a culture. We are always potentially in the dark when it comes to others' meanings – more so, no doubt, when the others share less with us than when they share a lot with us, but not to the extent that we can draw a bright line between us and cultural others, or temporal others. A lot has been made of *culture* in recent thought, as though it were simply self-evident that cultural difference is the main barrier to interpersonal understanding. But is it really? Perhaps an introverted Japanese aesthete in our own day is better placed than a nineteenth-century Parisian *flâneur* to understand what Proust was saying, and perhaps a map of communicativeness would not match up at all precisely with maps of spatial or temporal difference.

Perhaps, too, we need to question a phrase that was used above: do we work within *systems* of belief? That term, like the associated idea of (language) "games," may misleadingly suggest the idea that we operate with a determinate and consistent set of rules that fit together and reinforce each other. But if we look at such people as Las Casas or the witchcraft sceptics at Salem, a different metaphor may suggest itself, that of the *bricoleur* (Lévi-Strauss 1966, 16–36), who can work creatively with a repertoire of sources and devices and come to conclusions that are sharply at odds with the authoritative definition of cultural meanings. Cultures may better be thought of as miscellanies that permit adaptation and surprise. Because of this, those who adopt the standpoint of convention and authority have no defence against later judgments that they could have done better if they had tried. Being unthinkingly conventional is rather less bad, no doubt, than being an actual originator of novel evils, an Adolf Hitler or Charles Manson, and to that extent it should mitigate extreme blame, the connection with evil being mediated by all sorts of deficiencies that we are likely to recognize (without admiring) in ourselves. But given the open potential of cultures, which are best understood as resources rather than determinants, it cannot excuse the failure to use available resources in a discerning way.

IV

The above may recall – but is not equivalent to – some familiar objections to the idea of relativism; and of course, nothing has been said to meet the very long-standing arguments that have been marshalled, since ancient times, in support of that view. But the argument above says nothing about the status of systems of belief, as the full relativist program does. It has only been an argument about the discretion that agents enjoy within systems of belief. So it tries to show that systems of belief are less than fully deterministic, whatever truth-value an epistemic doctrine may ascribe to them. The argument would find some support, I believe, even in Bernard Williams's defence of a nuanced and qualified version of relativism, for his account acknowledges that "cultures, subcultures, fragments of cultures, constantly meet one another and exchange and modify practices and attitudes" (Williams 1985, 158), a view that, I take it, should lead us to recognize a degree of play or slack in the demands that cultures make of us, as suggested above.[7] Any definite conclusions that they sustain are necessarily made by agents, then, not simply given to them. But an important difference between the account offered here and Williams's account concerns the place of deviant or heterodox belief. According to Williams, we must make a "special case" of a "criminal or a dissenter," for "neither we nor his contemporaries see him as living entirely by the local values" (ibid., 162). Setting aside the case of the criminal, that remark seems very deeply question-begging in the case of the dissenter, who may well think that it is not he but his contemporaries who misinterpret the local values; and what "we" think of the matter, in turn, depends exactly on whether we take the dissenter's, or his contemporaries', point of view on what local values amount to, practically interpreted in the case at hand.

The classic modern defence of the approach favoured in this chapter is provided by Michael Walzer's work on interpretation, which places so much stress on the ways in which even dissenters draw upon and fashion the resources of their tradition. Walzer's most vivid example is Old Testament prophecy. Violent naysayers in the face of current social mores, the prophets nevertheless saw themselves as emphatic affirmers of their society's constitutive beliefs. They "disclaim originality," Walzer writes, they "assume the previous messages [from teaching]," and they assume also that "their words could be immediately understood and accepted" without esoteric addition (Walzer 1985, 71–2). The "repentance" that they called for draws on an etymological root implying return to "a previously accepted and commonly understood morality" (75).

But where Walzer's account becomes particularly apposite to the case made in this chapter is in rejecting the specialness of the prophetic dissenter's situation. We *all* interpret, in trying to make connections between inherited beliefs and the need to respond practically to our circumstances. So we "need to resist the portrayal of the prophets as peculiar, eccentric, and lonely individuals," for "they are no more alone when they interpret the Israelite creed than when they repeat the creed. Interpretation ... is a common activity" (ibid., 83). The conclusion that I draw from this – without wishing to implicate Walzer in it – is that those who conform to the prevailing interpretation of received beliefs are interpreting them with no less agency than those whose interpretations are heterodox and that the dissenter is not a "special case" of a free-floating and epistemically detached individual, but a standard case of an interpretive being faced with the task of bringing inheritance and practice into a liveable union.

Unlike relativistic views, then, the view advanced here says nothing about the status of cultures or frameworks: it is a view about the agency that people enjoy within the frameworks that they endorse or that history assigns to them. To recognize that people within frameworks other than ours exercised agency in judging seems no more surprising than it is to suppose that our own judgments are more than simple reflexes of inherited belief. If we believed that our own judgments were simple reflexes, it would be odd for us to suppose that they mattered any more than trivial cultural requirements such as table manners or dress codes matter. If we believe that important moral judgments matter more than that, we must, implicitly, be supposing that they have a value that is independent of our framework; and if we believe that, then it would be inconsistent – as well as deeply patronizing – to suppose that people making judgments within different frameworks were simply passive recipients of them. Relativism involves far-reaching epistemic claims, to the effect that all frameworks within which judgments are made are of equal value. The view advanced here offers no verdict on that. It simply claims that if we rely on our ability to make judgments that are more than reflexive, then parity of reasoning requires us to extend the like ability to others and to praise or condemn their decisions just as we praise or condemn the decisions of contemporaries or co-citizens. (Of course, if we shouldn't praise or condemn contemporaries or co-citizens, this argument from analogy fails: but the logical cost of denying others' agency while relying on one's own is, obviously, very high indeed.)

V

In her essay, "When Sorry Is Enough," Eleanor Bright Fleming quotes an Australian senator who, in 1998, resisted the movement for a public apology in relation to the policy of removing aboriginal children from their families. "Such an apology," he said, "could imply that present generations are in some way responsible and accountable for the actions of earlier generations, actions that were sanctioned by laws of the time, and that were believed to be in the best interests of the children concerned" (Fleming 2008, 102). Likewise, confronted with reparative claims made by present-day Namibia, in relation to violence against the Herero people in the former German colony of South West Africa, a spokesperson for the German government contended that reparations were inappropriate "since the international rules on the protection of combatants and civilians were not in existence at the time" (Lu 2011, 265). Here, then, as in many other possible cases, we have a clearly implied principle that the standards of past time must govern *what we now do about* past events. This is different from the principle that the standards of past time must govern *how we judge the past*. But like that principle, it trades on the temptation to see the people of the past as inhabiting a different world; and it then moves from that to political conclusions about what should or should not be done. This seems mistaken in at least two important cases.

One case is that of apology, perhaps a context in which anti-presentist objections are especially common. Since *they* didn't think x was wrong – whatever *we* think of the matter – what sense can it make to apologize for x on their behalf? Actually, it does not seem at all inconceivable that one should apologize for something that was not known to be wrong at the time. Suppose one borrows a close friend's hairdryer, not knowing that she has an important appointment, to which, as a result, she has to go with off-puttingly wet hair. Or suppose one gives some third party a completely innocent piece of information about a friend – his star sign, let's say – not knowing that, for totally idiosyncratic reasons, it's information he has very sensitive feelings about. But these and similar cases are ones in which one does not know at the time that an otherwise innocent act happens to fall into a larger category of wrongfulness. One wouldn't be apologizing, if one did so, for "borrowing from a friend" or "engaging in conversation with a third party," but for inconveniencing someone in the first case and for embarrassing them in the other. And since one knew both of those things to be wrong at the time, the standard of wrongness is not being retroactively applied. It is simply a matter of "action descriptions," of coming to see that something that one thought was adequately described in one way at the time in fact requires a more relevant description (Isaacs 2011,

100–2). And to apply that to the Australian senator's remark, surely at the time of the events in question it would have been generally agreed, as an abstract or as-yet unapplied principle, that it is wrong to destroy families and wreck children's lives for reasons that are entirely misconceived, even if for one reason or another that abstract principle did not come to be connected, in the minds of some, with practice.

But what is perhaps more relevant here is the difference between private and public apologies. One of the puzzles set by public apologies is how to make sense of the sincerity condition. It is, of course, essential to a private apology that it should both be sincere and appear to be. It is likewise important to a public apology that it appear to be sincere, and those who have studied public apologies have noted some of the conditions that are essential to this – especially who is present (both givers and receivers) when they are made. But who, in the case of a public apology, is meant to be sincere? Its entire point is that it is made on behalf of an institution – a state, or a church, or a university – for what the institution has done. And institutions are not the sort of thing that can be said to be sincere (or not). (It does not seem important how the person actually delivering – or writing? – the apology really feels, deep inside.) So it makes sense to replace the sincerity condition, in the case of public apologies, with a different test of seriousness: a demonstrated forward-looking resolve not to repeat the offence (Thompson 2008). The act of apology may itself make it more difficult to repeat it. That can be reinforced by creating an indestructible record of it; by legislation or (even better) constitutional changes; by accompanying the apology with substantial compensation, thus creating a precedent that would make repeat offences expensive. The point is to draw a line that marks an ending. Given that public apologies are essentially forward looking in this way, it is no objection at all that standards are different *now* from the way they were *then*. Or, if you like, showing that standards now are different from the way they were then is exactly the point that a public apology is meant to make.

The case of climate change is related, but significantly different. There can be little doubt that the generations that carried out deforestation and industrialization in the eighteenth and nineteenth centuries not only did not foresee the long-term effects on the global climate, but lacked the science necessary to foresee it. So in assigning responsibility for responding to climate change, an attempt is sometimes made to assign a date after which the effects became foreseeable and after which, consequently, a duty to respond could be placed on the countries most at fault. A convenient date is 1990, when the Intergovernmental Panel on Climate Change published its first report (Singer 2002, 34); after that, "It is hard to forgive governments on the grounds of ignorance" (Garvey 2008, 77).[8] If there is anything to be said for this approach, it does not confirm anti-presentism because climate change is an interestingly special case in which ignorance *may* in fact excuse. Setting one's air conditioner at eighteen degrees Celsius is an innocent act up until the point at which one becomes aware, or should become aware, of the aggregate and cumulative effects of millions of people doing so (Isaacs 2011, 100). In this it is unlike, say, actively participating in genocide, in which an individual act even taken separately may count as a wrong (murder), although all the individual acts taken together amount to another and greater wrong (genocide). The environmental case is special, then, in that awareness of the causal mechanisms involved actually *establishes* the wrongness of contributing to them, as opposed to adding a further, magnifying, dimension of wrongness to an existing wrong.

Now of course, the "1990" principle is open to challenge on the grounds of being overly generous to the developed countries that had been deforesting and industrializing for centuries before that date (Garvey 2008). For one thing, the burden of those processes weighs heavily on the whole world, developed and developing alike, and in some respects more heavily on the developing. For another, the benefits of those centuries of industrialization remain in the hands of the developed countries in terms of accumulated capital (see chapter 3 for consideration of this argument). And for yet another thing, if the remedy for emissions build-up is going to impose further costs in terms of forgone opportunities for growth, it is wrong to distribute those costs on a principle so massively favourable to its chief beneficiaries. But I don't think this counts as evidence *for* presentism. For the point in this case is not to assign blame or guilt for wrongful acts, but to establish a fair way to allocate costs or ration future access to the carbon sink. There is no implication that nineteenth-century polluters were affecting ignorance, that they should somehow have had scientific knowledge that they didn't have, still less that we are now reclassifying coal burners of the past as moral offenders like participants in the Armenian genocide or eighteenth-century slavecatchers.

Does that invalidate the idea of *climate debt*, in the sense of something that is owed, as repayment is? In environmental negotiations, spokespersons for developing countries sometimes claim that developed countries' prior history gives rise to an obligation akin to repayment, in the form of accepting more stringent constraints on their future use of the carbon sink or transferring resources to developing countries to enable them to adapt to the effects of climate change. The argument may seem to be undermined by the consideration that – before a certain point, say 1990 – the environmental damage was inadvertent. But Pickering and Barry (2012) attempt to rescue the debt view by detaching responsibility from any necessary connection with guilt. You may be responsible for fixing something even though you never meant to damage it. The cases in which this is most clearly so do not seem quite relevant, however. There is a private-law doctrine of *unjust enrichment* (discussed in chapter 3), according to which one is liable to return a good wrongly transferred to you even if there was no fault on your part. The doctrine has been put to use in the United States as a legal expedient for compelling institutions to provide restitution for slavery-related commercial activities. But insofar as it is more than a usable legal expedient, it seems valuable mainly as a way of drawing public attention to past wrongs; and of course, whether inadvertent environmental damage *was* a wrong is exactly what is at issue here.

Two elements seem sufficient to explain why developed nations have a duty to aid, without invoking the notion of debt. One is that the need of the global poor to enjoy development is more important than the need for the global rich to develop further – this is the issue of "subsistence emissions" versus "luxury emissions," as it has been called (Shue 2010). The other is that rich countries have more resources to spare for remediation – the "deep pockets" view, based on the duties arising from present capacity, not from the historical past. Given that a cost must fall somewhere, where is it most reasonable that it should be imposed (Caney 2010)?

In both cases, then, the fact that accepted standards and received knowledge have changed is beside the point, and anti-presentist views are simply a distraction.

VI

Above I mentioned Chris Brown's emphatically argued article on human rights as a particularly clear example of the sceptical view of intercultural critique. Its focus is temporal only in part; mostly it is about differences across global space rather than in historical time, but from the point of view of this chapter, there are important similarities between the critique of presentism and the critique of global moralism (see chapter 9). To conclude, I want to consider an issue that Brown's article raises particularly well.

After objecting to the critique of Athenian slavery, Brown immediately goes on, perhaps surprisingly, to claim that while practices can be judged only within the relevant moral system, moral systems as a whole are subject to evaluation. "The modern state represents a higher morality than the Greek polis" (Brown 1999, 113). This would make sense in terms of a theory of moral progress that relativizes judgments about particulars while licensing meta-judgments of epochs; Hegel's view of history appears to be the model. I think this gives the presentist much more than he or she wants or should want. In fact, it plays into the hands of anti-presentists by provoking their worst fears. That people naturally privilege their own way of life is a basic fact, and so it makes sense to be sceptical about attempts to elevate it above others by elaborate theoretical means. But judgments about whole ways of life are surely *suum cuique*. Is there any imaginable way to rank the lives of the Homeric hero, the pre-contact Choctaw Indian, and the nineteenth-century English Romantic poet?

Here the moral pluralists make their good point. All ways of life exalt some virtues and suppress others, there is no comprehensive ideal of life that embraces all possible virtues, and one cannot have the virtues (to use Joseph Raz's example) of both the nun and the mother (Raz 1988, 159). So we should resist rankings of ways of life, and this means that we should resist theories of overall progress that suppress losses for the sake of portraying eventual and inexorable gain. If possible virtues are incommensurable and can't meaningfully be traded off against each other, then overall gain can't be measurable. But we can still ask about the distribution of benefits and burdens, however measured, in a way of life, and here some ways of life will show up much better than others. We don't demean the intrinsic *virtue* of the Homeric hero, or of the Victorian entrepreneur, by pointing out that their virtue is developed on the backs of thousands of others. Our admiration for their skill may be undiminished, and perhaps we can imagine close analogies in our own society.

Now, of course, this at once invites the charge that we are applying "*our understanding* of human equality" (Brown 1999, 113; emphasis added). This phrase seems a bit loaded in implying that there is some less parochial understanding of human equality that we could use instead. But in fact there isn't one. The Homeric hero and the Victorian capitalist didn't invoke some rival idea of equality – that wasn't a value that figured in their aims. So in introducing considerations of equality into our evaluations, are we simply substituting our aims for theirs? This would be so if we took elite claims at face value, as we would be doing if we took the hero or the capitalist to speak on behalf of their societies. Why should we do so, though?

Critiques of presentism show a marked tendency to identify whole societies in terms of definitions proposed by their elites. When applied to the distant past, of course, there is indeed the problem that often it is the elite of the time that has left us the only records that we have (Moody-Adams 1994, 296). But even without this complication, it is all too easy to underestimate degrees of dissent and resistance. Anti-presentist views draw a bright line between us and them. The question may be, rather, which of *them* do you side with? And of course, and in addition, elites are often divided among themselves.

Here is final example. One of the most moving episodes in the sad history of mistreatment of North American aboriginal peoples was the Trail of Tears, the forced displacement of the Cherokee people in 1830, after repeated broken promises. The move was debated in the US Senate and passed by one vote (Evarts 1973). It is beyond imagination that anyone voting *could not have known* that it was wrong. Anti-presentism infantilizes the past and congratulates our own time for being the first to see things that earlier generations were too limited in their restricted imaginative powers to grasp. Paradoxically, anti-presentism falsely exalts the present. Only *we* know, it implies. But this is temporal chauvinism, and it prevents us, from the very outset, from seeing what we share, even if what we share is less than complete.

In a groundbreaking work of empirical moral psychology, Jonathan Haidt (2012) has proposed that there are five basic topics that trigger the sense that something of moral importance is at stake: when the value of care is threatened by harm, that of fairness by cheating, that of loyalty by betrayal, that of authority by subversion, and that of sanctity by degradation.[9] Whether sensitivity to these topics has been selected by human evolution, as Haidt believes, it is not hard to see them as matters that bear in an important way on preserving structures of human cooperation; if so, we may see them as comprising a sort of repertoire of concepts that together establish the possibility of a shared evaluative language. And all are repeatedly deployed by the opponents of the Cherokee removal. Care/harm: the Indians are said to be the "children" of the federal government (Evarts 1973, 16–17, 221); to be weak, defenceless, and dependent (176–7, 212, 227, 249); and for that reason must be seen as objects of special concern. Fairness/cheating: veil-of-ignorance arguments are freely used to discredit the idea that skin colour should make a difference to how one is treated (8), to question the assumption that the response to population pressure is available only to white people (54, 161), to require senators to think about how they would justify equivalent measures if applied to their own constituents (279), and, at the most abstract level, to reflect on the fact that names do not change cases (230). Loyalty/betrayal: supporters of removal are repeatedly condemned for betraying treaty commitments and for violating or trampling on promises (65), and they are reminded of the importance of good faith (67), particularly in contexts in which we have caused others to come to rely on us (143). Authority/subversion: the example of revered predecessors such as Jefferson and Washington is invoked (17–19, 221–2), and supporters of the bill for removal are invited to inspect their views in the light of the opinions of illustrious and upright ancestors (131, 227, 250). Finally, sanctity/degradation, which, interestingly, is the moral topic most commonly invoked: our nation will be dishonoured (23, 176, 179, 249), disgraced (99, 221, 227), disgraced in the eyes of the world (130) and of history (211, 250), and suffer stigma (167) if it tramples on the sanctity of treaty obligations (120, 132).

All this comes from men who cannot be supposed to have any (at the time) unusual predisposition to favour the cause of the Indians, men who freely describe them as backward or childlike, apply the word *savage* to them, look forward to their assimilation and Christianization, and remember (real or imagined) cruelties suffered at their hands. They are also men who recognize and even endorse the inevitable momentum of westward expansion at the Indians' expense. But none of this prevents them from understanding that the moral tropes that we all feel the force of, in the most ordinary contexts of everyday life, are brought into play by what their society proposes to do to people for whom they cannot be supposed to have any special fondness. Of course, our sympathy for the opposers of removal would be modified if the proposers were able to deploy the same basic tropes to different effect. But what we find, on the most open-minded possible reading of their case, is a narrow and morally impoverished legalism that induces a sense of almost physical revulsion (Lumpkin 1971). To say that this revulsion is just a feature of our time, and not of theirs, is in effect to say that we belong not just to a different time but to a different species. It is true that as the great sceptic Sextus Empiricus liked to point out, we would see things differently if we were some other kind of creature, such as a fish (Annas and Barnes 1985, 31–53); but we are not some other kind of creature, and some judgments are tied so intimately to the shared human condition that it is artificial and almost certainly self-serving to avoid them.

One classical point of reference that may come to mind here is the early modern philosophy of history of Giambattista Vico (1970), who believed that there were constants in human circumstances that successive epochs interpreted in different ways, so that human history could be seen as an interpretative adventure. Successive generations are divided from one another in that, of course, different themes and priorities are urgent at different times, but connected in that interpretations become remote and artificial if they fail to address what humans have in common (for Vico, the primal themes of birth, sexual relations, and death). Relativity in interpretation is accepted, relativism about what is interpreted is not. And, to repeat a point made briefly above, if we did not believe that societies disagreed about (and interpreted variously) at least some of the same things, we would hardly see their disagreements as important – as more important than, say, differences in etiquette or formal dress or punctuation, and as involving blameworthiness in a way in which gaucheness or bad dress sense or the improper use of the semicolon do not.

Beyond that important resemblance, however, Vico isn't definitively right as a point of reference for what this chapter has tried to suggest. Overlying the primal themes, Vico maintained, there were large epistemic dispositions that made each epoch distinctive from others – "poetic," "heroic," and "human." Whether historical periods lend themselves to these or (today, more likely!) other descriptions, to insist on the homogeneity of periods is to risk suppressing internal interpretative variety, on which this chapter has placed considerable weight. If presentism isn't a vice, it must be for two reasons. First, to make judgments about resemblance or difference in morality, we need to know what counts as a moral judgment, and so we must assume that there is an inventory, of however general a kind, of moral topics. Second, to offer judgments about people in other epochs, we must assume that, in their own time, there was an interpretative space that was open to them to explore. Here the fact that some explored it in a transgressive way, despite the pull of conformity, is taken as evidence that, in principle, all could have and that our retrospective judgments are not, always, or necessarily, out of place.

Chapter 2

The Question of [Anyone's] Guilt: Collective Liability to Punishment

Does backward-looking justice require retribution? Whether there should be punishment for past actions is a matter that is strongly related to, but importantly distinct from, the question considered above: the moral basis on which the past should be judged; for what ought to follow, practically, from any moral judgment is a further issue. In this context, Karl Jaspers's series of 1947 lectures, published as *The Question of German Guilt*, is a modern classic of critical self-reflection, and the first text in a literature that by now has achieved an impressive level of sophistication. Anyone who now wants to think about the guilt, or responsibility, or punishability of collectives can draw on a rich and nuanced discussion by political, moral, and legal philosophers. This discussion often pays tribute to Jaspers's seminal work. Here I do not mean to cast doubt on its historical importance or (still less) on the candour and self-reflectiveness of its author, two qualities that shine through in his lecture. But I do want to draw attention to the ways in which it lays a false trail and in which it inhibits rather than guides thinking about the hard topic of collective punishment. This chapter will argue that it sets the stage for too communitarian an approach, one that is not attentive enough to what, in the Introduction, was termed "justice among persons."

Jaspers sets out and discriminates among four kinds of "guilt," to use his term (although others, as we shall see, question whether that term is the right one). Later in his text, he entertains the thought that his distinctions create a net through which, as it were, real guilt passes. He then proposes a remedy, in terms of a connection between guilt and national identity, a connection that, he believes, captures forms of guilt that would otherwise slip through his own net. His self-critical thought is, I shall argue, correct: he has created a net that lets important forms of guilt slip away. And although he offers a remedy, I shall suggest that it is the wrong one because it extends guilt (or, better, responsibility) on the basis of national, rather than civic, identity. It is civic complicity, not national identity, that best provides a ground for, and also limits the scope of, collective punishment. But before we get to that conclusion, we need to take account of Jaspers's careful and nuanced case.

I

To get an issue of definition out of the way immediately, Jaspers uses the term "guilt" to cover issues of guilt in the sense of blameworthiness, the idea of causal responsibility for something blameworthy, and liability (through group membership) for something blameworthy having occurred. These are very important distinctions, but to impose them from the outset would get in the way of exposing Jaspers's view, so until further notice, let us take a relaxed view of the term that he uses for the four categories that he works with: criminal, political, moral, and metaphysical guilt.

Although they are familiar, his categories are important to this discussion, and so I quote them almost in full.

> (1) *Criminal guilt:* Crimes are acts capable of objective proof and violate unequivocal laws. Jurisdiction rests with the court, which in formal proceedings can be relied upon to find the facts and apply the law.
>
> (2) *Political guilt:* This, involving the deeds of statesmen and the citizenry of a state, results in my having to bear the consequences of the deeds of the state whose power governs me and under whose order I live. Everybody is co-responsible for the way he is governed. Jurisdiction rests with the power and will of the victor, in both domestic and foreign politics. Success decides....
>
> (3) *Moral guilt:* I, who cannot act otherwise than as an individual, am morally responsible for all my deeds, including the execution of political and military orders. It is never simply true that "orders are orders." Rather – as crimes even though ordered (although, depending on the degree of danger, blackmail and terrorism, there may be mitigating circumstances) – so every deed remains subject to moral judgment. Jurisdiction rests with my conscience, and in communication with my friends and intimates who are lovingly concerned with my soul.

> (4) *Metaphysical guilt:* There exists a solidarity among men as human beings that makes each co-responsible for every wrong and every injustice in the world, especially for crimes committed in his presence or with his knowledge.... If I was present at the murder of others without risking my life to prevent it, I feel guilty in a way not adequately conceivable either legally, politically or morally. That I live after such a thing has happened weighs upon me as indelible guilt.... Jurisdiction rests with God alone.[1] (Jaspers 2000, 25–6)

Of these, criminal guilt is the least controversial, the only issue being that of the law to be applied in defining criminality. This issue is, of course, itself open to controversy, given that the law applied to the Nuremberg criminals was not exactly standard black-letter law, particularly in defining (some) crimes ex post facto. But Jaspers does not want to raise that familiar issue, recognizing as he does that the atrocities of the Nazi state were novel and, given that their wrongness was transparent, that only the purest formalism stands in the way of their criminalization. His treatment of political guilt is more questionable because it implies that what is done to the guilty is, as a discretionary matter, not, for that reason, a matter of justice. His treatment of moral guilt is also controversial, implying that it is only in a person's own conscience that a sanction can be found. His treatment of metaphysical guilt is controversial mainly because, in my view, it is deeply ambiguous. I will now discuss the latter three kinds of guilt. The main point at issue is that they evade the clearest (most persuasive) idea of collective responsibility.

In connection with the political variety, the term "guilt" (in English translation) is particularly misleading,[2] for what Jaspers means is (what he also calls) "liability" – that is, being placed in a situation in which one is open to whatever are the consequences that happen to befall. Unlike anything that can be called guilt, it arises not from one's actions – as, for example, criminal guilt does – but simply from one's status as a member of a collective; in this case, it is as a member of a nation condemned as an aggressor. Likewise, the notion of punishment is out of place, not only because it is conceptually tied to guilt but also because, according to Jaspers, the consequences that are to befall Germany are entirely discretionary on the victors' part, and it is awkward to think of punishment as something that because it is discretionary, could range from murderous, vengeful elimination – *Vae victis* (ibid., 39) – to nothing at all, for it is a standard feature of theories of punishment that there should be some measured proportionality between offences and sentences.

To be sure, if the victors (as Jaspers hopes and recommends) exercise moderation in setting the consequences of aggression, it will bring their measures "into a form of right" (30); and while that term needs interpretation, it still does not mean that their measures will become deserved in the manner of judicial punishment, but, rather, that the victors' conduct will become consistent with their own conceptions of just or decent behaviour. So the effect of the stated idea of political liability is that collectives, while they must expect to bear the consequences of their actions, and cannot justly refuse them, cannot be held to be guilty in the condemnatory sense that applies to the wrongdoing of individuals. Jaspers makes the point explicitly. "For crimes one can punish only an individual, whether he was acting alone or in concert with accomplices" (34). He welcomes the frequently stated view – associated particularly with Robert Jackson, the US Supreme Court judge who served as chief prosecutor at Nuremberg (46) – that the criminal accountability of leaders at Nuremberg was an alternative to condemning a whole people (52).

Moral guilt clearly *is* guilt in the sense of this term in English; it is something that bears on one's conscience. What is immediately controversial, of course, is Jaspers's view that it bears only on one's conscience, leading to the "insight," "penance," and "renewal" that a conscientious person may attain. In terms of very standard conceptions of morality, the subjectivism of this view seems quite striking. Commonplaces have no special authority, but it is a commonplace meta-ethical view that to approve or condemn some motive or action in oneself is also to approve or condemn it in relevantly similar others, so that self-evaluation is inherently tied up, at a very basic level, with general evaluation. If that is so, then it cannot be true in any literal sense that "no one can morally judge another" (ibid., 33). It is also a very common ethical practice to worry about the justifiability or excusability of another's action in the very process of learning about it; for example, we may reach different conclusions about the cruel actions of the former camp guard in Schlink's novel *The Reader*, but it seems wrong to bar from the outset the very process of worrying about them on the grounds that her situation is not ours. Few if any situations are exactly like hers, or ours.

Now there is a qualification to Jaspers's claim. After writing, "Morally man may condemn only himself, not another," he writes, "or, if another, then only in the solidarity of charitable struggle," and "Where the other seems to me like myself ... the closeness reigns which in free communication can make a common cause of what finally each does in solitude" (ibid., 33). I think this reinstates the meta-ethical point that self-judgment *is*, after all, tied to the judgment of relevantly similar others, while narrowly restricting, however, the scope of "relevantly similar." I must situate myself only in relation to others who have been through the same thing. But this too seems to restrict moral imagination in a particularly unprofitable way. No one in the countries allied against Nazi Germany had been a member of the SS; but if they had been members of bomber crews in the US or British air forces, could they not have understood what it would mean to receive a horrific order? And conversely, if we confine the relevantly similar to one's own nation, is the experience of co-nationals relevantly similar enough? Has any of my co-nationals been through exactly what *I* have gone through? There are layers or webs of analogy and difference that do not map onto nations; and if Jaspers means to say that only Germans may discuss moral guilt (among themselves), his argument falls very far short of establishing this, for the relevantly similar group, from an experiential point of view, is of indeterminate size and implausibly identified with a nation as a whole.

Konrad Morgen – the subject of a remarkable study by Pauer-Studer and Velleman (2015) – was a judge in the SS court system who set himself the astonishing task of prosecuting irregularities (such as embezzlement and unauthorized killings) in the operation of the Nazi camp system; surely he had as unique an experience as anyone at the time. He may possibly have been the only person who felt himself to be confronted with such an odd blend of professional and ethical choices. But he obviously felt himself to be subject to moral scrutiny of a generic kind, offering explanations that he believed sympathetic others, placed quite differently from himself, would receive as justifications – justifications of a choice of action that was deeply troubling in its apparent blindness to the massive slaughter being perpetrated around him. He said, for example, that he did what he could, inadequate though it patently was, to impede things; he said that prosecuting illegal wrongdoing would bring to light the monstrosity of what had been legalized. Whether these justifications are retrospective or self-serving is beside the point; he clearly did *not* accept that only those (if any) who had been through what he had personally been through were the relevant evaluative audience for judging what he had done.

Metaphysical guilt is the most complex of the four categories, the one most closely tied to Jaspers's distinctive (religious) world view, and perhaps it cannot be given a fully secular rendering. There is evidently a duty arising from the "solidarity among men" to respond to "every wrong and every injustice," but we do so – if we respond at all – only conditionally – i.e., on the condition that we do not lose our lives. We may respond unconditionally in the context of "the closest human ties" (Jaspers 2000, 26) – those whom we love – but in other cases, we give our own life priority. We wouldn't do so if we were angels (27), physically unembedded in biological life, but we are not. So we choose to live and feel guilty. Presumably (here I am guessing), the guilt about surviving is metaphysical because it arises from the kind of beings (very non-angelic) that we are; and, presumably (here I also guess), it is because we cannot choose what kinds of beings we are that the judgment rests with God because we are liable for our choices only.

Although metaphysical guilt relates to the imperfect grasp of human solidarity on us, Jaspers notes that "historically we remain bound to the closer narrower communities" that provide "the ground under our feet" (ibid., 69). Perhaps this explains why metaphysical guilt, obviously universal in (at least) the first instance, is brought to the question of German guilt? An explanation may be provided by the initial formulation: metaphysical guilt applies to us "especially for crimes committed in [our] presence or with [our] knowledge" (26). If presence or knowledge is what connects us "especially" to crimes – other possible connections are discussed below – then the *German* connection seems tenuous. Some Germans were present, some were not. Some Germans had knowledge, others did not. Some non-Germans had knowledge. Jaspers himself notes the complicity of other European countries in permitting the Nazis' rise to power (85–6). Of course, one could say that they had little *fore*knowledge of what Nazism was to be, but exactly the same could be said of the population of Germany at the relevant time (when it voted Hitler into power).

Moreover, if we turn to the important consequences of metaphysical guilt, they are universal, not national, in their scope if they include the abasement of pride in being part of a species that can commit atrocity (ibid., 30), for our pride in being human may be abased by knowing about acts that are very distant from us in either space or time for the sole reason that they are committed by beings like us. Later in his discussion, Jaspers himself points out, quite rightly, that what a national tradition brings forth depends on the historical circumstances that confront it (82). So just why and how metaphysical guilt attaches to Germans, specifically, remains (for the moment) unexplained. We should all feel it if it is the case that historical circumstances have the potential to bring out the violence latent in our own traditions (and perhaps inseparable from our created nature).

II

If we look back at part I of Jaspers's text from the standpoint of later discussions of collective responsibility, we may have an uneasy feeling that what we are looking for has somehow been argued out of existence; there is no clear sense, it would seem, in which a collective may be held accountable, by others, for what it has done, even though the victors may arrange the world pretty well as they like and the losers (if honest) must indulge in self-examination. Has collective guilt (in something like a standard sense of that word) been evaded? But part II of Jaspers's text raises the issue of evasion in a forthright manner. May it not be, he asks, that the way in which the types of guilt have been framed could enable people to wriggle free? Could they not say, he asks, that political liability has merely external consequences that do not affect one's inner self, that criminal guilt affects only a few, that moral guilt leaves everything up to one's own conscience (so that one can excuse oneself), and that metaphysical guilt – if one believes in it – is something that no human can charge another human with (Jaspers 2000, 68)?

These potential objections are not the same as those raised above. The important objection to Jaspers's definition of political guilt, it was argued, is that something that is wholly discretionary cannot be called punishment, a notion that calls for proportionality between offence and penalty; if the response to political guilt were purely discretionary, then nothing done to offenders would be objectionable, unless it were in terms of prudence. The objection to his definition of moral guilt was not that one can refuse the claims of morality, an obvious truth, but that no one can stand in moral judgment of another, a claim that denies moral experience altogether, at least as it is standardly understood. The objection to his definition of metaphysical guilt was that it covers too much to allow us to affix blame anywhere in particular. Nevertheless, Jaspers's self-criticism at this point in his text leads him to exactly the matter of collective responsibility arising from the fact of membership in an organized society. And given his earlier and very clear opinion that only individuals can commit crimes, can he now explain how he came to speak of a "criminal state" (ibid., 46)? What is the idea of collective guilt that, in his own view, has slipped through the cracks among the four formal categories? I think the idea is elusive, that he points towards a good answer, but adopts an unpersuasive one.

"There is a sort of collective moral guilt in a people's way of life," he writes, "which I share as an individual, and from which grow political realities" (70). Jaspers's discussion at this point amplifies an earlier remark about his categories of guilt: although they are conceptually distinct, "Every concept of guilt demonstrates (or manifests) realities, the consequences of which appear in the spheres of the other concepts of guilt" (27).

Specifically, moral guilt in some sense flows into political guilt.

> Moral failings cause the conditions out of which both crime and political guilt arise. The commission of countless little acts of negligence, of convenient adaptation of cheap vindication, and the imperceptible promotion of wrong; the participation in the creation of a public atmosphere that spreads confusion and thus makes evil possible – all that has consequences that partly condition the political guilt involved in the situation and the events. (ibid., 28)

How should we define this "sort of collective moral guilt?" Jaspers clearly means it to add something to the notion of purely political liability – exposure to the consequences of aggression – that he has presented. But it does not seem the same as the (individual) moral guilt that he has presented, for two important reasons: it is condemnatory in a public way, and it is systemic in its focus.

It is condemnatory in a public way in that an account of the personal or psychological features that underlie political events is either valid or not, regardless of who offers it, and could in principle be offered by any observer, not just by participants. Even if there is a case for allowing that only an individual's conscience can adjudicate personal guilt (or that only individuals with closely similar experiences can co-participate in mutual adjudication, blaming, and excusing), it would still not follow that causal accounts of political processes, accounts resulting in the condemnation of actors, could be offered only by those who participated in the processes. What Jaspers now offers is also systemic, in two important ways. First, it brings into play a background situation, comprising "tradition and reality" (ibid., 29), that individuals inherit and do not choose. Second, it brings into play the interaction among many individual acts and omissions, an interaction with consequences that few, if any, individuals personally intended.

However exactly we are to define this variety of guilt, it is in something of a tension with Jaspers's account of both political guilt and moral guilt; with the former because, in condemning a system, it goes beyond simply recording its liability in a consequential sense; with the latter because it involves the normative judgment of a social and political complex and not a personal, conscientious judgment. But if it goes beyond these two models (and is neither criminal nor metaphysical guilt), how should we define it?

Two kinds of model are mingled together in a complex way in Jaspers's account. One, as we have already seen, invokes "a people's way of life" (ibid., 70) or what he elsewhere calls "a sort of collective morality contained in ... ways of life and feeling" (73) and may include national intellectual traditions (74). After the event, this whole way of life is opened to assessment and critique in light of its consequences and can be condemned for the influence that it exerted on people's behaviour. To the extent that members of the collective identify subjectively with their way of life, they feel about its failings in the same way that they may feel about the failings of a family (73). Perhaps we may call this the cultural-failure view. But bound up with this is another mechanism of a more individualistic kind, one that assigns causal force to the obedience of citizens. Jaspers speaks of the toleration, support, and submission on which the Nazi regime depended (29, 40, 72), and he caustically delineates the various forms of self-deception by which many citizens reconciled themselves, in their interpretations of their own political behaviour, to the oppression around them (59–64). We could call this the civic-failure view. To be sure, a cultural failure may lie behind, and partially explain, a civic failure; but the two views place the burden in significantly different ways.

Remarkably, what is wrong with the cultural-failure view is stated by Jaspers himself, at several points; and it strongly recalls the objections, offered in the previous chapter, to all-of-a-piece views of national cultures that represent them as organic wholes. There is, he says, no such thing as a "national character," for some differences among co-nationals make them as strange to each other "*as if they did not belong to the same nation*" (ibid., 34; emphasis added) – a striking affirmation of interpretative responsibility. The "genius" of a nation may give rise to many different potential outcomes (66). What we call national character is situationally influenced. "Other situations might bring entirely different, otherwise hidden character traits to the fore" (82).

This line of thinking draws our attention to a general weakness in the project of explaining political events using cultural features such as national ones. What cultural or national values *mean*, in the practical sense of *meaning*, is highly contested, and what one person sees as being required by those values, others may see as an outright betrayal of them. The conservative opposition to Hitler provides an example close to hand: what Hitler saw as Germanness, traditional patriots saw as plebeian vulgarity. Alasdair MacIntyre (1995) makes the same point very effectively in his well-known essay on patriotism. While the patriot must be unconditionally committed to the existence of her society "as a [continuing] project," she may take that very project to require the radical rejection of the policies that it adopts (ibid., 221). MacIntyre's example is, exactly, the opposition to Hitler's regime that was offered (at terrible personal cost) by von Trott and other patriotic, conservative, but temperamentally non-Nazi Germans. So we need to take account of what may be called the political mediation that occurs between background beliefs and commitments and the concrete actions for which some person or group can be held accountable.

Substantially the same point is made, in a different context and from a different perspective, by Chandran Kukathas, in his critique of collective responsibility (Kukathas 2003, 177–80). Not only is it the case, he argues, that it is implausible to suppose that a whole (national) society has the sort of homogeneity that allows us to count it as a single entity (except for the most casual referential purposes), but even if it were in some sense a single entity, it is not the sort of thing that – without institutional mediation – can be said to decide or form a will, and hence to be said to bear responsibility for doing anything. Nations can become responsible agents only as states because it is only under that description that they can have agency, if agency requires the formation of a will as distinct from the mere presence of some descriptive identity.

Thus, the civic-failure view is more promising, in identifying political organizations as responsible agents. But what kind of guilt and accountability does that view lead to?

III

A moral gap appears between the public and perhaps objective condemnability of a set of political relations and the supposedly private or personal status of the individual decisions that together bring that set into being. How can matters of personal conscience become, but only in their aggregate, a public wrong? The best case for seeing individual decisions as adjudicable by conscience alone is surely to be found in the idea of excuse. Jaspers rightly stresses the difficulty and the costs of refusing obedience to the Nazi state. Nazi Germany, as he puts it, became a prison after 1933, escape was impossible, and to hold the inmates responsible for what the guards did is unjust (Jaspers 2000, 76). Bearing this in mind, "a metaphysical guilt suggests itself" (44) – that is, the "guilt" of preferring life to death, a guilt that is inherent in human (i.e., non-angelic) embodiedness. A system that in its totality may be called criminal may be supported, then, and excusably, by the most ordinary human motives; and Jaspers's devastating catalogue of the emotional self-defences that people fell back on may be seen simply as a list of the ways in which people tried to conceal (above all, in the first instance, from themselves) their own "metaphysical" frailty.

But the civic-failure model introduces something other than non-angelic status. We fall short of angelic status in connection with all sorts of disasters and tragedies, the deprivations of people around the world, and not only in relation to the disasters that are due to our own political society. Failing to act in relation to those is a failure – even if an excusable one – to take on the burdens of citizenship. Being a citizen is an inherently risky business. The state is a human creation of enormous power, and its lethal potential is correspondingly enormous. The damage that it can do by way of military aggression is obvious. The damage that it can do to its own members – and especially to minorities – is no less terrible, and it is even more so, in fact, if we do the twentieth-century body count: more people were killed by their own states than by enemy states (Rummel 1994).

So to be a citizen is to be part of a system that can become a killing machine, a machine that one will have supported in (at least) innocuous ways, if only by forming part of a docile (majority) population from which the state derives its legitimacy and its revenue.[3] That one has not chosen to be a member of a state, or of a particular state, is, I believe, neither here nor there. One is part of it, it would not exist unless its members recognized its claims, and what it does implicates them. This is not, to revert to an earlier point, because of shared values that lie in the background of practical decisions, but because of support that counts as practical even if it is minimal. The civic-failure view, based as it is on facts about a population's political support of institutions, can be inclusive in a way that ideas about values cannot be.

The view's minimal character raises, of course, the issue of individual efficacy. We could only have resisted, Jaspers says, "without chance of success, and therefore to no purpose" (Jaspers 2000, 26). It is beyond doubt that the element of individual causality is minute and the effectiveness of refusal correspondingly negligible. But we can hardly leave the matter there without emptying all large-scale organizations of personal morality. It is a feature of a large-scale organization that it depends on the active cooperation of large numbers of people, while making any one person's non-cooperation futile and their cooperation thus causally negligible. The state exemplifies this on a very big historical canvas. It draws on the contributions of millions, while dwarfing individual resistance. But given the catastrophic results of obedience, we have to be able to say more than that obedience is a matter of personal conscience.

The "more" that we have to say can be only, I think, that as a citizen, you are blameable and can be held accountable, perhaps punishable (but see below), for what your state does, even though your contribution may have been excusable. The circumstances of organizations in general, and of states in particular, are such that we cannot intelligibly draw a line, as Jaspers proposes, between letting things happen and participating in producing them (ibid., 61) because the facts of political organization are such that letting something happen is to participate in producing it, and requiring the full equivalent of the criminal "guilty mind" is simply to leave out of account the ways in which a criminal state differs from an ordinary criminal. It becomes a criminal state by virtue – for the most part – of otherwise innocuous behaviour.

This thought is, of course, similar to, but not, I think, the same as, Hannah Arendt's (much contested) construct "the banality of evil" (Arendt 1977), for that applies principally to agents who, like Eichmann, consciously and conscientiously undertook professional tasks on behalf of the regime, believing themselves to be efficacious, while closing their minds to the nature of the ends that they were conscientiously serving. This isn't typical of the citizen experience, which is one of individual powerlessness, or ignorance, rather than of the professional deformation that the bureaucratic fragmentation of causality brings about, something that was central to Arendt's influential account of Eichmann. The much-discussed banality of evil may not lie in the personal moral vacuousness of figures such as Eichmann, but in the ordinariness of civic obedience.

The fact remains, though, that the object of accountability, on this view, is a whole system of organization, not the individuals whose contributions supported it, even though the system consists of their contributions. Even though their non-angelic nature isn't enough to exempt them – in light of civic responsibility – the fact of excuse weighs heavily; and here we must take account of the fact that any sanction directed against the system that is condemned is likely to fall on those who were excusably implicated in it. Here theories of collective responsibility face a dilemma.

On the one hand, what is to be brought to account is a set of interactions that are made possible by institutions and roles and of cumulative effects at a system-wide level, all of which make it possible even to think of collective agency. Within collective agency, it is certainly possible to pick out individuals who had a formative or initiating role and hold them personally accountable; we may see them, if we wish, as the closest thing we can find to the *mens rea* of a crime, a directive force akin to criminal motivation (May 2005, 154); but even in doing so, we must not lose sight of the fact that *their* agency was in turn made possible only by a network of institutions and roles and habits that depended on the non-criminal agency of many others. Exercises of state power are indeed things that depend on personal agency, but are equally things that are possible only within a framework of roles that cannot exist without public recognition of them. Unless ideas of accountability capture the systemic feature of a crime, they miss the mark. On the other hand, in imposing sanctions on a whole society, in recognition of the systemic nature of its agency, we inevitably extend their impact to its members. In either case, a serious form of what Tracy Isaacs calls a "normative loss" (Isaacs 2011, 97) seems to occur: if individuals pay the penalty, we miss the distinctive fact of collective agency, while if we exempt individuals from the penalty, we have no way of deploying system-wide sanctions.

One initially attractive, possible resource here is the long-established notion of *double effect*. In just war theory, it is a standard view that while some targets – such as purely civilian ones – are off limits, it is permissible to inflict damage on them if doing so is inseparable from attacking a military target that is sufficiently important to justify the collateral damage. Of the two effects that are caused, only one is intended; the other is regretted. We could apply this to the case at hand by saying that the intended effect of sanctions is to damage the collective agent, while the regrettable but unavoidable effect is to punish individuals for their membership in it. Another possible approach, parallel to that of double effect, is drawn from the facts of ordinary domestic criminal punishment. When an offender is imprisoned, family, friends, and employer are negatively affected, and we accept this as a sad by-product of the practice of imprisonment. So why, then, on either of these two models, should we hesitate to damage individuals in the course of imposing collective punishment?

The just war model fails to apply in this case, however, because it presupposes the existence of two quite separate targets, a legitimate one and a protected one, justifying the damage to the latter by the military need to destroy the former. But in the case of collective punishment, the effect is experienced *only* by a society's individual members. There is simply no one else around to whose suffering their own suffering is a necessary accompaniment and by which it is therefore justified, as the intended damage to soldiers is said, on double-effect doctrine, to justify the regrettable damage to civilians. David Luban makes the same point, employing Shylock's proposed remedy for a bad debt in *The Merchant of Venice*: the pound of Antonio's flesh that he demands is not, of course, separable from the blood that it contains, as Antonio's lawyer rightly points out (Luban 2011, 326). In the alternative model, that of domestic punishment, we can perhaps imagine that punishment falls on a single entity, the offender and her family, and to that extent the parallel works better. But we should not, I think, be too quick to use it, for the practice of incarceration, while widely accepted, is open to moral objection, in part, exactly because of its collateral effects in terms of destroying the social context in which, quite often, the offender's best hope for the future may lie. So punishing whole societies may not be all that different from domestic criminal punishment, but its justification cannot rest securely on that analogy if the analogy's ground is itself insecure.

An alternative may be provided, however, by a role-based solution. If a person suffers damage because his state is sanctioned, he suffers it *qua* citizen, not *qua* individual agent. It is as a citizen that one forms part of an organization that is capable of internal and external violence and aggression, and the effects of sanctions return to one in that capacity. Rather than there being two separate parties, as in double-effect doctrine, there are two distinct aspects of a person, and while one may experience the effects under both aspects, it is only under one of them that a person is the intended target. Here the closest parallel may be the discipline exercised by professional bodies. Suppose a lawyer were to misbehave and be disbarred; the penalty would be aimed at her only in her professional role. It is true that it would also affect her *qua* wage earner and consumer, but that would not be the point, and indeed, professional bodies have no jurisdiction over their members' wage-earning and consuming capacities. They cannot, for example, confiscate someone's Porsche, even though the exercise of professional sanctions may as it happens make it impossible to keep up with the lease payments on it. So by analogy, it could make sense to think of some process having jurisdiction over people only as citizens, even though one recognizes full well that any sanctions imposed will spill over into other aspects of people's lives. If a state is compelled to pay reparations, for example, the cost will be raised from general revenue and so constrain spending on other goods; but that would not be the intended *point*.

In explaining how people become liable as citizens, however, we face further distinctions and further choices. In particular, we could focus on what they have done, invoking their complicity in what their state has done, or we could try to derive an explanation from, simply, who they are, their status, invoking here the notion of a community of fate in which citizens simply as a matter of fact can expect to benefit from both the successes and the failures of their society. At first glance, the former alternative looks more attractive. After all, the argument above has sought to show that collective agency is possible only because of the support[4] (active or passive) that collective entities can secure from their members, and so a complicity view simply records the way in which the results of collective agency rebound on them. On reflection, however, two reasons present themselves for questioning this view. One is that it simply sweeps aside Jaspers's important concerns about the constraints on individual agency, especially under circumstances of oppression. After all, if we didn't give any weight to those constraints – either because we expected heroism or because we believe that people really contributed willingly – we wouldn't have to worry about the ways in which collective sanctions distributed down to the collective's members. They would simply be deserved. So the appeal to complicity may threaten to short-circuit the issue by implicating members too straightforwardly in state actions.

A second reason is that if complicity is the criterion, then we would expect liability to be calibrated, for complicity covers such a wide spectrum of engagement, ranging from approval through complacency and various forms of self-deception to fearful compliance. But if sanctions are applied to a collective, they will distribute in ways that bear no relation to a person's place on this spectrum. If they are financial, for example, they will depend on the structure of the tax regime. There may sometimes be no alternative to this moral randomness, as Avia Pasternak (2011) has pointed out in a careful study of the ways in which sanctions may distribute downward. But while that may be practically necessary, it should not be our first resort at the normative level.

What of the community of fate argument? This dispenses with the idea of complicity, and hence the problem of calibrating degrees of it, by simply asserting that as a member of a political society, one is not unreasonably expected to share in its gains and losses. One might, of course, object, right at the outset, that since gains are unfairly distributed, the moral issue is compounded if losses are also unfairly distributed because, for example, the well-off are better able than others to shield themselves from loss, having more readily moveable assets (capital moves rather more easily than labour) and skills that are more readily portable on the global market.

But before we even get to those issues, there is a problem connected with the very notion of fate. Fate is what isn't subject to human control, either because it is natural in origin (tsunamis) or beyond what humans are currently able to control (financial crashes). But punishment, the deliberate application of sanctions, is something to be decided. One option, after all, is that no one should be punished. So we need a reason to punish, one that takes account of its consequences, which are not "fateful" if they have been comprehended and accepted in advance.

Here, I think, we need to distinguish between punishment properly so-called and cases in which we face a forced choice between imposing a cost on one party or another. Suppose, given all the circumstances, we can try to protect citizens in country A by conducting a bombing campaign that (foreseeably) damages civilians in country B, which we deem to be the aggressor. Erin Kelly (2003), in a paper that I take to have been written against the background of such a real-world case (in the former Yugoslavia), argues persuasively that overweighting the suffering of the citizens of B entails underweighting the suffering of the citizens of A. I think that is right, if the case is correctly described, but the forced-choice scenario does not guide the optional infliction of punishment. That B rather than A should suffer is not to the point when the infliction of suffering is up to us, for then we have the option of imposing no new suffering at all, on anyone, and we need a justification other than a default justification for doing so.

IV

In light of the difficulties faced by these two views, I want to suggest a third model, one that we could call "obedience responsibility." The model for it is, of course, the established doctrine of *command responsibility*, which is applied to military commanders, and what it has in common with it is that it is essentially forward looking and so sidesteps issues about the role of (direct) agency in causation. Military commanders may be held responsible for crimes committed under their command even if they did not order them to be committed. The doctrine somewhat resembles the doctrine of *strict liability* in civil law, in that it foresees the need for unusually heightened care in situations of extreme risk. Its point is to flag a situation of great risk and incentivize attention to it. When stakes are very high, we want to give decision makers a reason to forestall crimes proactively and not just avoid committing crimes by their own direct agency. Knowing, in advance, that he will be on the hook, a commander will want to put safeguards in place, ahead of time, by fostering a culture of compliance with clear legal and moral norms. Likewise, a doctrine of obedience responsibility puts citizens on notice that the state that they support – even for innocuous reasons – may go bad, and if it does so, then the consequences will travel back to them. As in the case of command responsibility, the point is not to account for chains of causal connection, but to flag a warning and incentivize attention to it.

Like command responsibility, however, obedience responsibility is or should be defeasible. Regardless of what the Tokyo War Crimes Tribunal decided in 1945, if a theatre commander's communications have been destroyed so that he no longer exercises any sort of command at all, the doctrine is either inapplicable or overridden: for that reason, the Tokyo Tribunal's harsh treatment of General Yamashita has been roundly condemned by legal scholars and others (Walzer 2000, 319–22). Likewise, in cases in which citizens would face imprisonment, torture, or death for non-compliance, their forced compliance with state actions should defeat obedience responsibility. Here we reach the level of contextual judgment, at which we may find ourselves in agreement with Jaspers's depiction of the Nazi "prison" state, and so exonerate quite broadly. But before we get to this level, it seems not only unobjectionable but also important to give citizens a forward-looking incentive to appreciate that their compliance sustains the most potentially lethal institution that humans have so far evolved – that is, the state.

One kind of qualification, then, will involve judgments about the cost of noncompliance, a familiar but important line of enquiry that goes back at least to Hume's critique of Locke on "tacit consent." Another kind of qualification, perhaps less familiar, involves the kinds of punishment available. For certain purposes, this may be a second-order question to be addressed after the issues of justification have been settled. But here the case at hand is sufficiently unusual that modes of punishment become a first-order issue that needs attention before we start assessing liability. If the purpose is admonitory rather than retributive, there is a strong reason for caution in imposing damage. And if the damage is to be inflicted on people in a specific capacity of theirs – that is, on people *qua* citizens – then some kinds of penalty will clearly be more defensible than others. To revert for a moment to the analogy to professional discipline: the disbarment of a lawyer strikes at him in his professional capacity, albeit with diffuse results, whereas incarceration would strike intentionally and pervasively at his freedom. Curfews, suspension of driver's licences, writs of trespass, gag orders, and so on are other examples of targeted penalty that do not pervasively deprive people of freedom. Are there similar examples of penalty that could target people *qua* citizens?[5]

The oldest and perhaps most common example of collective punishment, that of war reparations, is not a good example of this because financial penalties obviously inhibit other uses of resources in a diffuse way. A state compelled to pay to repair damage to another state's infrastructure would have correspondingly fewer resources to spend on repairing damage to its own assets, with direct consequences for the conduct of ordinary life by its citizens. Here, perhaps, it would be easier to accept a transfer-of-costs argument based on fairness than a justification in terms of punishment: given a forced choice, it is understandable that those who have been aggressed against should not be required to bear the further burden of paying for the damage.

But any notion of punishment, as was noted above, requires the stronger justification that any deliberate imposition of a burden calls for. And the kind of burden that is available to us will affect our willingness to accept that it is justified. A declaratory judgment of guilt – such as the International Court of Justice's ruling in the case of Serbia – is a clear example of a burden that citizens of an aggressor state may be called on to bear. Preventing the use of symbols such as flags and anthems and requiring changes in school curricula would be somewhat stronger measures. Imposing constitutional change, as in the case of post–Second World War Japan, is stronger still, as is the restriction imposed on the development of Japan's military capacity. The division of a country into two, or its absorption into another state, would be the most decisive possible blow against civic identity. All these burdens would rightly be classed as *qua*-citizen punishments that strike at people insofar as they identify with their state and/or its former policies. Whether one is willing to go further, imposing punishments that damage people in, say, their economic capacity, is likely to depend on judgments about the degree of (uncoerced) complicity that was typical of members of the society; here we would need to have measures of significant levels of consent.

What does this add to Jaspers's category of political liability? First, it involves a denial of his claim that how victors treat losers is a purely discretionary matter, limited only by prudential considerations, on the victors' part – considerations about future cooperation with the defeated society, its place in the global market, its use as a potential ally, and so forth. It suggests that how the defeated are treated is a matter for moral enquiry. Second, and correlatively, it suggests that the moral judgment of citizens is not a private matter or a matter of personal conscience alone, that there is a moral relation between citizens and their political society that generates public and possibly objective judgments of desert, albeit of a limited sort.

This liability to judgment, it was argued, arises from the specific nature of membership in states, institutions that transform minute quanta of individual power into a capacity for great violence, and not from the morally open or indeterminate nature of one's membership in a nation, membership whose meaning lends itself to such radically different practical interpretations that to condemn some interpreters, however vehemently, cannot be to condemn all who value it. Collective liability does not depend, then, on shared identity, but on the distinctive structural features of the state – in particular, its violent capacity to lever unexceptional motives in the service of atrocious ends. That capacity brings into play attributions of blame so different from those that make sense in ordinary experience that the message of collective punishment can be only this: you have been warned.

Jaspers's lecture was entitled *The Question of German Guilt*. No one is guilty by being German; no one is guilty by *being* anything. Liability arises only from doing, and in the context of citizenship, what one can be said to "do" is open to a stringent assessment unlike anything that applies in other contexts of behaviour. What we do, in the most ordinary acts of civic belonging, may open us to liability in ways that have no parallel, and to be a citizen is to be exposed to the searching judgments of later generations.

Chapter 3

For Benefits Received

Being complicit in an institution that does wrong may merit (limited) retribution, the previous chapter claimed – but does *receiving benefits* from that wrong amount to another kind of complicity and expose the recipients to claims of redress? Many people think so. According to Plato, Socrates thought so too. Offered an opportunity to escape confinement and execution, Socrates, in the *Crito* dialogue, refuses on the grounds that he has been condemned by "the laws," from which, he says, he has received many benefits. Imagining a dialogue between himself and the laws, Socrates has the laws ask, rhetorically, "Did we not give you life in the first place? Was it not through us that your father married your mother and begot you?" Receiving Socrates's agreement, the laws continue, "Are you not grateful to those of us laws which were instituted ... for requiring your father to give you a cultural and physical education?" And Socrates again agrees (Plato 1961, 35–6).

Some commentators believe that (Plato's) Socrates is, uncharacteristically, a bit of a pushover in his own dialogue (Woozley 1979), for several objections to the personified laws come to mind at once (see below). But there is a core idea here that is not so easily dismissed. Gratitude for benefits received is surely a basic requirement of personal virtue: we have already seen that the philosopher-psychologist Jonathan Haidt includes it as one of the core elements of morality, so that, on his view, to give no weight to it is to lack one of the five essential moral senses (Haidt 2012, chap. 6). On a more political level, it is not at all uncommon to find that the receipt of benefits by one party is pressed as a major reason for aiding another party – especially, perhaps, in the post-colonial context: the obligations of the North to the South are sometimes represented as fundamentally reparative just as the obligations to descendants of slaves are sometimes represented as a return of the benefits extracted from their ancestors. As Ali Mazrui said in an interview in this connection, "For as long as you are accepting the asset side, you should accept the other side, the liabilities" (quoted in Howard-Hassmann 2008, 33). This discussion hopes to honour what is valuable in these intuitions and demands. But its main purpose is to question the moral weight that is given to the fact of receiving benefits at the hands of another person or institution. When examined, it will be argued, what is ascribed to the fact of receiving benefits is, generally, better explained as something else.[1]

I

Let us return, for a starting point, to the *Crito* dialogue. At least two things seem at once wrong with the demands that the laws are supposed to make of Socrates. One is that the laws – continuing to personify them here, as Plato does – were doing what they ought to do. Another is that they impute unlimited scope to the gratitude that they claim to deserve. Let us consider these in turn.

First, the laws base their claim on having done two things that, it is assumed, laws should do: instituting a marriage regime and prescribing education. Had they based their claim on some wholly discretionary benefit (such as providing tax refunds or public entertainments), their claim would have had negligible intuitive force; but as it is, they argue on the basis of two provisions that are taken to be essential tasks of the state. We are led, then, to the question of whether gratitude is due to some agent for doing what her role required of her in the first place. If there is a familiar analogy, it would be with the established but anomalous practice of tipping wait staff in restaurants and hotels. This practice is justifiable (if it is) only on the basis, surely, that since it is in existence, it enables employers to pay wait staff less than would otherwise be necessary, so that the practice has a sort of self-sustaining justification. If there is a general principle involved, it is that people who benefit from the performance of a service should contribute to paying for it if that is understood to be part of the market cost.

How this might apply to the laws' claims is mysterious and cannot even be thought about without dismantling the fiction of personification. What could it mean to give laws a benefit? If anything, it would mean contributing to their authority through one's behaviour, which is another – distinct – argument that Socrates advances through the laws' voice. "Do you imagine that a city can continue to exist and not be turned upside down, if the legal judgments that are pronounced in it have no force but are nullified and destroyed by private persons?" (Plato 1961, 35). This is a better argument – but not a benefits-received argument. It's an argument – of a kind that was to be elaborated by the social contract tradition – about the collective conditions necessary to the fulfilment of individual purposes.

Second, the laws require rather a lot of Socrates's gratitude – in fact, they require his life. Taking someone's life does not normally seem to be a power that one acquires by giving someone life, of course; think of mothers, or surgeons in emergency rooms, or firefighters who rescue people from burning buildings. Surely they don't get that power by virtue of what they have given. But even if we stick with less extreme demands, there would still seem to be important limits. Perhaps Socrates had already made a commensurate return by serving in the army, as he did? And even if he had not, we would have to ask about the reasonableness of the demands. What can states reasonably require their citizens to do?

This is, of course, a central question of political theory, and there are many answers to it. But it does not seem that apportioning requirements to benefits is at all a promising approach. It would mean, for example, that states that provided relatively more of some good – freedom, let us say – would be justified in removing relatively more of it; this would be self-defeating. It might seem to lead to the possibly attractive principle that those who benefit more than others do from a state should contribute more than others do: but it seems more convincing, on reflection, to base regimes such as progressive taxation on the principle that what the rich pay is worth less to them, not more, than what the poor pay. The logic of this view is based on the compelling doctrine of diminishing marginal utility – the rich miss a dollar lost less than the poor value a dollar gained – while the idea of soaking the rich, for its own sake, would seem to owe more to unattractive motives such as resentment.

But Socrates's dialogue with the laws leads directly to an actual and contemporary case, that of parents and children. The laws say to Socrates, "Can you deny … that you were our child?" (Plato 1961, 36). This claim would, of course, tend to displace the claims of actual parents to their children's gratitude by substituting metaphorical parents for actual ones. Jean-Paul Sartre offered a famous moral fable about a young man who was torn between staying at home to look after his ailing mother and going away to join the Resistance, thus serving his country. Sartre (1948, 35–7) denied that there was a right answer to this, but on Socrates's argument, it could not even have been a right question – the state *is* your parent, and it apparently absorbs or supersedes what is owed to biological parents.

What happens, though, on the benefits-received argument, if one has received benefits from multiple sources? Does the nature of the benefits determine the outcome, regardless of one's relationship to the parties involved? If the young man's mother had done more for him than France had done, would that mean he shouldn't join the Resistance? (There is, of course, quite a close parallel in Athenian culture itself, that of Sophocles's *Antigone;* and the question there would seem to resolve into one about obligations that are quite independent of anything to do with benefit. They have to do with the demands of traditional piety, set against the claims of political obligation and state building.)

But let us stay with the question about parents and children. The same two initial questions recur. Do we owe a debt to people for doing what they have to do? Parents do a lot for their children, and the benefits of good parenting are enormous. But do obligations arise? Let us imagine, for the moment, the case of foster parents, who, although well intentioned, take in children for financial reasons. They are, in their own view, adequately compensated. What would their foster children owe them? If they were to learn that they were fostered purely for money, they could well decide that they owed them nothing at all. If they felt they owed something, it would be because natural bonding effects moulded their feelings about their foster parents, or their foster parents' feelings about them, or both. Then anything owed would be due to the affective quality of a relationship rather than to a receipt of benefits.

Could we not say that the affectively charged relationship is itself a benefit, given its great importance to the formation of identity? Of course we could, but let's modify the example to make a distinction. Suppose the foster parents were perfectly scrupulous (but no more) in carrying out their responsibilities, but that it was with their own live-in parents, or with outgoing and friendly neighbours, that a child bonded more strongly? Then it would be to *this kind of benefit* that gratitude attached, and if we want to call it a benefit, it would be a relationship benefit, rather than a benefit that creates a relationship – the topic of this chapter.

Do parentally conferred benefits confer absolute obligations? Of course they don't, but rarely, if ever, are we thinking of parents who, like Socrates's laws, demand the ultimate sacrifice. (It would, as noted above, be an odd demand.) Obviously, there are limits to what parents may and generally do require of their children. The question that is worth pursuing here is whether the legitimate extent of parents' requests has anything to do with the extent of the benefits that they have conferred. Consider two cases. In the first, wealthy parents buy private schooling for their only child, enabling her to enter an elite university and attend a costly professional graduate school, thus launching her on a career that is enormously lucrative.[2] The sacrifice on the parents' part is (relatively) small. In the second case, working-class parents divide their limited resources among three children, enabling them to defer entry into the workforce and complete apprenticeships, thus launching them into modestly rewarded trades. If anything governs what is due (morally speaking) to parents here, it is not the benefit received – even if we aggregate, and the three children in case 2, let's say, make less than the child in case 1 – but the sacrifice made by the parents in question. To push the point further, suppose parents made a considerable sacrifice to provide a child with an opportunity that didn't, as it happened, pay off – they were wrong about his talents, or the market for them suddenly and unexpectedly dried up: are they owed nothing because no benefits accrued? Or does their intention count for something?

In one of her discussions of so-called filial obligation, Jane English aptly contrasts the parent-child case with the paradigm case of obligation-generating benefits, the case of favours. Waiting in line at the supermarket checkout, a shopper remembers some forgotten item and asks her neighbour in the queue to keep her place while she dashes off to get it; and then her neighbour calls in the favour by asking her to reciprocate (English 1991, 149). What characterizes the paradigm case is that (a) no sort of relational obligation precedes the initial request, and (b) the initial request is voluntarily acceded to. As English points out, this is entirely unlike what happens in the parent-child relationship, in both of those relevant respects.

But it is the parent-child relationship, rather than the supermarket-queue transaction, that better fits the cases in which the receipt of benefits is invoked – not, of course, in the sense that one party is like a parent, the other like a child, but in the sense that one generation is thought to acquire obligations by virtue of what a previous generation has given it. And if this connection fails even in the intimate familial case, it surely looks still more unpromising in the more diffuse intergenerational case.

II

An important distinction is sometimes made between receiving and accepting benefits (Simmons 1979, 126–7, 130). The context is not that of the present discussion, for it involves reciprocal relations among citizen contemporaries. We have obligations to support the scheme of relations that we share with other people, it is sometimes argued, because we receive benefits from it, and so must lend our support to it so that it can confer like benefits on others. It is a matter of simple fairness, of not claiming a privileged position whereby I can claim to receive what I refuse to others. The argument has been much discussed, and one core objection is that receiving a benefit may fall short of entailing a duty to return it.

Robert Nozick's famous and elaborate example concerns a fictitious neighbourhood entertainment system, whereby everyone within earshot of loudspeakers can hear music and local news broadcast by local activists. One day, the activists come to your door and tell you that it's your turn to provide the programming for next week. Must you agree? Nozick says no, appealing to the objectionableness of an implied principle that we could thrust obligations on people by thrusting services on them unasked. Can I oblige you to mow my lawn by mowing yours when you're not looking (Nozick 1974, 90–4)?

Of course, the people who refuse to contribute to Nozick's neighbourhood broadcast system could simply be shameless free-riders who want something for nothing. But they need not be. Suppose my ranked schedule of preferences is (1) listening to the broadcasts without having to take time to contribute, (2) not listening at all, and (3) listening and contributing. I may prefer (2) to (3) because, for example, I have some other valued activity – working out on my elliptical trainer, say – that I can combine with (1) but not with (3). In that case, when the neighbourhood activists come to my door, they cannot tell me that listening necessarily requires contributing, as a matter of consistency on my part.

Now what makes it impossible to distinguish in practice between the shameless free-rider and the person with nuanced preferences is that the benefit provided is non-excludable. The inexcusably shameless and the excusably nuanced alike may listen in. We can neither tar the nuanced with shamelessness nor give the shameless the fig leaf of nuance. It is here that the distinction between receiving and accepting benefits becomes important. If we could show that some had (passively) received benefits, while others had (actively) accepted them, then we could make distinctions with significant moral consequences. Receiving benefits would include, for example, enjoying the security provided by an effective police force. One would then *accept* that benefit if one called the police for protection against an intruder. Richard Dagger has pointed out that there are probably more instances of accepting than one might suppose. "There is reason to believe, in fact, that almost all citizens of [modern] states have taken some steps that count as accepting the benefits of the rule of law" (Dagger 1997, 74). Moreover, the benefits arising from a public infrastructure are taken willingly; no doubt few, if any, people reflect on the full extent of the public arrangements that are necessary to enable one to cycle to work, but one does, after all, have to mount the bicycle to do so, and so it is wrong to think of the benefits being literally "thrust upon" people as opposed to being assumed in some minimal, although real, sense (75).

So – depending on how one interprets "accepting," exactly – the enjoyment of benefits may have moral force after all. On the other hand, it may be better to see this argument as an argument about membership in a set of common arrangements and, hence, one that is fundamentally about who one is rather than what it is that one has received. After all, the same considerations could sustain the view that simply being part of a set of arrangements makes one liable for one's share in its losses, and so it is compatible with suffering the (net) *dis*-benefits that go along with belonging to it. If so, it's not the benefits, specifically, that count.

Richard Arneson (1982) once made an even stronger case that dispenses with the need for demonstrating acceptance in some sense. He appealed directly to the value of fairness and argued that people who benefit from non-excludable public goods while refusing to contribute are simply free-riders. If they excuse themselves by claiming that the goods in question fall like manna from heaven, then they are simply mistaken, or if they maintain that the costs should be paid by some racial group other than their own, they are unreasonable bigots, and, in either case, we would rightly discount their excuses.

But surely there are reasonable objections to a (moral) obligation to pay one's share, whatever the law may say. In the case of national defence, for example, a pacifist may believe that military establishments are the cause of war and should not be supported. Or, in the case of social services, for example, a libertarian may believe that a principle of personal responsibility makes it inappropriate for states to provide things that individuals or families should provide for themselves and that state provision is corrupting of personal responsibility or family ties (Oldenquist 1982). In requiring such people to pay their share, we would essentially be discounting their view of what a benefit is by officially endorsing a contested view of what states are and what they should do. So it would seem wrong to describe such people as free-riders if a free-rider is someone who agrees that something is a benefit, enjoys its receipt, but refuses to pay their share (Vernon 2010, 44).

What should we conclude in the case of benefits inherited from past generations? On the acceptance argument, the diffuseness of benefits often creates a difficulty, in that it becomes impossible to separate receipt and acceptance. The benefits from, say, slavery include the creation of capital that fed general economic growth in North American and European societies in ways that must by now affect pretty well every institution in them. Every deliberate act within their borders would count as acceptance, and we would need a good reason to think of something so diluted as being morally significant. The analogy would be with the much-criticized doctrine of "tacit consent" in Locke – criticized because acts to which there is no real alternative offer a very weak basis, if any, for holding agents liable (Hume 1947, 156).

Now there are less diffuse cases of transmitted benefit – as, for example, in the case of institutions, such as universities, that hold a historically tainted endowment. Then it makes a lot of sense to say that those who choose to participate in them "accept" a morally questionable benefit. There is a case for redress of some kind, or at least acknowledgment, on the part of participants. But one may wonder whether it is the benefit as such that counts or simply the taint arising from association. Suppose the endowed investments went bad and evaporated. Or suppose the university simply took its name from some great person who was subsequently shown to be a racist or just an awful fraud. No benefits would be in play, but the institution might well wish to dissociate itself by symbolic and/or material acts. The case would be somewhat analogous to that of North American sports teams that had long ago taken the names of Native American tribes and come to be pressured to change them, not because they benefited from them, but to distance themselves from something – i.e., in this case, what comes to be seen as an act of racist appropriation.

As for the fairness argument, I think the same considerations arise as in the original case. The issue of redress arises because some past practice, from which profit was derived, comes to be seen as indefensible. But some members of the society that has profited may abhor not only the original practice but also the uses to which the profits were put. Perhaps they would much prefer not to be part of a society that used the profits of colonialism, say, to build a society in which luxurious consumption was promoted. They would not be like free-riders, hypocritically enjoying goods that they refused to support; they would be unwilling recipients of circumstances thrust upon them. They might well be among the strongest supporters of redress, they would likely favour a transfer of (to them unwanted) resources to make redress, but their position would have nothing to do with receiving *benefits*.

Now in addition to what may be a minority of austere refusers, there will also be numbers of grateful consumers, who do enjoy the long-term benefits of a colonial past. If material redress takes place, both austere refusers and grateful consumers will be called on to pay whatever the taxation regime assigns as their share. But the simplest way to justify this is in terms of the collective liability of a state for past actions that now stand condemned as unjust. Profits come and go, are absorbed indistinguishably into a general pool of resources, and are viewed in different ways (valued or disvalued) by different members of a society. States, however, claim to be and are treated as transgenerational actors that retain their identity despite changes in their economic fortune and despite internal dissent (Kukathas 2003). In the twenty-first century, states do not feel the need to justify occupying the territory that they currently own by virtue of what happened in the eighteenth or twelfth century or whenever. This fact alone signals a desire to claim identity, as a continuous occupant, that connects what one is with what happened long ago. So for that reason, we can say of a state that *it did* something before any of its present members were born, and what is owed on the basis of what it did is rightly assessed in terms of what it was that it did, rather than in terms of whether and how it benefited.

III

It may be hard, however, to escape the sense that receiving benefits, even involuntarily, gives rise to a certain sort of moral pressure on the beneficiary. Nozick's famous example derives its plausibility from the suggestion that it would be wrong to *compel* someone's assistance on the sole grounds that they had benefited. But the force of his example certainly diminishes if we set the element of compulsion aside and consider only what we may call moral appropriateness (Butt 2014). Doing so moves us one step away, to be sure, from reaching conclusions about what can be coercively enforced as a matter of public policy and so may very sharply diminish the topic's political saliency – interest in the topic stems from debates about what can be imposed on people by way of policies of affirmative action or restitution or redistribution. But it clears away what may be a complicating factor in assessing what may follow from receiving benefits, considered to be a topic that is moral rather than political in the first instance.

That certain obligations are not appropriately enforced does not, of course, mean that they are not important. In between what is appropriately enforceable and what is purely discretionary lies an important realm of moral requirements that one clearly does wrong in failing to meet. Whether we should call them *obligations* or whether we should reserve this term for the appropriately enforceable duties is something that language does not settle. But what is to the point is that there are clearly requirements that we would hold people seriously blameworthy for neglecting or refusing. Into this category we would place omissions that result in serious damage to others, even though omitting to prevent the damage is less culpable than violating an enforceable duty in voluntarily causing it. For example, failing to rescue a vulnerable person, when one could do so without great cost to oneself, is less bad than deliberately inflicting pain on a vulnerable person, but it is still blameworthy.

This paradigm example, however, at once suggests two ways in which it may fail to illuminate the receipt-of-benefits case. First, the without-great-cost proviso will work against cases in which the benefits are significant and their return therefore costly. Second, the example's persuasiveness depends on its connection with wrongdoing and so does not help with cases of innocent benefit. Of course, one (often) comes to do wrong by failing to return an illegitimately acquired benefit; but to deal clearly with the cases at hand, we will need examples in which the initial receipt is innocent, but retaining the benefit is blameworthy; otherwise, it is an initial wrongdoing, not the possession of a benefit, that is doing the persuasive work.

Carefully constructed examples can be deployed as a way of evoking an intuitive sense that receiving benefits gives rise to a moral pressure to make restitution, at least sometimes. One such example involves involuntarily benefiting from expert topiary (Butt 2014). Your neighbour has commissioned a topiarist to transform his hedge into the ornamental form of a peacock. But the topiarist mistakes the address, working instead on your hedge while you are away and presenting the bill to your neighbour. Should you not refund the cost? As in the case of Nozick's example (setting aside the question of obligation), we may wonder about priorities: although you may like the peacock well enough, you may well have something else more urgently needed in mind, and reimbursing your neighbour would disrupt your budget. (Perhaps you need funds to pay your tax bill right now.)

But we can dispel this sort of problem by refining the example, as Daniel Butt does. Suppose you had already decided to commission the topiarist, that very week, had in fact written out an order for the work, but had forgotten to mail it. Simultaneously, your neighbour reaches the same decision, mails the order, and, as before, the topiarist mistakes the address, and you benefit from the work. *Then,* surely, you should foot the bill when your neighbour brings it to you. I think you certainly should, but I also think that refining the example in this way strains the idea of involuntary benefit. It was your settled will that your hedge should be topiarized that week, regardless of other budgetary demands. But something very unusual went wrong with the normal causal chain. Two errors disrupted it, but happily cancelled each other out, so that your intended result occurred. It is far from clear that the benefit is involuntary: you actively pursued it and received exactly what you wanted because someone else's incompetence just happened to cancel out your own.

It would seem quite right to reject the view that writing a letter (even if one forgets to mail it) amounts to a sort of contract, given that the standard idea of contract involves bilateral exchange, not unilateral intention (Butt 2014, 348). To fend off the contractualist line, however, the example is further refined in a way that re-invites the objection outlined above. Suppose you didn't write a letter; you simply came home one day, saw that the topiarist had (mistakenly) sculpted your hedge, but you mistook it for your neighbour's hedge, and said to yourself that you wished you could have that done to your hedge for less than $1,000; and then your neighbour comes by to explain the whole sorry story to you and to ask for your $900 cheque. Surely *then* you should give it to her? Again, surely you should, but it is because your own will was clearly engaged in such a way that the whole idea of *involuntary* benefit has no purchase on the situation.

Another sort of example concerns appreciation of what one owes to others' voluntary efforts. Say the local Girl Scout troop cleans up the neighbourhood park, removing unsightly litter. Members of the troop then distribute leaflets around the neighbourhood, drawing attention to their work and asking for contributions towards their next camping trip (Butt 2014, 346). There is clearly a reason why this evokes intuitions different from those evoked by Nozick's famous thruster of unsought services, and it is, surely, that supporting camping trips by diligent young people is a good cause. It is one that many people are predisposed to support, and the litter drive is more plausibly explained as an affective trigger than as a benefit demanding requital. A Cosa Nostra litter drive, even if (one imagines) very much more rigorous and effective and therefore more beneficial to the neighbourhood, would surely trigger quite different responses on the residents' part.

A third and perhaps more promising case *would* involve wrongdoing – but not one's own. Take the case, for example, of someone who is awarded a place at an elite university, such as Harvard, thanks to his father's having bribed an admissions officer (Goodin and Barry 2014). Having won the place, he goes on to enjoy all the benefits of being a Harvard student and alumnus, becoming rich and successful, only to discover, quite late in life, that his getting the place meant that there was no place available for the next candidate on the list, a person who, deprived of a Harvard education, was doomed to a life of failure and crime. Now something should surely be done to respond to the injustice. But something should be done even if the successful candidate hated Harvard and flunked out, while the unsuccessful one, thanks to the stimulus of penalization, went on to great things. The example does not, I think, even begin to tell us enough to decide what should be done and by whom. One can imagine that there would be circumstances in which, yes, the successful applicant would owe something to the unsuccessful one – for example, if his later success was great (assuming him to be successful), while the unsuccessful one's condition was awful, and if no other agent was on the scene to help him out. But then we would be invoking a capacity-based argument, combined with a welfare-based consideration about relieving distress.

We can also imagine a case in which a malevolent scheme by some third party went wrong in such a way that one benefited from it, while another party suffered a complementary loss (Butt 2009). Butt's well-constructed proposal is as follows: B suffers a loss because of an injustice perpetrated by D, D is no longer around to compensate, C (innocently) benefits from the injustice, and so, intuition suggests, C has a duty to make (some) compensation even though a fourth nearby party, A, has greater resources. We can make this concrete by imagining four inhabitants of an island, one of whom, D, devises a scheme to divert water away from B's land, but it goes wrong in such a way that C benefits. D dies and so isn't available to pay compensation, while, all the while, A is unaffected by the whole thing and enjoys more prosperity than any of the others. Shouldn't C transfer her innocently acquired benefit to B? Initially, at least, this seems right, but I think this intuition is complicated by another intuition arising from the fact that C's extra resources, unlike A's, are unearned, and we might think that C would have a duty to compensate if she had received some recent windfall unconnected with the injustice.

If a pickpocket had just stolen $50 from you, and by chance, I had just found $100 on the sidewalk, I would feel compelled to make up your loss, even though my benefit was unconnected with what had caused it. What would be doing the work, in that case, would be a sense of human solidarity in the face of terrible bad luck and a desire to stand together against misfortune. Of course, that interpretation is challengeable, and in the nature of things, disagreements about the thinking of imaginary people are going to be untestable. But even if we adopt a benefit-based interpretation, we will be left, I believe, at some distance from any of the real-world events that inspire the question at hand, for in real-world cases (such as, for example, colonialism), benefits to C would rarely, if ever, be a consideration standing entirely free of anything C had done.

Once again, then, we arrive at the same conclusion as before. Even if we adopt premises favourable to the benefit-based case, both setting aside the enforceability issue *and* acknowledging that there is moral pressure that definitely exceeds the realm of pure discretion, the case cannot be separated cleanly from other reinforcing considerations without which it would be unconvincing.

IV

What, though, of the free-riding thesis? "A free-rider obtains a benefit without paying all or part of its cost" (Gosseries 2004, 42). This account of free-riding has a bearing on at least one important case, that of *climate debt*, already touched on in chapter 2. Setting aside for this purpose the question of who is *currently* polluting what and at what rate, it is surely clear that the countries that are currently comparatively rich became rich by (e.g.) emitting CO_2 in quantities that had long-term effects, effects that include enduring damage to poorer countries, effects such as drought and rising sea levels. Although the current inhabitants of richer countries did not do this – and so were not causally responsible for the damage – they continue to enjoy the resultant benefits, for the pollution caused by their ancestors' practices enabled the creation of capital that contributed in a real, though no doubt complex, way to wealth that they are currently enjoying. So current generations of people in rich countries may be said to "obtain a benefit without paying all or part of its cost" and so to free-ride on the costs borne by poorer countries. If so, that would seem to give us a compelling benefit-based case for redress.

While this description of what a free-rider does is clearly true, I do not think that it can be taken as a definition of what free-riding is. Or if it is so taken, then free-riding becomes too inescapably endemic to be culpable. Consider case 1. You teach a third-year seminar that draws on material that students are deemed to cover in second year. The colleague who teaches the second-year course does a terrific job, from which, of course, you greatly benefit. But suppose it turns out that the second-year teacher throws himself into that course so enthusiastically that he rather skimps on the time available to his first-year students – not to the point of unprofessional neglect (which would introduce distracting questions of wrongdoing), but significantly all the same, and it affects the first-year students' learning experience. It seems implausible that because of this, you would acquire a duty of redress to your colleague's first-year students.

Or consider case 2. Both country A and country B produce a certain good for sale on the global market – let's say a collapsible bicycle. Then country B's engineers slip up and design a very unsatisfactory new (much too collapsible?) version of their bicycle, with the result that sales for their product slump and consumers flock to the machine manufactured by country A. The industry in country A certainly "obtains a benefit without paying all or part of its costs," and it is a free-rider if the account of free-riding above is to be taken as a definition of it.

Now the relevance of both cases could be challenged for the following good reason. In case 1 and case 2, there is an established and taken-for-granted background of expectations that excuses the beneficiary of obligation. In case 1, there is a background of an established division of academic labour, which excuses participants from responsibility (whatever concern they may nevertheless have) for what happens in other courses. In case 2, a background endorsement of economic competition necessarily entails acceptance of outcomes with differential effects. All this is true. The cases that engage concern are ones in which there are no secure background expectations – they take place within the flow of historical cause and effect and ask us to arrive at just solutions, rather than appealing to agreed-upon background justice.

This, however, makes it even more improbable that we can separate justifiable outcomes from distributively just criteria. Working within an orderly division of labour or an economic market, the defects of particular outcomes can be overcome by considerations about general systemic needs. This kind of justification isn't available, however, when outcomes flow from historical sequences rather than systemic necessity and the kind of evaluation is less narrowly focused. We cannot but be swayed by distributive considerations – how well or badly did people do?

If we weren't swayed in this way, then we would, I think, be led, eventually, to objectionable conclusions. The model of redress is sensitive only to correlative benefits and losses – that is to say, to benefits I enjoy that entail your corresponding losses. But suppose that country A builds two dams. Dam 1 is a big success and produces huge quantities of energy, from which A benefits. Dam 2 is an engineering mistake and produces nothing for A, while, as it happens, inflicting losses on country B. B's losses are not correlative to A's gains (A would have received the gains even if B hadn't suffered the losses). So if you have any sense that A owes something to B, it cannot be for restitutive reasons, for what is owed in reparation for harm is, in this case, independent of what is gained from it.

V

Of course, it remains true that the predator states that are called on to make redress are among the world's richer states, while victim states are, for the most part (though not entirely), among the world's poorer states. This raises a distinct issue: that of ability to pay. And, of course, if a state committed an injustice that brought profit, and still had the profit on its hands, then the issues of receiving benefits and ability to pay would significantly overlap. It would be like a simple case in which I stole your bicycle and retained possession of it, so that my possession of it would signify both my responsibility and my ability to make good the loss. No doubt there are clear cases – notably, the removal of culturally valued objects – a topic to be addressed in the following chapter.

In less clear-cut cases, the capacity to make good some loss would seem to be a necessary condition for making good, on the ought-implies-can principle. A currently impoverished former colonial power such as

Portugal is not in a position to do anything for a relatively prosperous former colony such as Brazil. In fact, it has been provocatively (but seriously?) proposed that it is Brazil that should aid Portugal, given their historic colonial-era association coupled with their currently very different economic circumstances (Ypi, Goodin, and Barry 2009). So incapacity is an excusing condition. But what, if anything, does capacity itself add to obligation?

There are, first of all, purely Good Samaritan obligations that arise from capacity, but have nothing to do with receiving benefits. The whole point of the Good Samaritan story, after all, is that there is no sort of background connection (benefit-based or otherwise) between the Samaritan – who is a stranger, from another country, Samaria – and the injured man. The virtue displayed is that of sheer humanity. If there had been a problems. It is to everyone's benefit that those passengers who are seated next to the emergency exits on airliners know how to operate them, but only because convenience dictates this, not because being seated there confers a duty-conferring benefit.

In practice, however, it will be artificial to separate historical considerations from critical considerations about present global arrangements, for only rarely could we deny that the ways in which arrangements work to the disadvantage of some is path-dependent. A system in which wealthy countries with many options prosper at the expense of poorer countries with fewer options is obviously one in which a country's starting point is crucially important. Poorer countries and their advocates are unlikely, then, to rely on events that happened in a historical past separated from the present; they are more likely to appeal to "enduring" rather than "historical" injustice, to employ a useful proposed distinction (Spinner-Halev 2007). And this will shift the argument very largely to contemporary terrain and to the benefits that are currently extracted thanks to a very one-sided global economy. The argument is an indisputably powerful one; but once again, one may wonder whether it is centrally one that depends on the receipt of benefits.

At the time of writing, a recent news story concerns a clothing factory in Bangladesh that collapsed, killing over a thousand workers. The building was substandard, and the operation was obviously conducted without basic regard for the safety of its employees. The clothing produced there is (or was) sold by a major North American retail chain in its grocery stores. Now everyone concerned, including, to a minor degree, individual customers, may have shared in some degree of complicity once the conditions of the Bangladeshi workers became known. (Others, somewhere in the chain of responsibility, would have had a duty to acquire knowledge of working conditions *before* the event took place.) And obviously, the substandard working conditions in Bangladesh translated into a benefit for North Americans, in that they made it possible for the local employer to produce items at a lower unit cost. But to apply a benefits-received model to customers, we have to assume, first, that it was necessarily *that* benefit that motivated them. It may well have been the convenience of buying clothing in a grocery outlet, especially in view of the fact that even cheaper clothing was available elsewhere. Or possibly the clothing was more attractively designed than other lines of less or comparable cost.

But regardless of whether a person's particular benefit was causally connected to substandard factory conditions by way of the low prices that those conditions made possible, any decision to switch brands is most plausibly ascribed to a sense of distaste for the callousness involved and a desire to avoid the taint of connection with it – what Iris Marion Young (2006) calls "social connection." It is not having benefited in the relevant way – i.e., by saving money – that would motivate this, but having to some very small degree been part of the process once it comes to light. Perhaps more important, it is a type of fetishism to attach special significance to possessing an item of clothing, when all members of wealthy societies are complicit to (typically) an equivalently tiny degree, regardless of which store they buy clothing at, in a global economy radically skewed towards injustice. To attach guilt to the benefit of buying children's clothing along with one's groceries is to miss a larger issue.

Young makes the valuable point that those who are relatively benefited by global injustices may have special remedial responsibilities "because they are able to adapt to changed circumstances without suffering serious deprivation" (Young 2006). The ability to adapt may, in many cases, be the most important element of capacity, for capacity can be expressed either in the positive contributions that one could make or in the forgone advantages that one could accept. Young continues, "Lower-income clothing consumers, whether in the developing or developed world, may be less able than more affluent consumers to spend more for clothing to ensure that the workers who make it are treated fairly" (ibid., 128). An implication is that those who benefit most, lower-income consumers who would otherwise be unable to afford the items, have more of a responsibility to support remedial change than the more affluent who have benefited less. Given this argument, then, either we transform the benefits argument into a special form of the capacity argument or conclude that it leads to intuitively unfair results.

Along somewhat parallel lines, Norbert Anwander (2005) distinguishes between "benefiting" (from) and "contributing" (to) injustice, two elements that, he argues, are sometimes wrongly conflated in critiques of the global economy. It is contributing, he argues, that counts, the point often being obscured by the fact that contributing and benefiting generally occur together. "Situations of pure benefiting are very rare in the real world" (ibid., 40). To separate out benefiting and contributing, he constructs a fanciful case in which we (earthlings) somehow benefit from Martians' persecution of Venusians – perhaps, for example, earthling academics get tenure by writing about the emerging field of "planetary injustice." The beneficiaries are not, Anwander says, acting wrongly.

In the real world of the global economy, though, benefits flow from various processes to which we are, to some degree, complicit in contributing. His point could be reinforced by noting that while there may be few real cases of benefiting without contributing, there are quite a few cases of contributing to injustice from which the perpetrators do not benefit, either because their intention was purely malevolent or because they intended to benefit, but it didn't pay off. In such cases, it seems completely implausible that we would see the lack of benefit as somehow mitigating their guilt. It would, though – absurdly – if receiving benefits held distinct moral force, as something separable either from one's contribution to the injustice involved or from one's capacity (in one of the two senses distinguished above) to make good the loss.

VI

There is, however, one context in which the receipt and possession of benefits is very clearly held to make someone liable for restitution – that is, the context of the law regarding *unjust enrichment*. The example that is standardly used is that of accidental overpayment. If you cash a cheque for $100 and the teller mistakenly gives you $110, you have been unjustly enriched in the amount of $10, and the bank can require its return. The contrast – in this particular case – with the topic immediately above is clear. You, the recipient of the extra $10, are not even minimally complicit in the enrichment. You may be entirely unaware of it, in fact. So *this* example of benefiting runs no risk of eliding with *contribution*.

Moreover, the potential merit of the unjust enrichment doctrine is that it dispenses with difficult questions about the transmission of responsibility, questions that repeatedly plague the topic of historical redress. Accepting that some act by some predecessor of mine towards some predecessor of yours was unjust, how do *I* come to bear the responsibility of making good, and how do *you* come to be entitled to recompense for something you never suffered? The unjust enrichment doctrine cuts through these issues. The injustice resides simply in the continued possession of a benefit that was not justly (not unjustly) gained. The original owner may have left the scene, and the original possessor may also have left the scene, but the thing itself subsists, and its very subsistence in someone's hands is enough to create liability for return.

As we shall see in a moment, it is this temporal aspect of unjust enrichment that explains its recent political use, but first it has to be said that, all the same, the moral force of the idea[3] – whatever the courts make of it – is clearest in the case of contemporaries, where it remains the case that an extant person benefits from possessing something and an extant person suffers from losing it. An important Canadian case, *Peter v. Beblow* ([1993] 1 SCR 980), concerned partners' contributions to a common-law relationship. The Supreme Court ruled that the male partner had received and continued to enjoy material benefits arising from his partner's unpaid contributions to their joint household and so was liable for restituting their value to her in the division of assets. The woman, the court ruled, had no legal obligation to make those contributions, so that her partner (or his lawyer) was mistaken to claim that they were required – there was "no juristic reason for the enrichment"; and so he had no claim to justly continue enjoying the subsisting benefits that had arisen from them.

Setting aside, again, the strictly legal merits of this judgment, it seems clear that those who find it congenial do so because it responds to basic considerations of equity. The outcome corresponds to an egalitarian sense that if contributions to a joint arrangement are insufficiently valued, then a way should be found to compensate them; and if a court can find a way to do so by interpreting the unjust enrichment doctrine, then all is well and good. It is quite hard to believe, though, that what is doing the moral work here is one partner's enjoyment of a material benefit, rather than a belief that the relationship had inequality embedded in it. In this sense, we may be reminded of the global justice case discussed above: really – from a moral point of view – we're talking about equality, and on moral grounds, we tend to like restitutive arguments if and to the extent that they reinforce our egalitarian values. The parallel with Tan's argument about colonialism, quoted above, is clear. Add-on arguments are only that, even if they are moving ones.

As noted above, though, one principal use of unjust enrichment arguments today and in the recent past does not bring the focus to bear on the moral relation of one person to another; it involves, rather, the subsistence of a material benefit that absolves us of the need to think about what it is that one living person owes to another. It may be possible to trace what an institution, such as an insurance company, profited from in the nineteenth century – for example, by providing slave owners with insurance on their human property. Perhaps we can work out roughly – the exactness of the sums wouldn't seem to be a basically important issue – how much of the company's current assets that profit represents. Do the descendants of slaves have a case for the recovery of that portion of the company's assets?

The view that they do is implied in legal actions mounted in the United States that have sought redress for the unjust enrichment of existing institutions by slavery in previous centuries. No attempt will be made here to convey the complexity of these actions, which is considerable. They appear to have been politically rather than legally consequential, in that whatever their lack of success in the courts, they helped to force the issue of compensation for slavery onto the public agenda. Moreover, of course, the context here is a moral one, not a legal one, and an important question is whether such unjust enrichment suits correspond to any strong moral intuition, as opposed to being simply an ingenious use of legal doctrine. And the moral message that they express has been objected to (Sebok 2000). The objection is to the monetization of a grievance. It is related to, but not the same as, other objections to monetization, such as the opposition of some Israelis to accepting compensation payments from the former West Germany. It is different, though, in that it connects with the fact that slavery, specifically, was a system of unpaid labour; and demands for the return of benefits could be taken to imply that it was the absence of payment that comprised the evil of slavery. That implication, critics said, missed the mark. Slavery was evil because it was violent, cruel, and racist – not because slaves weren't paid. It wouldn't somehow have redeemed itself if slaves had been given money.

There is an important counter-objection to this (Klimchuk 2004).[4] Without denying at all that slavery was evil for other reasons, the case can be made that construing restitution as payment for work has a major and very relevant symbolic bearing. Slavery was evil in all its aspects because it reflected the belief that some people were of no account and that their voluntary cooperation with others' arrangements didn't have to be sought or induced. A wage payment represents a recognition that a worker is an agent whose independent interests have to be given satisfaction by an employer if his agency is to be engaged. So material compensation to the descendants of slaves, if understood as restitution for unpaid labour, marks the difference between being treated as property and being treated as an agent, and so it can be seen, after all, as picking out something distinctive to slavery and not as a distraction from what needs to be said about it.

I think there is a lot be said in favour of this argument, which, valuably, rescues unjust enrichment suits from being mere legal devices and ties the receipt of benefits to moral consequences. Two rather disparate sources may be quoted in its support. One is Lincoln's Emancipation Proclamation of 1863, which called on slaves in the Southern states, despite their emancipation, to continue to work for their former masters for pay. "I recommend to them, that in all cases when allowed, they labor faithfully for reasonable wages" (Witt 2012, 218). We might take this to imply a view that the evil of slavery lay in its unpaid character rather than in the conditions specific to it. But Lincoln's political motivation is obvious – he needed to fend off the charge, from anti-war opinion, that he was fomenting a slave rebellion – and so nothing of a conceptual nature can be drawn from his recommendation. Besides, even if we suppose the ex-slaves' (now paid) working conditions to be unchanged, it is still the case that they would now be free to leave their employers, so their circumstances would have changed in that crucial respect too.

A second possible source is Marx, who wrote, in *Capital*, that the wage relation comprises the sale of labour-power for a definite period only, for if someone sold his labour-power "once and for all, he would be … converting himself from a free man into a slave, from an owner of a commodity into a commodity" (Marx 1977, 271). But that distinction is rather undercut by the more familiar reference to "wage-slavery" in the *Communist Manifesto*, which, although only metaphorical, throws the comparison between the two forms of labour back to the question of working conditions, suggesting that the distinction made in *Capital* has only a limited and formal purpose in a general critique of oppression.

On balance, then, there are reasons to be sceptical about the moralized view of unjust enrichment, in the present context at least. It may require us to set too much store by *one* of the differences between slavery and subsistence-wage labour. Slavery was a complex system of atrocity that rested on racism and extreme physical brutality, and if we want modes of redress to capture that, then it seems desirable that they should reflect what was distinctive about slavery, rather than how it was different from the contemporaneous exploitation of millions of unenslaved workers, something that was wrong for a different if sometimes parallel set of reasons. Moreover, though, even if we remain unpersuaded by the counter-objection above and believe that the symbolic point of payment does capture a crucial difference, the fact remains that the restitution of benefits is being used, symbolically, to express rejection of a system of oppression that we already know, on independent grounds, to be morally repulsive. It still has not been shown, then, that it is the receipt of benefits that *creates* an obligation – it has been shown only that the return of benefits can be a powerful way of making a point in a context in which we can assume people to have strong assumptions about the moral necessity of rewarding people for the work that they do.

VII

In the *Peter v. Beblow* case, the unjust enrichment that was at issue formed part of an ongoing and supposedly reciprocal relationship between two parties, and one partner's unjust benefits corresponded to a simple unfairness in that relationship. The Supreme Court's ruling is supported by very common moral intuitions. And it is in the context of ongoing relationships, justified by ideas of reciprocity, that the receipt of benefits finds its most natural place. In a famous paper, H.L.A. Hart argued that "when a number of persons conduct any joint enterprise according to rules and thus restrict their liberty, those who have submitted to these restrictions when required have a right to a similar submission from those who have benefited by their submission" (Hart 1955, 185). Those who have benefited have obligations that are strongly parallel to the obligations arising from consent. It is important to this argument that there is something resembling a "joint enterprise," at least in the sense that agents can be expected to adjust their behaviour according to the principles of reciprocity that govern successive actions over time. (So what is implied, it may be noted here, is not really much like the one-off situation, discussed above, that Nozick employs to discredit the notion of fairness.) The model would seem, initially at least, to run into difficulties if extended into the intergenerational context. For it is too late for previous generations to adjust their behaviour; and while future generations will be able to adjust their behaviour, that will come too late to confer benefits on the presently existing generation. So the basic notion of reciprocity, according to which all agents are called on to adjust their behaviour by virtue of receiving benefits, does not seem to work.

We could rescue the notion by introducing a three-party rather than a two-party version of this argument. Generation B receives benefits from generation A and "reciprocates" by conferring benefits on generation C. (Terence Ball [2001, 104] calls this "punctuated reciprocity.") We should think of a society as being defined not only by contemporaries but also as an intergenerational entity – a "joint enterprise" extended in time. Here is a compelling example, supplied by Annette Baier (1980). Suppose one has benefited from an excellent university, founded by previous generations who had profound beliefs in the value of advanced education. They wanted to create an institution that would preserve those values for future generations; they did not intend any particular generation (such as our own) to benefit exclusively. If, then, a generation benefits from the university and declines to take or support steps to ensure its future, it is unfairly taking advantage. What it owes to future generations doesn't arise from what future generations can do for it, but from what past generations have already done for it. Future generations are, as it were, the beneficiaries of a debt owed to past ones.

The general idea of an intergenerational polity will be discussed at greater length in a later chapter. For the moment, let us focus on the work that is apparently being done here by the receipt of benefits. That we value the transmitted good in question is, of course, a condition of its being called a benefit. Perhaps we could contrive cases in which something could be called a benefit because it was valued not by us but by the person transmitting it (an ugly heirloom?), so that we valued it only as a mark of her favour; but that would simply turn it into a benefit of a different kind, valued for its provenance rather than its own properties. If we value a good for its own properties, it would seem to be a sufficient reason to transmit it to others that we believe it to be good.

But there are, of course, many sorts of things that we believe to be good, and if we observe what we take to be the right priorities, we should not be blamed for failing to transmit a good if we decided that other goods were more important. Having inherited a good of the sort that Baier describes, however, makes us blameworthy if we fail to transmit it in turn; it becomes significantly less optional. Here we might distinguish between (a) failing to preserve the University of Otago, a fine going concern; and (b) failing to build another university for New Zealand (one for which, let us assume, there would be an urgent need). On Baier's argument, (a) would be a wrong in a way in which (b) would not. The former would be a moral failure, the latter only a policy failure.

But it would be a wrong to the founders of the University of Otago, whose trust in us we would be abusing, not a wrong to future generations. And it would be a harm to future generations, a setback to their interests – we would be depriving them of a valuable institution. But we would also be equivalently depriving them by failing to build a badly needed new one. So one question is, why would we think the *wrong* to past generations would be more morally salient than the *harm* to future generations if we were condemning the university's closing? To test this, let us contrive an example in which the wrong to the past and the harm to the future come apart instead of converging. Some previous generation, let us say, left us a very beautiful though sadly fragile temple, intending that we would enjoy it and preserve it for the future. We agree that it is beautiful – so it counts as a benefit – but given the primitive construction techniques of the time, it is rapidly becoming decrepit, it is hopelessly energy-inefficient, and the cost of reconstructing and maintaining it is colossal. Meanwhile, our society faces terrible economic problems and, without drastic savings, we cannot hope to maintain minimally decent health and education provisions. Without dictating the right answer to this dilemma, it would surely be defensible to put the needs of future people first and let the temple collapse. (We should take pictures first.)

If that is at least a defensible choice when avoiding wrong to the past and harm to the future diverge, why would we insist that when justice to past people and benefits to future people happen to converge, it is the former that is the morally salient element? Of course, we cannot simply ignore magnitudes. Avoiding a huge wrong to past people might justify a less major harm to future people. But if we engage in that kind of balancing, we are implicitly rejecting the view that intergenerational reciprocity of the kind outlined has any sort of general primacy in determining what we owe to the future. And surely what we owe is established, or for the most part established, by what we think is good.

VIII

In every case that we have touched on in this chapter, having received benefits means something. It may be a sign of an injustice that demands a remedy; it may be a sign that we have the capacity to remedy it; it may be an opportunity to employ restitution as a symbol of regret; it may be a reason to carry on a fine tradition that we value. In no case, however, has it turned out that receiving benefits gives us, by itself, a morally weighty reason to act. It's certainly something that should open our eyes, however, to something else that *is* morally weighty, and the claim made above is that the importance of what it leads to can lend misleading importance to its own normative merit.

Chapter 4

Giving Back: The Case of Stolen Art

"Of particular justice and that which is just in the corresponding sense," wrote Aristotle, "(a) one kind is that which is manifested in distributions of honour or money or the other things that fall to be divided ... and (b) one is that which plays a rectifying part in transactions between man and man" (Aristotle 1941, 1005–6). The first – *distributive* – kind of justice takes a non-historical baseline, and it leads us to ask how, given a certain population and a certain set of valued goods, and giving no weight at all to any prior claims that may have been made, the latter should be allocated to the former. The answer could be, as Aristotle himself advocated, "on the basis of merit," but alternative answers such as "on the basis of need" or "on the basis of equality" would follow exactly the same starting-from-nothing pattern, although more congenially, of course, to many readers today. The second – *corrective* – kind of justice, however, follows a different pattern altogether. For the baseline adopted is historical – it is the way things were before a wrongdoing took place, and the object proposed is that of returning, in some sense, to the way things were, not to a ground-zero baseline at which every good is taken to be initially unassigned and to await its starting-from-nothing justifiable distribution, as in the case of the first kind of justice.

Now there are several ways of understanding what it could mean to *return*, some of them quite complex. As we saw in chapters 2 and 3, even retributive justice can be understood as a kind of *return*, it has been claimed, in the sense that in penalizing the wrongdoer, it returns (civic or human) status to the wronged person whose equality has been implicitly and practically denied; but by far the simplest and most direct understanding of *return* is expressed by the idea of restitution.

If I wrongfully take something of yours, thus causing a loss, I can remove the loss by returning the very thing that I took, undamaged, and perhaps, also, by compensating you for expenses or lost income or inconvenience that you suffered during the period of loss.

Although the idea is simple, we can easily introduce complications if we wish – and as we must if we take some of the more obviously difficult cases under consideration. For most cases are complicated in at least four ways. First, there is the issue of the identity of the two parties concerned. A standard view of morality is individualistic, in the basic sense that only individuals can be held either to be responsible for things or to deserve them: how then can either the responsibility to return something, or the deservingness to receive it, be attributed to groups? Country A may have taken something from country B a century or more ago, but the present inhabitants of A are not the ones who took it, and the present inhabitants of B are not the ones who lost it. We cannot, for moral purposes, subsume them under their collective identities. And of course, even the collective identities may have changed, making the subsuming of individuals doubly problematic. Then there is the question of the thing itself: it may no longer be extant or extant in its original form; and whatever interest the original possessors had in it may have been "superseded"[1] by important interests that later generations have come to have in it by virtue of settlement and development. Further, it may not be, exactly, a thing, but something intangible that cannot literally be returned, and what is relevant is something more along the lines of memorial events, which are discussed in the following chapter.

But if there is such a thing as a relatively uncomplicated case, it must surely be the return of artefacts to a group from which they were taken. As Nahshon Perez points out, returning such things is, among the various standard cases of return, the least likely to face the problem of "supersession" (Perez 2012, 22) or the problem that because of changed circumstances, return would simply compound injustice. Compare, for example, land claims, cases in which the land in question has been densely settled by successive newcomers, who have built up expectations of continued use, or a restitution claim on such a large scale that meeting it would divert revenue from other important projects of great value to a society. In such cases, it may well be thought that concern about harm caused by redress would supersede concern about the original harm. But in the case of art objects, that fear is a distant one unless we place quite exaggerated weight on the interests of art lovers in metropolitan centres and on their loss of convenient viewing opportunities.

Only a little less directly, art objects largely escape the challenges that are posed by the commitment to moral individualism. Taking those who suffered the loss first, it is, of course, true that their successors are, from a moral point of view, differently situated with regard to the loss. But they may still be tied to the object in one of two ways. Suppose an item's return is demanded because of its cultural importance to a group: then the group in question is, obviously, *identifying with* earlier members who were deprived of the item, not because of some dubious ontological proposition about continuous *identity* but because of continuously shared values (Appiah 2005, chap. 4). Or suppose return is demanded by or on behalf of a family, a case in which the object in question is valued for reasons that are personal rather than cultural: then what is being demanded is very closely related to the familiar practice of inheritance. Depriving a family of a possession is like improperly blocking a legacy. Turning now to the case of the current possessors, who, on a moral-individualist conception, must likewise not be ontologically fused with an earlier generation of wrongdoers; they are nevertheless in possession, and even if – following the argument of chapter 3 – we do not agree that the possession of a benefit generates a case for return, it remains the case that if there is an independent case for return, it is the current possessor who is naturally picked out as the agent who should return it.

But there are other cases that, while complex enough on their own terms, do not raise these kinds of issues and so enable us to focus more undistractedly. Among these is the case of stolen art, perhaps the most straightforward and compelling real-world example of corrective justice in its most strictly restitutive sense. Valuable things, with an important local cultural meaning, were taken, without warrant, by outsiders. Their return is demanded by societies[2] that are continuous with those from which the things were taken – it would be too much to say that they have to be *identical* to the original society, for few, if any, jurisdictional boundaries remain entirely constant, and important ties of culture and history remain despite intervening changes in boundaries. (And perhaps it is *identification*, in the sense of a subjective connection, that matters rather than *identity*, understood in an ontological way?[3] Or in an anthropological way that is important only to anthropologists?) Finally, return is possible because the things that were once taken can be demanded only because they are extant. What, then, if anything at all, stands in the way, in the clearest possible case, of the most obvious solution – restitution? What could be a more basic moral requirement?

Perhaps nothing stands in the way. In this chapter, I want to discuss a particularly well-known exemplary case of stolen art, that of the Elgin/Parthenon Marbles, and my conclusion will be that they should indeed be returned. But before we get there, some issues need to be discussed. And after we get there, I hope to show, generalizing from the case discussed, that there is a view of the matter that, interestingly, muddles Aristotle's distributive-corrective divide and suggests a different approach, one that could be better described in terms of political justice of a forward-looking kind.

I

There are two important approaches to the question of return that rely on entirely distributive principles: cultural nationalism and cultural cosmopolitanism (Merryman 1986). The former is the view that cultural artefacts have some essential connection with the social context in which they were produced, of such a kind that they should be held by or returned to that society. The latter is the view that what, precisely, it is that makes works of art valuable also makes them valuable to all people indifferently, so that where they are physically located makes no difference – unless, of course, they could be located in some other place that would permit a larger number of people to view them, a consideration that would naturally tend to favour a metropolitan venue over the works' original home. (As we shall see, this point would be defeated if their presence in their original home was, for one reason or another, essential to appreciating them, but supported if their presence in their original home was inconsistent with their preservation.)

With regard to cultural nationalism, one can accept a strong claim for the importance of cultural contexts without thereby accepting that everything that goes into an artefact is essential to its appreciation. Some hypothesize that the work of painters of the later nineteenth century (Turner in England, the French Impressionists) was affected by the industrial pollution of the atmosphere, which made the outlines of objects indistinct and so facilitated painting in such a way that the distribution of coloured mass replaced the depiction of distinct things. While this may perhaps be so, it would seem to detract from appreciating the paintings if we substituted a causal story about their production for an aesthetic account of what makes them compelling.

And it isn't immediately clear what it is that would distinguish a causal account based on physical facts (atmospheric pollution) from an account based on cultural influences (admired *points d'appui*). One important thing that would separate the two, of course, would be a distinction between *influence* in a causal sense and *influence* in the sense of something that an artist consciously modelled his work on; and influence in the latter sense would be something that should incline us to situate an artist's work in the milieu from which it drew its inspiration, without in any sense substituting a determinist account for aesthetic understanding.

Now it may well be true that, in some cases, artists drew their inspiration entirely from local sources (histories, landscapes), and in such cases, I can see no possible objection to gathering together works of art that are essentially connected to a locality, for here influence and aesthetic meaning would seem to be inseparable. The work of the Canadian artists known as the Group of Seven, for example, being so referentially tied to local landscapes, as well as emblematizing Canada's cultural coming of age, should surely remain, mostly anyway, in its national home. Picasso's *Guernica*, on the other hand, while no less tied to context in its inspiration, would seem to reference the topics of war and violence in general, and while it might gain effect by being displayed in an appropriate venue, it hardly seems likely that it would lose meaning if it were not. It could also actually gain *effect* if it were to be displayed in another venue in which civilian populations had suffered from terror bombing. In fact, a particularly complete and meaningful story would be told if it were to be displayed in, for example, Dresden, where what the bombing of Guernica effectively began reached its horrific culmination. What better place could there be to appreciate the painting's moral point?

One might wonder, though, in how many cases the local-reference model would apply, given the cosmopolitan (and transhistorical) influences that permeate modern, globally influenced artistic production. If the French Impressionists admired Turner, then at least some of his canvases should be in Paris, on the same argument that says that Group of Seven works should stay in Canada. Likewise, the African works that inspired Picasso should be in Barcelona. Perhaps, as one writer has argued, the very idea of locating a definitively proper context is, in general, a lost cause. To attempt to fix a limited context of meaning and appreciation is to "conspire against a greater understanding and appreciation of the world's many diverse cultures. No culture of any consequence is free of influences from other cultures. All cultures are dynamic, mongrel creations, interrelated such that we all have a stake in their preservation" (Cuno 2011, xxxv–xxxvi).

Moreover, even in cases in which the localist model could plausibly be made to apply – because, let us say, the artefacts in question were produced by an insular community for local use – there are important objections of a practical kind. No doubt items of pottery, for example, could be better understood in the local context of their production and use. But if the country in which they were produced lacks the means to do anything more than warehouse them – let alone showcase them in replica villages in which their use and meaning can be conveyed, as rich North American societies can do in the case of both native and pioneer artefacts – it is not clear that the available context is meaningful in the sense of communicating anything or that preserving it is meaningful enough to outweigh the preservation of objects taken separately in their aesthetic meaning.

A final point here. The nationalist view cannot possibly attribute merit to a bare connection between place and artefact, at least not without some implausible metaphysical view connecting creative genius with local soil – a sort of geographical determinism that treats social, cultural, political, and demographic discontinuities as being of no account.[4] The nationalist case for return is surely plausible only if understood as a case for connecting works of art with a society that is best placed to appreciate them.[5] We may wonder about the plausibility of this, even, since appreciative capacity cuts across national identities here, and the graduate of an elite American art school would surely grasp the deconstructive value of, say, Marcel Duchamp's famous urinal, displayed provocatively on a gallery wall, more fully than the average user of an actual Parisian urinal. Setting that aside, though, what would follow from a viewership-based case for return? Surely it would altogether forbid the private ownership of art. A privately owned work anywhere is, in most cases, more unavailable to any viewers (other than its owners) than a publicly displayed work anywhere, whether in the owner's country or some other reasonably accessible one. Of course, though, this consideration does not apply to pieces of public monumental art, where the goal is to return them to their place of display; and in such cases, the localist point about the value of context applies anyway – we have to return the pieces simply to see what they *are*, for their very meaning is tied up with their display to one public rather than another.

As for cultural cosmopolitanism, its attraction is so manifest that objections to it are very likely to be oblique. If the back-and-forth flow of artefacts between countries were more or less even, it is hard to suppose that people would be radically upset by the presence of Anglo-Saxon brooches in Nigerian museums and Nigerian necklaces in British ones. What, in fact, could be better than an arrangement whereby every museum visitor in the world could get a sense of the rich differences and sometimes startling convergences of different cultural production? But the reality is, of course, different, and this surely motivates the anti-cosmopolitan view. The movement of artefacts is overwhelmingly unidirectional, from developing countries to developed, with the result that cultural cosmopolitanism is overwhelmingly likely to be interpreted as a veil for cultural imperialism. And this is correct: while we should evaluate principles on their merits, we should also be sceptical of principles that, given the facts of history, can have only a one-sided application, with the result that, given the world as it was and is, museums in developed countries hold Nigerian and Colombian artefacts, while collections in developing countries do not hold Anglo-Saxon canoes or Viking weapons, even if in an ideal world they would.

But the available remedies are only limited. "Source" countries – poorer countries with an abundance of artefacts – can now forbid or restrict exports. The damage has long since been done, however, and no museum in a developed country would now even contemplate transfers on the nineteenth-century scale. (They would also be clearly illegal.) Moreover, it is not at all clear that preventing export is the best thing to do from the point of view of either the artefacts themselves or those who may potentially appreciate them. Again, if a supply of local artefacts is kept hidden in a warehouse, it is not of much, if any, significance that the warehouse is a local one; surely some discernible interest would be better served if the artefacts were displayed in a much-visited museum in some metropolitan capital.

These broad distributive principles, scholars have persuasively argued, are unattractive because they are too insensitive to context. The nationalist principle is too insensitive to questions about the actual capacity of institutions and the public to display things and appreciate them. The cosmopolitan principle abstracts from the real-world conditions under which artefacts are actually transferred from one part of the globe to another and the inequalities of power reflected in this transfer. We can't, then, settle the issue by appealing to a principle that, on Aristotle's merit-based view, required us to distribute the best flutes to the best flautists or, updating his line of argument, a principle that requires us to distribute welfare to the most needy or allocate voting rights on the basis of equality. There isn't a good distributive principle in this case. So should we return, then, to corrective justice? To making good, not in relation to some general principle, but simply in relation to how things came to be wrongly redistributed?

II

On both of the distributivist views mentioned above, it is important to note that how a work of art was acquired, in one way or another, is neither here nor there, for on these views (unlike the corrective view), what matters is where things end up, rather than how they got to be where they are. The Elgin/Parthenon Marbles were acquired by (at best) dubiously legal means. Other artefacts were acquired by entirely legal means or else by sheer force; still others could have been sold by cash-strapped governments. Cultural nationalists could, if necessary, make their case for return without regard to the means of transfer (although they are not obliged to be conceptual purists!). But the circumstances of transfer are often accorded great significance. The excellent book by the late Christopher Hitchens (1987), for example, devoted over half of its space to the manner of Lord Elgin's appropriation of the Marbles, and it is hard not to assume that the manner was supposed to contribute to the matter of redress or the response of those sympathetic to their return. To quote another source,

> Elgin's men removed cornice blocks from the Parthenon that were still *in situ* (after some 2,250 years) and forcibly extracted sculpted metopes from the exterior and blocks of the frieze from the interior wall; in addition, they levied [*sic*] out much of the remaining pedimental sculpture. Some of the sculpture and several cornice blocks were dropped or smashed in the process. A few years later, one whole shipload was sunk on its way to England. (Miles 2008, 309)

All this would, of course, have no significance if where things ended up *wholly* occluded the matter of how they got to be there in the first place.

If there were legal issues, of course – or, rather, extant legal issues – that would make an important difference to the question, and Hitchens's book could well lead the reader to believe that what was involved was theft – not exactly barefaced theft, but theft thinly disguised by irrelevant formalities. However, a more measured article by John Henry Merryman (1985) fairly clearly lays any (extant) legal issues to rest. International law unambiguously recognizes the Ottoman Empire as enjoying sovereignty, at the time in question, over the territory of Greece. Had its officials unambiguously allowed Lord Elgin to remove what he removed, then matters would, legally speaking, be simple. Unfortunately for Elgin's case – and hence for Britain's case for possession, for unless Elgin enjoyed title, Britain could not legally have purchased the Marbles from him – the permission given was, to say the least, hazy in its details. The original document (a *firman*, in Turkish) has disappeared. An Italian translation of it survives, and it would seem to fall short of permitting the sort of wholesale removal that Elgin's crew carried out. But later permissions were issued, amounting (as far as one can tell) to retroactive approval of what had been done, and agents of the Ottoman Empire certainly had opportunities to block Elgin's export of the Marbles had that been its intention. Moreover, formal application for return, on the part of the Greek government, was a very long time coming, and both legal practice and common thinking about what law should do recognize that, at some point, a delayed demand for remedy becomes implausible because it is untimely. At the very least, if a legal claim is long deferred, we may reasonably conclude that considerations other than legal ones have by then entered into its revival and that, correspondingly, considerations other than legal ones may be relevant to resisting it.

Of course, issues of legality are not the only ones that come to mind in reading the accounts by Hitchens and others. What Elgin's crew did could well be described as a brutal affront to an iconic and irreplaceable monument. Pieces of marble were sawn down to reduce the shipping weight; the structure of the Parthenon itself was damaged in the process of removing panels (metopes). Bearing in mind the unique and historic dignity of the building, one can hardly read an account without the word *vandalism* coming to mind. But even if we want to be judicious rather than sympathetic to Elgin, we also have to bear in mind the mindless vandalism to which the Parthenon had already been subjected. We do not have to take it to be self-serving on Elgin's part that he drew attention to the terrible damage that the Marbles had suffered and the risks that they continued to be exposed to. Hitchens, by no means an admirer of Elgin's, notes that "since its original dedication to Athena the Parthenon has undergone many indignities" (Hitchens

1987, 36), and he notes in particular the period of suzerainty by Venice in the seventeenth century, when the Venetians bombarded the site and caused the Turkish magazine stored in the Parthenon to explode. And it is perfectly clear that, in Elgin's own time, the Ottoman occupiers took no interest at all in the building's protection.

Even Melina Mercouri, the Greek minister of justice who lent her star-quality charisma so effectively to the case for return, acknowledged that Elgin may have had a preservationist case for removal, while also quite rightly denying that this alone would amount to a case for permanent retention; the right response to such a case, she said, would be, "You have cared for them ... we thank you ... please give them back" (Mercouri 1986, n.p.).

That remark, of course, implies a clear separation between the circumstances of removal, and whatever it is that justified it, and present circumstances of separation between object and source. It suggests that there is a case for return that is quite independent of the history of removal, and in the next section, I shall state what I think is the best version of that case. But before we get there, I think we have to come to terms with an aspect of initial removal that gives history a much stickier and less dispensable connection with what should now be done.

To understand this, let us turn to another sort of case, one in which society A's possession of object x arises from A's oppression of society B. An example would be the possession by museums of artefacts taken from native populations or conquered peoples. A's possession of x would thus amount to a standing reminder to B of its subjugation. If members of society A had any concern at all for fostering a new relation of equality with B, then the return of x would be very high on the list of useful things to do. The higher the symbolic importance of x, the higher on the list its return would be. Very high on the list, of course, would be human remains, considerable quantities of which have been held by museums in settler societies in North America, Australasia, and the metropolitan centres of European settlement. To return these remains is an important gesture in the direction of the human equality that European settlement denied. In Tony Hillerman's novel *Talking God*, a white lawyer is representing a museum that faces demands for the return of native remains and artefacts. One day, she arrives at work to find that her own grandparents' skeletal remains have been dumped on her desk by a protesting native group (Hillerman 1989, 7–9). It is hard to think of a more vivid way to make the point about inequality: what we would find outrageous we can somehow overlook when it is suffered by the Other. That radical inequality is contained, in a powerfully symbolic way, in the victor's continued possession of the spoils of past victories; and the point of demanding return, and of returning, is an expressive one.

This amounts to a very compelling case for return. But it doesn't apply in the case of the Elgin/Parthenon Marbles. For Britain has never been Greece's oppressor, and so the return of artefacts cannot be seen as a way of restoring equality between oppressor and oppressed. In fact, to make the contrast sharper, British policy has twice taken on the role of Greece's protector, in the nineteenth and twentieth centuries – and in the former case, paradoxically, as a result of exactly the philhellenic attitudes that led Elgin to undertake his highly questionable rescue project. Whatever his views about the inhabitants of Greece at the time and their capacity to look after their own heritage, he was most certainly not motivated by anything resembling contempt for the idea of Greece.

The contrast between the removal of aboriginal and Hellenic artefacts could hardly be greater. The former were up for taking, it was assumed, because they were the curious products of a savage society; the latter could be taken, it was supposed, because, on the contrary, they contained a great aesthetic power that would stimulate the development of the fine arts in the materially advanced but aesthetically underdeveloped society of Britain. Much like ancient Rome, the new Rome of imperial Britain looked to Greece for the aesthetic cultivation it thought it lacked, and appropriation of its artefacts sprang from profound admiration rather than contempt or condescension, or mere anthropological curiosity. The Marbles' presence in London, then, expressed a deep-seated view about the Western world's profound cultural and intellectual debt to the city that created them. When the British Parliament discussed the purchase of the Marbles from Lord Elgin, one enthusiastic supporter claimed that their acquisition would "animate the genius and improve the arts of this country" (Parliamentary Debates 1816, 34:1036).

Of course, whatever British attitudes were to Greece, removal of the Marbles depended on, and was legitimated by, imperial consent – that of the Ottoman Empire. And so while Britain never subjugated Greece, the removal of the Marbles, we might say, made Greece complicit in its subjugation by another empire. But here I am simply unsure about what it is that justice requires. Suppose we accept that an empire has a duty to make good the losses suffered by those whom it has conquered and that this duty includes a duty to return stolen artefacts:

does this mean that one empire has a duty to return artefacts stolen by another? Practice, of course, hardly supports such a view. To cite just one example, when Major-General Sir Garnet Wolseley defeated the Asante Empire in 1874, he seized the contents of the imperial museum, contents that had been gathered – rather poignantly – in imitation of the British Museum, as an emblem of imperial status and reach (Wilks 1975, 200–1). But a notable counter-example, in actual historical practice, is offered by the forced return of looted artefacts after Napoleon's final defeat by the allied armies in 1815.

The looting carried out by Napoleon's armies was unprecedentedly systematic, and it was to be improved on, in scale and thoroughness, only by Nazi Germany. In the course of the invasion of Egypt, for example, "large quantities of antiquities were collected by a team of 167 scientists, scholars and artists shipped over to Africa by Napoleon" (Evans 2011, 17–18). Artefacts were also removed on a large scale from Spain, Italy, Prussia, and the Netherlands. The Treaty of Paris (1814), signed after Napoleon's initial defeat, permitted France to retain its plunder. But after Napoleon's escape from exile and his second defeat at Waterloo in 1815, the allies required it to be returned.

Wellington is generally thought to have had an important hand in this decision, and a letter of his to then prime minister Lord Castlereagh (dated September 23, 1815) is enormously revealing about the reasons. When the Treaty of Paris was signed, Wellington writes, the object was to "consolidate the reconciliation [of France] with Europe," and permitting French museums to retain plundered art was justified in that light. But, he writes, "the circumstances are now entirely different." After Napoleon's return, the French army again gave its support to "the common enemy of mankind" – here he applies to Napoleon a term conventionally applied to pirates – and so there must be punitive consequences. In his letter, Wellington makes it clear that the underlying moral belief is not restitution, but retribution – i.e., that what basically drives the decision is not the (restorative) benefit to the loser but the (retributive) loss to the gainer.

> It is ... desirable, as well for their own happiness as for that of the world, that the people of France, if they do not already feel that Europe is too strong for them, should be made sensible of it; and that, whatever may be the extent, at any time, of their momentary and partial success against any one, or any number of individual powers in Europe, the day of retribution must come. (quoted in Miles 2008, 375)

Wellington concludes by noting that in recovering the plundered art, we have "the opportunity of giving the people of France a great moral lesson" (ibid.). It would also seem that another contributing factor was his hatred of plunder. Having fought the very campaign that gave rise to the term *guerrilla warfare*, he strongly believed in the importance of securing the hearts and minds of local populations and so strictly forbade pillaging from them. So I think we can conclude that the exceptional policy of return that he favoured sprang from a doctrine of military necessity, coupled with the purely retributive idea of making France regret its second chance, rather than from any principled idea that artefacts should go back to their original home.

Among the most notable items repatriated by Wellington's decision, it is interesting to note, were the statues of four horses, which Napoleon had removed from Venice and displayed next to the new Arc de Triomphe in Paris; they were returned to the Italian city – with great rejoicing – in 1815, and there they are still displayed. But the statues had previously been looted by the Italians themselves, from the Hippodrome in Byzantium. The example poses a serious regress problem. When we recover a stolen object, do we leave it in the hands of its possessor, or return it to the previous possessor, *or* return it to the party from whom the previous possessor stole it? Should Major-General Wolseley's army have returned the Asante museum's contents to their original owners or, rather, have seen them as plunder subject to prevailing standards of current possession? I see no possibility of a stable answer to this question as it stands. There may be too many layers of ownership without there being a decisive way to weight them.

III

But neither present possession nor some point (which?) in previous possession may be decisive. The issue, regardless of possession or priority of possession, may be one of relative stakes in the present. The case of aboriginal artefacts may be best placed to make this point. Settler societies appear to have been entirely unrestrained in their expropriation of items of aesthetic, curiosity, or scientific value to themselves. Despite many significant acts of return in the past decade or two, museums around the world continue to hold items such as masks and pipes used in native religious rituals, as well as human remains, which themselves have religious significance, of course, given the beliefs of many aboriginal societies.

The cultural nationalist view seems to me to entirely miss the case for return of such items, and no sort of cosmopolitan view can sustain any case against return. This is because an incommensurability comes into play. Suppose, to simplify, that you and I both lay claim to some item that is imperfectly described in an ancestor's will and that my attachment to the item is sentimental (grandfather held it in his hand while he wished me all the best in life), while yours is mercenary (you can get $1,000 for it). The claims of sentiment and profit meet an apparent impasse, inviting either fight or compromise. But neither fight nor compromise seems the right solution, for the former will reflect brute strength, while the latter will substitute convenience for right.

The only solution is to bring into play the question of mutual stakes. As just described, the example would, I think, suggest to most people that if you inherited the item, I would suffer an irreparable loss, while if I inherited it, you would suffer only a reparable one. The item is connected to my specific repertoire of values, while for you its value is only of a generic or fungible kind. Things might change if you were in desperate financial straits, perhaps being hounded by loan sharks for a $1,000 debt. Even in that case, however, it seems that I should be given the option of paying off the loan sharks, on your behalf, rather than losing something of irreplaceable value. So what we might think of as a fair solution would depend on (a) the nature of our respective attachments to the item in question and (b) our respective resources and thus our capacity to compensate for loss. These two features would define our respective *stake*.

The stakes principle is well recognized in game-theoretic theories of fair division (Brams and Taylor 1996) as well as in practical applications such as the Australian Family Winner software program, designed to realize fair and pacific divorce settlements. In these applications, assets are divided by a procedure that allows those concerned to prioritize their attachment to particular items, to expend resources (in an auction-like manner) in a way that expresses their respective degrees of attachment, and to suffer the least possible damage (given the priorities of the other agent). This process cannot work, of course, when there is just one (indivisible) asset to be either gained or lost, but ideas of fair division nevertheless testify to the general importance, in allocative issues, of giving weight to the relative strengths of attachment.

IV

The Victorian writer Frederic Harrison got this point exactly right when he wrote, in "Give Back the Elgin Marbles" (1890), "The Parthenon Marbles are to the Greek nation a thousand times more dear and more important than they can ever be to the English nation, which bought them" (quoted in Hitchens 1987, 67). Taking this view in favour of return has the great merit of avoiding the fear that once a precedent for its application had been admitted, cultural nationalism, or some other indiscriminate principle of return, would empty the world's great museums, a serious blow to a global public that takes a strong interest in the artefacts in question. "The Elgin Marbles," Harrison wrote, "stand upon a footing entirely different from all other statues" (ibid., 68), and so the metaphors of slippery slopes and thin ends of wedges are out of place. The slope isn't slippery, and the wedge's progress can be blocked, by bringing relevant considerations into play. The view has further merit, however, of a more theoretical kind: that is, it brings the matter of return within the reach of a potentially valuable theory of democratic justice.

The issue of relative stakes has not played much of a part in the history of political thought, but there is an apparently curious exception in John Locke's *Letter Concerning Toleration* that implicitly brings out its potential importance. Considering the question of what states can properly require subjects to do, Locke distinguished between state directives that could be compensated for if they went wrong and state directives that could not similarly be compensated for; he imagines and contrasts two situations, one in which a "prince" directs a merchant to engage in a risky business venture, another in which the prince compels a subject to subscribe to a particular religion. If the former doesn't work out, the prince has the resources to make good the losses, while if the latter turns out to be the wrong choice, the loss is beyond all human remedy (Locke 2010, 19).

Now we cannot apply this directly to the subject at hand, of course, for it depends in part on Locke's views about the conditions for salvation; but we can derive from its argumentative structure a principle that is relevant – regardless of the goods in question – to the relations between the powerful and the powerless, whether the powerful are "princes," or parties in de facto possession of a disputed good, or democratic majorities. In pursuing some policy, the powerful should be constrained by considering the uncompensability of the losses that they may impose. They have more legitimate freedom of action in relation to compensable losses than in relation to uncompensable ones, and the uncompensability of a loss is among the strongest reasons not to impose it.

There are, of course, other and rival ideas of politics in which it is supposed to be legitimate that the winner takes all. Carl Schmitt, a German jurist of the Nazi period, must be the clearest example: politics, he claimed, is a struggle of friend against enemy and ends with victory and defeat (Schmitt 1996). Failing to recognize this is said to be the liberal illusion. At the other end of a possible spectrum of views here, we might well place Ronald Dworkin's belief that, in a liberal polity, agents should not seek to promote their "external preferences" – that is, preferences about how others should behave – but should limit themselves to placing their legitimate interests into the electoral balance with others (Dworkin 1978). From a point of view such as Schmitt's, it would, of course, be quite incomprehensible that anyone should feel inhibited about imposing their beliefs; and from a point of view such as Dworkin's, it would, of course, be incomprehensible that anyone should aim at the political elimination of the other. But both views seem basically unfaithful to what actually happens in politics and are questionable for that reason alone; and I would like to end by suggesting that the idea of compensable loss provides a third and more plausible alternative.[6]

The winner-takes-all view leaves out of account the prior legitimacy of whatever process it is that identifies winners and losers. Adopting the standpoint of a potential citizen in a polity that can make life-changing decisions for me, I cannot see that I would agree in advance to arrangements that make likely the total defeat of my interests. Your right to impose that defeat on me would depend on my prior agreement to accept that kind of defeat or else on your assuming my willingness to accept it without considering my prior agreement to be important.

For simplicity's sake, let us take the case of majoritarian democracy. That mode of decision making does not justify itself. Any plausible justification – any justification that is not patently self-serving – would have to take account of the potential losses of outvoted minorities and build in constraints on either the mode or the outcome of decisions. But we would go too far, I believe, in prescribing a mode of decision that barred political actors from seeking to impose on others policies that expressed their views of what it is important to pursue in framing the institutions that we have in common. For one thing, politics would be scarcely recognizable if they did not; it is an activity in which agents "set forth … the just," in Aristotle's phrase (Aristotle 1941, 1129), but we do not need any appeal to Aristotle's authority to recognize that people take an interest in how other people live and want to shape it.

For another thing, it is hard to see how we could separate interests in having social amenities from ideas of the good connected with them. (Is wanting green space to be protected, for example, to be seen as an expression of personal interest, either because it enables those who favour it to give their own children a place to play or as an external preference, on the grounds that it contains an idea of humans' need for connection with the natural world?) And for yet another, it will inevitably happen that the decisions and preferences of majorities will shape the environment in which minorities live, regardless of what we take to be the final explanation of those decisions; and should the lives of minorities be wholly subjected to majority preferences, even those of an innocently self-interested kind?[7] As Brighouse and Fleurbaey (2010) point out, an idea of relative stakes is already implied by two familiar features of modern political societies: decentralization and personal rights. Decentralization makes sense if we believe that localities have more to gain and lose in local issues than national constituencies have. Personal rights imply that individuals have so much to lose in certain areas that are essential to their lives that those areas are marked out in advance for an especially high level of protection, one that doesn't depend on recurrent justification in case after case.

The more we recognize all this, though, the more we will need to take account of the ways in which, when outvoted, one is compelled to adapt and so to think of ways in which the adaptive burden can be justified in political morality. One way – resembling Locke's case of the failed merchant – would involve those with power giving some form of compensation or accommodation to those on the losing end of a policy. (If religious sects such as the Hutterites believe that photo ID is a violation of the fourth commandment, for example, could fingerprints, or retinal scans, be substituted, so that the security objectives could still be met well enough?) Another way – resembling the Family Winner software – would involve those who lose managing an internal shift of priorities such that their resources are engaged by one of their attachments rather than by another. (If your town doesn't get a professional hockey team, can't you still pour your enthusiasm into amateur hockey?) My suggestion, then, is that total defeats should be avoided when available solutions permit one or other kind of compensation. And if we see a stakes view of this kind as being part of a democratic political morality, the question of the return of stolen art should not be seen as a marginal or outlying one, a fragment of the past annoyingly surviving into the present, but, rather, as all of a piece with a good way of conducting politics. In fact, it could be a test case for the political morality in question.

This conclusion is interesting because, as noted above, the return of artefacts is or appears to be among the purest examples of restitution, uncomplicated by issues about continuity, and so it is a case to which one might suppose backward-looking considerations to apply most purely. But the argument above has sought to show that, even in this case, we are driven to forward-looking considerations that bear on the present and future relations among the parties concerned and the affirming of a political morality of fairness. This morality, considered from a theoretical point of view, may be less than conclusive in its outcomes. It cannot tell us to return, or not to return, the Elgin/Parthenon Marbles, although my own interpretation of what it calls for will be clear from the above. But this is part of its point. This morality defines a field of political argument that would be meaningless if decisions could be justified without reference to an honest examination of the stakes involved.

V

The approach defended here could be called distributive, if we had to call it something, in that it establishes a general basis for allocation. Or perhaps a bit more naturally, it could be called corrective, in that it addresses a past wrong and the solution to it. But it goes without saying, surely, that the approach defended above eludes any sort of formula, of the kind that either distributive or corrective justice may lend itself to. It has to be driven by what we may term an ethos of mutuality, one that awakens us to disparities between our needs and others', and leads us to an obligation to be open-minded in making comparisons that could so easily be distorted by self-preference. Distributive justice tells us, according to Aristotle, to give the flute to the best flautist. Corrective justice tells us to give it back to whomever it was taken from, good flautist or not. On the view defended here, we need to know a lot more about the flutes and the flautists before we can make decisions about who should receive it. We need to know what it means to the two parties in order to assess their respective capacities to sustain its loss. That we may be one of the two parties in question makes the honesty of this assessment all the more necessary because, obviously, it is more personally difficult.

In chapter 1, the model of the *bricoleur* was introduced, in opposition to the (profoundly depressive) notion of unitary controlling paradigms that stand in domination over us. On the *bricoleur* model, agents come to terms with the world, and make claims on it, by identifying with and deploying available themes and items in often unsettling ways that express their freedom. Contemporary agents in very different societies, or even in the kinds of societies that anthropologists term *segmented*, may perhaps lay claim to quite distinct themes and items; if so, this gives us a recipe for an isolationist kind of peace in which groups manage to coexist only by disvaluing others' domains. This works when domains are differently valued, but more often than not, agents lay competing claims to the same items. The same symbols of authority and community may be put to rival uses, and the very same artefacts may figure in rival projects of self-identification. Either it must be that one of these projects is summarily defeated, or there must be a process through which the parties come to understand that the same thing bears competing social and political meanings, that others draw on it for rival purposes, and so come to recognize that this may profoundly modify the strength of their own claims. This is exactly what the idea of stakes expresses, and, given that agents do not typically live in self-enclosed worlds with points of reference that are unique to themselves, and of no interest to others, it may be possible and, if so, the only basis on which reciprocal respect can replace summary coercion.

Chapter 5

Bad Memories

More basic than restitution or punishing, perhaps even more basic than judging, is the topic of remembering. Recent years have seen greatly increased philosophical interest in this topic in the context of moral and political issues. This interest has accompanied a powerful real-world movement to advance what we may term *practical memory*, taking various forms of apology and reconciliation that involve the recovery of past injustices, cruelties, and also subsequent culpable neglect of them. Commentators have, on the whole, been sympathetic to this movement. Memory is thought to have therapeutic value at the personal level, to be essential to the public denunciation and repudiation of past wrongs, and to the overcoming of long-standing suspicion and hostility.

Memory's premier instrument, in the public context, is the truth commission, one of the later twentieth century's most notable institutional creations and one widely used to bring about "transition" from unjust to more just regimes. It is either a complement[1] or a rival (depending on one's point of view) to another twentieth-century innovation, the international criminal trial, also put to use in transitional contexts. But it is rather emphatically distinguished from the criminal trial on the grounds that memory is different from punishment, perhaps better than punishment; that it is more victim-friendly; that it is better suited to bringing out and recording a whole narrative of oppression rather than the misdeeds of a few.

So there is much to be said in favour of memory and the institutions that promote it. But first, can we say that there is a duty to remember? Second, what kind of memory can institutions such as truth commissions provide? And third, is memory always good?

I

In its most ambitious form, the idea of a duty to remember is tied up with the idea of identity itself, an important connection in that identity is, in turn, tied to the idea of accountability: for only an agent that remains *the same* can be called to account for earlier acts. Memory is often called on to underwrite sameness, one notable classical case being John Locke's account of personal identity in his *Essay Concerning Human Understanding*. "Had I the same consciousness, that I saw the Ark and Noah's Flood, as that I saw an overflowing of the Thames last winter, or as that I write now, I could not more doubt that I, that write this now, that saw the Thames overflow'd last winter, and that view'd the Flood at the general Deluge, was the same self" (Locke 1975, 340–1). This personal identity, founded on continuity of consciousness, is all that makes ideas of reward and punishment possible: we do not punish the madman for the sober man's actions, nor the sober man for what the madman did, Locke claims, "thereby making them two persons" (342).

Now much has been written about Locke's view of personal identity and its problems, but in the present context, what matters is the parallel use of his model of identity in thinking about collective responsibility: the claim that here, likewise, it is the continuity of memory that "makes possible the community as a subject for justice" (Booth 2008, 237). And here two issues arise at once. The first is that while Locke, in thinking about individuals, can (despite his best efforts, he says) find nothing but continuity of memory to ground identity – thus posing classic problems – while, in the collective case, several other candidates come to mind without much effort at all. (We share territory and institutions with the past members of our society, for example.) The second is that Locke's remarks about the discontinuity of memory raise quite a problem in the collective case: since collectives *do* rather often forget, turning their backs on the past for one reason or another, do they thereby cease to be accountable? Or what is even more worrying, could they cause themselves to be unaccountable by deliberately cultivating forgetfulness? Indeed, governments often do this by discouraging memorial activities and destroying or concealing the evidence on which memory could be based. In an especially telling episode recounted by Milan Kundera, a Czechoslovakian party official who kindly lent his hat to the party's general secretary at a chilly May Day parade was subsequently airbrushed out of history, with only his hat remaining – on the general secretary's head – in the official photographs as a now-undecipherable token of his act (Kundera 1980, 3).

With regard to collective identity, we might think first (as chapter 2 recommended) of political institutions or states, and their capacity to bear intergenerational responsibilities, as well as the claims that they make based on their transgenerational continuity: they do not, for example, have to justify to the world, with the passing of each generational cohort, their entitlement to control the territory that they have. Continued possession is enough, and so consistency of reasoning would suggest that they need to assume the unwanted burdens as well as the desired benefits of possession. We might think, second, of negative cultural traits that may have been implicated in past events and that persist today. We might think (in a more positive mode) of gratitude for what we have inherited from our ancestors. We might think of unresolved problems that persist in our present. None of these, as far as I can see, require us to depend on memory in grasping who we are. We might, after all, be immigrants, or the children of recent immigrants, and whatever importance any of the last three considerations may have would depend on their independent weight; it would be good to know, for example, that one had come to live (or caused one's children to live) in a society with an authoritarian culture, without that culture being in any sense part of one's own past, in the way in which possessing a family photo album is. Authoritarianism, if latent in a political culture, is a political liability, regardless of whose past it is. But if this is true and a sufficient consideration for immigrants or the children of recent immigrants, why would it not also be true and a sufficient consideration for *n*th-generation native-born people too? What additional value is there in thinking of memory as something constitutive of identity as opposed to thinking in terms of responsibilities flowing from one's current situation? In a single politically salient situation, people may self-identify in different ways, and identity is unnecessarily and unhelpfully restrictive as a starting point.

Of course, if there were such a thing as a basic duty to remember, we would need to think of it as underived from any of its present desirable spin-offs. And if, in this case, a society failed to remember, it would do wrong as well as (as it happens) perhaps causing damage. But here there seem to be problems of both priority and circularity. In terms of priority, is it the damage itself, or the failure of memory, that grounds the response and the remedy? As for the circularity issue, if there is some being whose identity is literally composed of memory, it becomes difficult to ascribe to it a duty to remember. It would amount to saying that it had a duty to exist, or to be who it is, a supposed duty that necessarily lacks a pre-existing bearer. Discussion of memory sometimes seems to involve a paradox of this kind. By virtue of being a member of a family, recalling familial memories "has something of a duty-like character" (Booth 2008, 243), as though it were the case either that membership came first or that one had a duty to become a member by taking part in memorial events. But of course, the paradox would be averted if memory did indeed, as a matter of fact, come first: if it was memory itself that defined a current act or policy as oppressive.

There are certainly some supporting examples. These are examples of symbolic acts that obtain all their meaning from history – burning crosses, flying Confederate flags, using Nazi insignia, and so on. It is indisputably true that, without their history, such things would be meaningless. But it is no less true that they would be meaningless, or virtually so, if the oppression with which they are connected had been entirely expunged from the contemporary world; if, for example, the oppression of black people had become a quaint memory akin to the persecution of Druids in some early phase of British history or the long-gone (and now risible) pre-modern hatred of ventriloquists. The same consideration applies to cases in which oppression currently exists but is magnified by the remembered past, something vividly discussed in the literature on memory. James Baldwin is quoted. "The man does not remember the hand that struck him, the darkness that frightened him, as a child, nevertheless, the hand and the darkness remain with him, indivisible from himself forever" (Booth 2008, 244). A victim of cerebral palsy, who suffered discrimination in his own life, is quoted, to the effect that he related his own experience to that of "century upon century" of abuse suffered by the disabled, his own protest against mistreatment "resurrecting" the experience of past generations (Williams 1998, 182). These moving references certainly enhance or magnify our sense of what was suffered. But what exactly is it that is magnified? The evil of the act itself? Or, rather, given the long-standing nature of the problem, the urgency of finding a remedy? Urgency would seem to be more sensitive to accumulation than evil itself is (unless we are prepared to discount occasional evil quite radically).

Take the famous case of the sadistic beating of Rodney King by officers of the Los Angeles Police Department in 1991, an event recorded on the cell phones of passers-by and broadcast on television and that led to widespread protest and (eventually) to the trial of the officers involved in the event. It would not, obviously, have been a relevant legal consideration, in terms of the officers' culpability, that black people had been repeatedly exposed to violence for many years. (If we thought it should affect the officers' sentencing, it would support only the remedial view.) Would it be a relevant moral consideration with regard to culpability? I can't see that it would be, unless we are supposing (as we may be) that history entered into the offenders' consciousness in the form of some racist account of their society's history, so that (an interpretation of) the past became relevantly present in the form of a motivating theme for them.

Without this, or something like it, the memory theme does seem to court the sort of circularity mentioned above, in figuring both as a constitutive element in who one is and as something that given who (having it) one is, one should have. Can it be *both* that "the duty-like facets of memory are ... obligations in light of ... identity, of the persistence of the group over time" *and* that "memory ... makes possible identity as the persistence of the subject" (Booth 2008, 248)? William James Booth writes, "A person who does not remember, who declines to recall, who in short escapes his past by imagining a caesura between his present and past, is (we think) deficient as a responsible subject" (239). Here, despite the claimed dependence of identity on memory, someone without memory is identified, nevertheless, as a subject and, by a double paradox, is held to be blameworthy for, exactly, lacking it. To be sure, the sentence may be ambiguous between making passive ("does not remember") and active ("declines to recall") attributions, and we would have to adopt very different readings depending on which of those we stressed: it is one thing to have no memory at all, quite another to have one and take steps to suppress it. On the latter reading, memory may indeed come first, and a sense of shame about it may well be what drives its suppression from one's public presentation of self. But the attempted suppression of memory seems best viewed as an additional failing, additional to whatever it was that an agent did, not because his memory is needed if he is to be connected to the past, and getting rid of it could somehow get him off the hook, but, rather, because we already know him to be connected to his past by virtue of what he did and would view his effort to rewrite his past as a bad-faith compounding of the wrong by denial.

II

At the most basic level, it would seem that whether one remembers something is a matter of fact rather than obligation. It is not, after all, a failing of a moral kind that one cannot remember where one left one's keys. (If so, aging would, oddly, be a process of moral as well as mental decline.) When the forgetfulness is directly other-regarding, of course, it is a different matter – one can rightly be blamed for forgetting a loved one's birthday, for example. Even in such cases, however, it may not be clear that it is actually the forgetting itself that is blameable. It could be that one has allowed other priorities to crowd something important out of one's mind, so that what are really blameable are one's previous choices about what to pay attention to, not the forgetting itself. Or it could be that what is blameable is the failure to take steps to ensure that something is brought to mind. If, for example, you have a history of forgetting something important to someone else – such as an anniversary – then surely you should be blamed for not taking steps to enter the date into your diary or computer calendar. For this reason, forgetting something important a second time may be much more than twice as bad as forgetting it once, as indeed intuition very strongly suggests.

What is called *public memory* resembles both of the personal cases just mentioned. First, it's a matter of recalling priorities that are likely to be forgotten – we enjoy the benefits resulting from previous generations' sacrifices, life moves on, there's only so much one can attend to. Second, public memory is best thought of in terms of institutional arrangements that prompt recall, rather than (as in the personal case) the event of recalling itself. Public memory is a sort of memorial apparatus, comprising memorials (properly so-called: statues, etc.), official histories, school textbooks, museums, days of commemoration, and formal public enquiries, such as truth commissions, which are designed to give events and experiences a prominent place in the public record.

What kind of *truth* can truth commissions record? The most basic kind and for some the most important kind is factual truth. When people have lost relatives or friends to political violence, it comes to be important to them to know when and how they died and where their remains are to be found. In Spain and Cambodia, for example, forensic archaeologists are at work exploring mass graves and identifying the remains of the victims of General Franco and Pol Pot, respectively. The role of truth commissions may be limited in this regard, but the foot soldiers of the old regime will be more open to revealing facts about what they have done than if they were subject to criminal penalties for having done it. (The South African Truth and Reconciliation Commission [TRC] offered an ingenious incentive structure here: admitting the facts about what one had done was a condition of immunity from prosecution for those particular acts [Boraine 2000].)

The second kind of truth is what we may call expressive truth: the expression by victims and the relatives and friends of victims of what violence meant, subjectively, to them. (This is akin to the victim-impact statement permitted in criminal trials in some jurisdictions.) These expressions will contain factual truths, but may also contain false impressions, interpretations, and value judgments, and a hardened positivist will not want to attribute truth to them. But it is nevertheless true, a fact about experiences, that the experiences were felt ones, and, in the context of political transition, there is as strong a case for deferring to the second kind of truth as there is for acknowledging the importance of the first. Deferring is the least one can do, at least in the context of the impossibility of doing more.

There is a third kind of truth, whose status is more problematic, but before turning to it (in the section below), I want to raise the question of justice. Recovering and making public the first two kinds of truth seems clearly important, for many reasons; but in what sense is it just? This seems to be an unsettled topic. On the one hand, a standard and authoritative collection of essays defines the issue in terms of *Truth v. Justice* (Rotberg and Thompson 2000), no doubt because, taking its cue from the South African experience, it examines the truth commission model as an alternative to the (retributive) justice that any criminal trials (of apartheid's architects) could (hypothetically, but improbably) have offered. On the other hand, truth commissions, such as South Africa's TRC, are central fixtures in proposals for justice, of either a restorative or a transitional kind. The use of terms is path-dependent here, and it is not really problematic if an institution is seen as being part of justice promotion from one path-dependent point of view but not from another. But if we are considering whether public memory is a duty, then how we are to relate it to justice is important.

After large-scale atrocities, there are sure to be several practical reasons for abandoning retributive processes.[2] Acceptably reliable criminal trials are methodical, time-consuming and costly, and simply unworkable when (as in the case of the Rwandan genocide) the number of perpetrators is enormous. There may be no effective and uncompromised judicial system in existence. In the case of oppressive regimes, significant levels of culpability may fall short of the ordinary criteria for criminal offences, particularly in relation to the distance between conception and implementation – the implementers may have known little about the overall plan. Finally, the threat or fear of retribution may deter leaders from giving up power or else lead them to negotiate amnesty in advance. If these are the motivating reasons for adopting alternatives to retribution, then a "second-best" justification clearly applies. We can give victims the chance to be heard, establish a documentary record for posterity, even subject perpetrators to the indignity of public shaming – but we would be regretting, all the while, that we cannot do what justice would ideally require – that is (on this view), punish offenders.

But in addition to practical reasons that weigh against punishment, there are also conceptual ones. We can consider these reasons in terms of both scope and scale. The standard view of retribution implies a set of background beliefs and practices that constitute a society's basic, publicly established moral order. It implies a society that is for the most part law-abiding, comprising schemes of expectations that depend on trust and basic mutual respect. Consequently, criminal offences are rightly viewed as exceptional disruptions, and so criminal punishments can be viewed as reaffirmations of the importance of the background order. In a society where the rule of law is effective, and where law itself recognizes the equal moral status of individuals, the rules constituting the order can be considered universal in scope, applying equally to all members of that society; moreover, all members have (in principle) access to the law to secure redress for violations that disrespect their moral worth.

When moral order and the rule of law coincide in this manner, a society is able to make provisions for the relatively low incidence of rule breaking that will unavoidably occur. Trial on an individual basis is possible because the society is capable of isolating the rule breakers from the order that they damaged by their crime. (On the isolation of the suspect in a trial, more will be said below.) As for the isolating circumstances of punishment, surely imprisonment would have been rejected long ago if the case for it rested entirely on its supposed deterrent or rehabilitative virtues, the system's promotion of which is so weakly supported by evidence. That it survives as a taken-for-granted remedy suggests that it responds to an intuitive idea that offenders must be excluded, even if temporarily, from an order of relations for which their actions are unfit. Their exclusion is an "expressive" affirmation of that order's value, as is the understanding that their wrongdoing must be addressed in some manner – consequential or not – before they are permitted to return to full membership.

The criminal process, then, seeks to isolate, contain, and cancel a transgressive act that violates widely shared norms embedded in a society's practices. But this model of exception can hardly capture what is wrong with atrocities and oppressive regimes. Atrocity and oppression occur when respect for the rule of law is compromised, or absent, or where the laws themselves are distorted. In cases where respect for the rule of law is compromised or absent, the scope of the legal order can no longer be considered universal: although the law may formally recognize the equal moral status of individuals, widespread disrespect operates to nullify merely formal recognition. The wrong to be corrected is not that of disrespect but, still more far-reaching, that of denial – denial that victims even have a moral claim to be regarded as victims at all. Disrespect is something that occurs against a background of acknowledged practices of respect for other people. But widespread atrocity and systematic oppression amount to practical denials that whole categories of people have any moral weight whatsoever.

This is accomplished by denials of the humanity, or membership, or presumptive innocence of their victims: they are described in dehumanizing language; they are outsiders, not part of our moral community; they are traitors, they stabbed us in the back or plan to do so. Or else this is accomplished by denials of the facts of oppression: there are no death camps, no systematic torture, no mass starvation. It is hardly a mere accident that such denials accompany major evils, which require either mass participation (Rwanda) or broadly diffused support (apartheid) and thus depend on the successful mobilization of opinion against their targets. We do not need a particularly sanguine view of human nature to see that, for the most part, people are incapable of sustained participation in causes that they themselves regard as straightforwardly criminal in nature. Harm, to be sustained by large numbers of people, must be normalized (see Glover 2001). When the laws themselves are distorted and do not afford all members of society equal moral status, then the model of isolation becomes inappropriate and even misleading. The scope of the moral order becomes restricted and particular, and this narrowness of scope allows for widespread rule breaking. In contrast to the rule breaking in societies where rule of law is respected, rule breaking in this second context may not even be acknowledged as such. In fact, what would be considered to be rule breaking where the rule of law is the norm may actually be justified on the basis of the now-prevailing order: it is a wrong that has entered into the actions or omissions of thousands, perhaps millions, of people, becoming, in effect, a counter-norm of its own. And insofar as the laws conform to this counter-norm, there will be no need for isolation of perpetrators because their actions are condoned, even encouraged, by the ethos of the law itself.

It is for this reason that recourse to legal means, while not without value or a role to play, is not enough to meet the challenge facing post-atrocity societies. If retribution seeks to encourage acknowledgment of wrongdoing at the individual level, and moral education at the societal level, it cannot achieve these goals if acknowledgment of a primary moral order that dictates rules is not first secured. The victims suffered what they suffered because a wrong assumed a systematic, typical, and normative character, and it is that character that needs to be uncovered and condemned. This is not inconsistent with calling individual perpetrators to account, whatever practical or political obstacles may obstruct that, for reasons explored in chapter 2; and the process of uncovering and condemning the larger pattern of wrongdoing may, for example, coexist with a criminal process that takes account of levels of degree and responsibility. To the extent that the truth-recovery process affirms a status that in the victim's case was violently denied, its aim is identical to that of retributive justice, whether it replaces or supplements punitive practice itself. It takes a different form because of the difference – a morally significant difference, not merely an empirical difference – between abnormal disrespect in a system of law and normal denial in a context in which the operation of law itself has become systematically exclusive; in which the state itself, as Jaspers and others have put it, has become criminal.

Above, it was noted that the circumstances of a criminal trial serve to isolate the suspect: her communications with others are curtailed, her actions are subjected to a level of scrutiny to an unparalleled degree, and at the same time, quite exceptional safeguards are extended to the admissibility of the evidence that may be brought against her. Trials are concerned with facts as they pertain to a particular and damaging interaction between particular individuals. Martha Minow points out how trials "interrupt and truncate victim testimony with direct and cross examination and conceptions of relevance framed by the elements of the charges. Judges and juries listen to victims with skepticism tied to the presumption of the defendants' innocence" (Minow 2000, 238). The suspected offender is taken seriously as an agent; this point is particularly stressed in James Rachels's defence of retributivism: in ways that ignore familiar kinds of restraint on agency, she is taken to be the sole authentic author of the actions that the trial process allows to be attributed to her (Rachels 1997). Any larger context of events is excluded from the attribution of responsibility, even if, as with remorse, it may mitigate sentencing. One person is on trial – not the group that she belonged to, the incentive structure that she was exposed to, or the influences, however powerful, that entered into her motives. The suspected offender is, so to speak, decontextualized in the name of establishing individual agency, as a prelude to individual acquittal or punishment. All sorts of considerations that, from a purely moral or historical point of view, might be relevant to understanding the offender's acts are rigorously excluded. All that is included is evidence about what, within narrowly circumscribed parameters, can reliably be attributed to the offender's individual agency.

All this is clearly justified in light of the point urged by Larry May – that it is the accused person who has the most to lose in any criminal trial; the victim's worst potential fate, after all, is disappointment, not incarceration or death (May 2005, 70, 77). But all the same, there is clearly a lack of fit between such narrow parameters and what is called for in the case of massive atrocities or oppressive regimes. What is called for may be described, in fact, as re-contextualization. For in the situations that we are considering here, the place of decontextualized individual agency is extraordinarily problematic. The final report of the South African TRC, published in 1998, argued that the narrow focus of the Nuremberg and Tokyo tribunals meant that "many perpetrators and co-conspirators remained in obscurity. The structures of society and its most formative institutions remained unchallenged" (quoted in Dyzenhaus 2000, 480). Such a situation would be unacceptable in cases like South Africa, where the apparatus of apartheid was propped up by numerous mechanisms at the disposal of the state.

In chapter 2, we considered Hannah Arendt's classic discussion of the issue of responsibility. Great evils may not necessarily express the aggregate of greatly evil individual acts. Instead, they may express an aggregate of banal acts, especially in the context of bureaucratized systems in which power is diffused, and accountability rendered impersonal and opaque, in such a way that few individuals can be described as intending the overall result; what they intended, or had in mind as a deliberate purpose, may have been quite mundane. Rather different considerations are advanced by David Cooper, who discusses a case in which participants *can* be considered to have intended the overall result, but in which their agency was diminished by what he terms a "cognitive model" (Cooper 2001, 211). Cooper asks what difference it should make to our judgments, as observers, that we were not in the participants' shoes and have been lucky enough never to have faced the choices that they faced. The question we must consider, he says, is not whether we, with our existing beliefs and commitments, would have done as they did; the question is, rather, "whether I, if brought up in a very different climate of beliefs and values ... would have acted as they did" (ibid.). He concludes that the cognitive distortions of perpetrators should make a difference to our judgments, even though we may hold the perpetrators themselves morally liable for acknowledging responsibility.

Arendt's and Cooper's approaches bring out different ideas of diminished agency, which we may call causal and cognitive. In the first idea, agency is diminished because causal connections between act and result are so fractured, while in the latter idea, agents are submerged in a climate of fear and prejudice that systematically clouds their sense of reality. But in both cases, what needs to be done is to recover the social, organizational, and ideational context that surrounded agency and to record its origins and results. This is just what a trial does not do. As before, however, the objective is entirely continuous with that of a trial in terms of moral education and equilibrium. A social context, it is obviously true, cannot be prosecuted or punished in the way that an individual perpetrator can be, but if we consider the matter in relation to victims, rather than perpetrators, then truth processes and trials more nearly converge. If the aim is to uncover and condemn the violent loss of status inflicted on victims, then in cases of mass atrocity and systematic oppression, a contextualized account will accomplish this much better. We can see a further or related aim of re-contextualization.

Allen poses the question thus: "What kind of disposition must be widespread if evil and unjust social arrangements are to be identified and resisted?" (Allen 1999, 335). The social, organizational, and ideational context in which atrocity and systematic oppression occur is not only a matter of diminished agency; it is also, and importantly, a matter of a greatly diminished sense of injustice. Where atrocity and oppression have become systematic, recognition of the consequences as unjust has important implications. As the TRC final report stated in 1998, "A sense of injustice is important if government during a transition is to preserve legitimacy and a commitment to the constraints of the rule of law, constraints which make it possible for citizens to call government to account for injustice" (quoted in Dyzenhaus 2000, 484).

In this way, then, re-contextualization will more accurately represent, and hold up for judgment, the processes from which victims suffered. It will establish that those processes were not, as it were, aggregates of crimes that happened to occur in parallel, but processes directed against people identified and deprived of moral status, on the basis of their group membership, and that fact has to be central to the recovery and condemnation of the wrong that was done. In accomplishing this, truth commissions, unlike trials, can draw in the context in which perpetrators acted, draw out the common elements in victims' experiences, and in some cases, investigate the involvement of whole institutions.

While there is an obvious sense in which criminal trials are concerned with the truth of the matter before them, they can be regarded as truth-seeking processes only in a qualified way. First, they can consider, not all the evidence, but only admissible evidence: since, as noted, the overriding consideration is the just application of the law to the suspected offender, procedural safeguards stand in the way of constructing what for other purposes would be a true account of the matter, such as a historian's account. So, for example, an accused's previous record – which historians would regard as particularly rich material, indispensable, in fact, for constructing an explanation of his act – is inadmissible, as is evidence gathered by means that are forbidden for reasons that have nothing to do directly with the truth-value of what it may reveal.

There is also the issue, noted above, of *expressive truth* – that is, the victim's own subjective experience of events. As Minow points out, the adversarial feature of trials – itself justified as a procedural safeguard of the rights of the accused – does not lend itself at all well to the recounting of narrative that victims often seek (Minow 2000, 238). Cross-questioning and procedural challenges interrupt storytelling, reducing evidence to an atomic registry of carefully sifted factual claims; and yet facts "do not stand alone but have to be understood in order to function in discourse – which is always understanding in a certain way, one that is not necessarily shared by others" (Parlevliet 1998, 145). In the process both of writing history and of the trial, "the narrator – single or collective – arranges testimonies in an order that seems self-evident, but is necessarily artful" (Maier 2000, 271). Especially in trial proceedings, although witnesses have stories to tell, their stories are not valued as stories of experienced loss but as contributions to the larger narrative that either the defence or the prosecution is attempting to project.

So truth commissions may differ from trials in these two ways, at least. The former difference is most easily accommodated: where no one is on trial, demands for procedural safeguards can be set aside. These safeguards are not based on any view that truth is unimportant; they are based on a principle of overprotection that reflects a moral view that the punishment of the innocent must be avoided, even at the cost of truth. There is, then, a difference of aim, but not a conflict of aims, for the principle of overprotection does not in any way conflict with belief in the importance of truth-recovery. It is the second difference that may seem harder to accommodate, for it is the virtual exclusion of the victim's perspective that is often taken to be among the greatest weaknesses of criminal trials. Conceived of as encounters between the accused and the sovereign, they marginalize the victim, whose own subjective suffering is implicitly conceptualized as nothing more than a by-product of the offence itself. Victims' rights initiatives attempt to remedy this by seeking to give victims the right to have their perspectives made directly present to the court. Such initiatives are, however, very much an add-on to a process that is still at heart *Sovereign v. the Accused*; and if truth commissions give a central privilege to victims' narratives, they may well seem to diverge quite radically from the ideal type of a criminal trial.

At a level of abstraction that is only one step higher, however, the difference tends to dissolve. In a functioning, rights-respecting system of law, victims suffer wrongs that the system takes upon itself to acknowledge by coercively insisting on the importance to the public of the violated right. The victim can call on the system to act, and her moral standing is acknowledged in her access to the police and to legal advice. Her subsequently marginal role is a procedural artefact that has nothing to do with a denial of her moral standing. But as we have seen, in post-atrocity contexts, it is just that standing that needs to be reaffirmed. It needs to be authoritatively and publicly established that classes of people were wrongly denied standing. And the importance of *personal truth*, or the recounting of narrative, in such circumstances can be readily understood: it expresses the fact that those whose humanity or citizenship was denied were agents and patients with a subjectively experienced view of the world that atrocity or oppression sought to obliterate.

This justification, which builds on the notion of recognition of standing that is implicit in criminal trials, may have advantages that other justifications lack. In particular, it is immune to the problems faced by the once popular appeal to cathartic effects. That those who have suffered wrongs experience release by retelling – the famous "revealing is healing" hypothesis – has a priori elements, or perhaps religious assumptions, that experience may not bear out (Shaw 2005). People may be too different for any such psychological generalization to apply, and in any event, the process of personal recovery is likely far too extended to be accomplished by way of a single institutional event. The claim advanced here is that the opportunity for personal narration is the exact and appropriately recast equivalent to the enjoyment of legal standing in a functioning system. It may look very different, but the affirmative aim of restoring equality is no different.

III

The affirmation of a victim's point of view, then, is a purpose that can be seen as being continuous with "ordinary" justice; and perhaps the continuity suggests ways in which trials and truth commissions could be seen as institutionalizing, in their different ways, a broad conception of justice, rather than rival conceptualizations of it. But there is a third ambition of (some) truth commissions, which is more problematic from the standpoint of justice: the project of creating a master narrative that is to serve as a sort of founding story for a new regime.

It is perfectly understandable that, in addition to recording discrete facts and bringing individual experiences to light, the circumstances in which truth commissions are set up will prompt demands for holistic condemnation – the root-and-branch rejection of a whole political system. This condemnation will take the form of a narrative in which right triumphs over wrong. Such narratives are familiar and play an important role at the cultural level – examples include the story of Exodus through Shakespeare's history plays to Spielberg's movie *Lincoln*. National and cultural groups that celebrate triumphalist beginnings may be better off, and less potentially toxic, in fact, than groups that fixate on past disasters. But all the same, the narrative of right defeating wrong is problematic when we move from the cultural to the political level.

Considering this from the sort of standard liberal point of view made familiar by Rawls, it is troubling if a state signs on to views of the world that some of its members will reject, for this disrespectfully diminishes their status. *Views of the world* obviously embraces many things, but among them would certainly be interpretations of recent history that cast some groups as right and others as wrong, some as (legitimate) winners, others as (deserving) losers. But truth commissions can generate narratives that do exactly that – they give official sanction to a view of a regime and claim to do so in everyone's name. Of course, doing so may simply be to set the stamp of approval on the idea of justice that the regime endorses. But stories can be exclusive in ways that ideas of justice are not. They can set a standard of what is rightly called "aptness" (Blustein 2008, 190) and in doing so, may render some memories inapt. It is one (necessary) thing to compel the Afrikaner community in South Africa to accept a regime of racial equality. It would be something else, and illiberal, to compel it to sign on to a narrative that begins with the ANC's struggle with apartheid when it already has a well-developed narrative that begins with events that displayed great determination and resourcefulness, such as the Great Trek, and stubborn resistance to a foreign enemy (i.e., Britain).

Not just whole narratives, but even discrete details may fail the aptness test. Bernhard Schlink makes the point in relation to the Holocaust. "Even if there might have been a funny moment in Auschwitz," he writes, "even if there might have been a decent concentration camp guard, even if there might have been a fairytale element in someone's rescue from persecution and horror – couldn't a novel, a play, a comedy about this make the reader or viewer forget that the full reality was profoundly different?" (Schlink 2009, 119–20). Another example could be the Truth and Reconciliation Commission that the Canadian government instituted to respond to the issue of residential schools, schools that formed part of a cruel and stupid effort to assimilate indigenous peoples. Everyone knows that the purpose of the commission was, quite rightly, to bring out "the full reality" (in Schlink's words) of the system's terrible effects on children and families. It was not an opportunity to insist that the policy, though cruel and stupid, was seen to be well intentioned, or to prominently celebrate the work of any kindly and devoted teachers who happened to be part of it, or to note equivalent cruelties suffered by non-native persons. Of course, in one sense, "the full reality" would include all sorts of atypical details, but what Schlink means is perfectly clear. There are times when we want people to see the forest, when it's politically urgent, in fact, to see the forest, and looking at trees gets in the way of seeing it.

Now in the Holocaust case, and in the Canadian case – for quite different reasons – the issue of exclusiveness is unimportant. In the Holocaust case, competing narratives would fail the justice test as well as the aptness test, whereas in the Canadian case, there are no competing narratives, and even people who think assimilation is a good idea recoil from the means used to promote it. But consider other cases: Israel/Palestine and Ireland. Does peace in either of these two (or four) places depend on acceptance of a jointly agreed narrative or on the acceptance by one party of the narrative endorsed by the other? I think this makes the liberal point. Or consider the evidence of Hutu resentment at the enshrinement of a Tutsi narrative by the government of Rwanda. If a just and workable political order is to be created and sustained, it may often be better to identify the order with an abstract principle rather than a narratively rich and "thick" idea of identity. For the thicker the idea of the identity that is supposed to unite people, the more likely it is that it won't.

Suppose we look at the matter in terms of another influential political ideal, that of democracy. It is sometimes argued that after the fall of an oppressive regime, a truth commission can be a sort of prototype of the democracy to come (Gutmann and Thompson 2000). We can easily see how such an idea might arise. Oppressive regimes stifle oppression, democratic regimes welcome it, and a truth commission is certainly a device that enables and embraces expression. So truth commissions and democratic regimes are alike in this regard. But they are unlike in the kind of expression that they need in order to work. A truth commission, in the third of the three roles distinguished above, is committed to finding a verdict. Of course, democracies too need to reach decisions, but it is important both that a commission's decisions are provisional and that minorities are not proved wrong when they are outvoted; they are minorities because they don't have the vote right now, and, whatever Rousseau said, there is no implication that when defeated, they have to change their minds. Moreover, on some important views of democracy, public discussion is supposed to be constrained by the requirements of public reason – that is, proposals are to be put forward in ways that invite the understanding and assent of others, as in a conversation. But this does not sit well with the project of conferring moral victory on one side. Nor does it sit well with the expressive-truth aspect of truth commissions or with the invitation to give full disclosure to subjective memory and the emotions associated with it. To be invited to say one's piece without inhibition is a different matter from being urged to find common ground.

So on both liberal and democratic grounds, some of the ambitions of truth commissions need to be resisted. But as we have seen, there are also reasons to value them that go far beyond regarding them as a poor cousin to trials. To that extent, memory's most striking recent instrument is given a limited vindication, although one that falls short of what is sometimes claimed on its behalf.

IV

But now let us turn from bad memories, victims' experiences, of the sort that truth commissions have some claim to deal with effectively, to bad memory – to the failures and distortions of recall. What is called the "ethics of memory" goes far beyond a demand for truth commissions; it amounts to a general disposition to believe that societies are better off for being more fully in touch with, and responsive to, their remembered past, just as individuals are. But memory, notoriously, is bad. Should this fact serve as a corrective to valuing collective memory?

The badness of personal memory is explored by psychologist Daniel Schacter in a series of studies culminating (so far) in an illuminating book, *The Seven Sins of Memory* (Schacter 2001). Our recall of the past, Schacter shows, is systematically hampered in seven ways: by transience (occurrences fade after being registered), absent-mindedness (occurrences fail to register because of inattention), blocking (inability to retrieve items on demand), misattribution (making erroneous connections between past events, persons), suggestibility (misattribution deliberately induced by another party), bias (the construction of events to match expectations), and persistence (the unhelpful obtrusiveness of memories). Among the most interesting features of Schacter's book is his demonstration that these "sins" of memory are the (probably inevitable) counterpart of memory's virtues. Selective attention (e.g.) is a good thing; otherwise, we would be completely overwhelmed by experience. But absent-mindedness necessarily follows; persistence is a good thing, for it is important to remember past traumas if they are to be avoided in future, but the corresponding cost may be a burden of deep apprehension.

Schacter's book is written strictly at the individual level, but to read it with collective memory in mind is to be struck by many intriguing parallels that, taken together, may inspire doubts about a more remembering society. First, though, the positive aspect must be noted: societies, like individuals, need memory, for all its potential defects. A case in point is that of constitutions.[3] A constitution may be seen as a record of worries about remembered events, remembered either directly or through the study of texts recording others' worries combined with prospective remedies. Constitutions such as that of the United States are shot through with fears about tyranny, fears inspired by a high-handed colonial master and also adopted from known authorities such as Locke and Montesquieu. No one could say that these fears are definitively outdated. But equally, few would deny that the safeguards built in against tyranny now amount to severe constraints on political capacity. An institutional parallel to the issue of persistence?

The first three sins of memory bring to mind the most mundane incidents in daily life: the inability to recall events at which one was present, forgetting where one has left one's keys, the frustrating way in which a name that one knows just will not come to mind readily enough. But analysis of such things brings to light a mental phenomenon that may be obvious enough but is disturbing all the same: the way in which memory systematically favours the generic at the expense of the particular. The phenomenon of *change-blindness*, for example, means that once we have coded someone as a member of a group (student, worker), we tend to perceive them as interchangeable with other members of that group (Schacter 2001, 49–50). It is apparently the case, for example, that proper names slip from the mind much more readily than general descriptors, so that we are more likely to remember that someone is a baker than that someone is called Baker, for the description is likely to create multiple links between sign and signified, while a proper name creates only a single, "fragile" link (66–7).

One thinks at once about the political relevance of this basic disposition to attend to and record group properties rather than personal ones. The sin of misattribution – picking out the wrong person from a police line-up, for example – is exacerbated both by motivation – e.g., wanting to help the authorities (ibid., 91) – and by expectations arising from familiarity (103). Suggestibility – perhaps we may loosely define it as induced misattribution – can play havoc with recollection; suggestive techniques bring it about that "present influences play a much larger role in determining what is remembered than what actually happened in the past" (129). On the political plane, we are now clearly in the territory of demagogues who can induce "memories" of insults and assaults by other groups, events that, to the extent that they have a factual basis, are dissociated from context and inserted into a current political program.

But worse is to come. Stereotyping figures prominently is the sin of bias. "Because it may require considerable cognitive effort to size up every new person we meet as a unique individual, we often find it easier to fall back on stereotypical generalizations that accumulate from various sources," resulting in "inaccurate judgments and unwarranted behaviour" (ibid., 153). Outcomes include the fabrication of incidents to bring perceived reality in line with what the received stereotypes tell us it should be like (156). Finally, there is persistence, or the constant intrusion of past traumas into present decision making – the political relevance of which hardly needs to be pointed out.

In *The Ethics of Memory*, Avishai Margalit (2002) entertains the thought that perhaps there is a case for forgetting historical memories that obtrude depressively, but decides that there isn't – the solution is not to forget but to come to terms with, and defuse, the depressive emotions (resentment, etc.) that accompany them (208). This seems right, in the case that principally concerns him, but is it always so?[4] Would it be a loss if the Protestant victory in the Battle of the Boyne (in 1690) were to be forgotten or the Serbs' defeat on the Field of Blackbirds (in 1389) were to fade away – two historical memories that apparently retain their potency? Schacter writes, "For all its disruptive power, persistence serves a healthy function; events that we need to confront come to mind with a force that is hard to ignore" (Schacter 2001, 183), but, of course, in the political context (at least), what we *need to confront* is a contestable matter and hardly free from demagogic suggestion. The agenda of things that need to be confronted is politically set.

Schacter continues. "The seventh sin – just like the other six – is not merely an inconvenience or annoyance, but is instead a symptom of some of the greatest strengths of the human mind" (ibid., 183). Given this complementarity of sins and virtues, the idea of a duty of memory needs to be accompanied by another duty: memory is so prone to mislead us, while doing its important work in our political as in our individual lives, that there must also be a duty to suspect it. No doubt there will be periods in which it is deeply insensitive to suspect memories that are important to people – the most basic human decency requires that. But those periods must surely reach a sell-by date. Just because memory is so powerful, the case for suspicion is exactly as strong as the case for recovery if what we believe to have happened is supposed to bear on what should be done now.

If memory is valued for its therapeutic importance, it is hard to see what would separate therapeutically important memories from therapeutically valuable myths. Some political theorists, indeed, resolutely bite the bullet here and decline to reject beneficial myths. David

Archard (1995), for example, suggests that we should weigh political benefits against historical veracity, while David Miller proposes that we should do so in some cases – that is, cases in which beliefs about the past have only a "background" as distinct from a "constitutive" standing (Miller 1988, 655). But take Archard's own apparently benign example – that of Britain's Dunkirk story – a story about an encircled army being successfully returned home, to fight another day, with the patriotic help of hundreds of individuals who contributed their small boats to the rescue operation. The story became an inspirational trope in appeals for British people to pull together in the face of setbacks. So far, so good. But it isn't hard to see how the story could deflect attention from the political and military failures that lay behind the setback and so, correspondingly, deflect accountability for whatever current setback the "Dunkirk spirit" is urged as a remedy. Or, to change the example, the well-meaning embellishment of an ethnic heroine's life story may overshadow other life stories of even greater and more relevant significance to questions of ethnic relations today (McDonald 2013).

This sort of objection may seem to be effectively met, however, by Miller's distinction between kinds of belief. A background belief is one that could be replaced without loss in terms of the practical conclusions that are derived from it, while a constitutive belief is one that is necessarily connected to its practical implications. An example of a constitutive belief might be the belief that someone loves you for who you are, a belief that leads you to conduct your life in a certain way, a way of conducting it that would be devastated by discovering that the person in question loved you for your money or your birth sign. An example of a pure background belief seems harder to find, for one or more reasons, I think. In part, no doubt, this may be because of ingrained intellectual traditions inspired by pure science: even if the background geocentric belief could (at the time) do everything that the heliocentric model could do, we have learned to applaud the Copernican revolution for itself – but, of course, it begs the question to suppose that we can simply transfer the applause to political truth.

In part, as one critic has argued, it may be because, in the context of democratic deliberation, it is hard to sustain the claim that anything can be sheltered, even provisionally, from enquiry (Abizadeh 2004). But perhaps the strongest objection is that almost any background event could turn out, in one way or another, to have a constitutive relation to some practical question. Miller's well-chosen case concerns a couple who, as a result of some mix-up in the maternity ward, go home with the wrong baby, but bring him up lovingly as though he were their own. When bonds have become established, the mix-up hardly matters anymore. Now if the mix-up is ever discovered, it certainly doesn't mean that the couple's child should automatically be returned to the birth couple (with presumably a complementary transfer in the other direction), and the example sustains that point very well.[5]

A real-world example may make the point even more effectively. During the repression in Argentina in the 1970s and 1980s, babies were taken from imprisoned dissidents (who were then murdered) and given for adoption to people who were deemed friendly to the military regime. The successor regime has adopted a policy of systematically tracing the parentage of the adoptees, a policy advocated by the famous human rights group Grandmothers of the Plaza de Mayo. But not all adoptees welcome the policy, regarding it as a further act of state oppression, one that disrupts established bonds between children and caregivers.[6] That case should lead us, common sense suggests, to consult the most directly affected individuals about what solution they would prefer. But it is not clear, when we move from the personal to the political level, that truth-finding can be equivalently optional, for remembering and forgetting are no longer purely self-regarding. Shared beliefs about the political past are constitutive ones, using Miller's important distinction, to the extent that they typically have pervasively framing effects. The belief that the good side always wins, for example, or the belief that one's own side is always good, or the belief that one's side has been victimized are politically destructive, and it is important to replace them, for forward-looking reasons, with historical truth. This idea is elaborated in chapter 10, which discusses the interests that future people have in becoming clear about what happened to other people, with whom they claim a connection, in the past.

PART II

Going Forth

Chapter 6

The Prior Question: Assessing the Benatar Thesis

Before we begin to think about what may be owed to future generations, we need to think about whether, morally speaking, there should *be* any. Barring some disaster – and there we have to turn the matter over to political and environmental scientists – there *will* be future generations. But this, for the most part, is because people don't ask themselves the prior question, or else they have reasons of self-regarding kinds,[1] or sometimes religious kinds, that persuade them that procreation is legitimate. We can't refuse to consider the question, though, once we're aware of it; self-regarding reasons simply beg the normative question, and here I'm going to bracket out reasons of a religious kind. So, should there be future generations?

A small number of moral philosophers have argued for a negative answer. David Benatar (2006) offers a book-length argument forwarding the claim that life is a harm, to humans and to other sentient creatures, and that the only way to rid the world of harm is to pursue a policy of humane extinction. Those who are already alive, he says, might as well make the best of it – the reasons for continuing a life being significantly different, he says persuasively, from the reasons for beginning it – but they do wrong in bringing new generations into the world to suffer the harms of life. What are we to make of what is called, on the back cover of his book, "a thesis that virtually no one accepts"?

I

The most challenging feature of Benatar's book is that it offers a provocative *asymmetry*, as he calls it, between the moral force of pain and that of pleasure. That asymmetry is supposed to have logical force of its own, but it is also reinforced by four sub-asymmetries, as we may call them, which bring into play intuitive judgments that, he believes, we will share. The initial asymmetry is on page 30: after asserting that (1) the presence of pain is bad and (2) the presence of pleasure is good, he continues,

(3) the absence of pain is good, even if that good is not enjoyed by anyone, whereas
(4) the absence of pleasure is not bad unless there is someone for whom this absence is a deprivation. (Benatar 2006, 30)

Regarding (3), it is, of course, natural to ask, "good for whom?" Christine Overall, in a thoughtful critique, entertains the possibility that Benatar may hold a non-person-affecting idea of good (Overall 2012, 97–103), and she offers an ingenious refutation on that basis. The refutation involves imagining an angel who guilts God into putting an end to suffering, but who is then saddened when God's response is to roll back time and eliminate all humans, both the sufferers and the happy. It's understandable that the angel should be disappointed about this since God had the option of rolling back time and re-creating the happy people and re-creating the unhappy people as happy ones.[2] Sharing the angel's point of view, Overall believes, we would think that a net loss had occurred, for we would think better of a world of happy people than we would of a world with no people at all. Of course, we may object to this thought experiment on the grounds that although it dispenses with a person-affecting perspective, it introduces an angel-affecting perspective from which the withdrawal of happiness is recorded and regretted. Overall then supposes that we can remove the angel's causal influence from the story. But the angel appears to have a cognitive role as well as a causal one, and for this reason, I think we have to side with Benatar here and agree that a loss recorded and experienced by no one at all (human or angelic) is unlike anything that we usually think of as a loss.

But I am not sure that he bears the burden of defending a non-person-affecting view. Immediately after the passage quoted above, he writes, "Claim (3) says that this absence [of pain] is good when judged in terms of the interests of the person who would otherwise have existed" (Benatar 2006, 31) – that is, we imagine a counterfactual. In my view, this move is required by the very notion of "pain," which we could hardly use without anticipating that it could be experienced by some potential sentient creature. ("The pain of seeing birds flying," for example, could amount to a pain only if we envisaged someone who, strangely, would be pained by it.) So claim (3), thus expanded, seems to me to be quite right. But why does the expansion not similarly modify claim (4)? The "someone for whom this absence is a deprivation" need not be, absurdly, an already individualized but ghost-like being waiting to be afforded or denied pleasure by virtue of being admitted to or excluded from the world, but exactly like the potential pain-sufferer, only an unindividualized possibility. I do not think we could consistently say that pain counts on the debit side *for the reason that* it would be suffered by as yet indeterminate people, while pleasure fails to count on the credit side *for the reason that* those who might come to experience it are not yet determinate. There could, of course, be other reasons.

Benatar's first intuitive sub-asymmetry comes to the aid of his argument and is undeniably impressive, at least at first. In support of the view that pain counts on the debit side, while pleasure doesn't count on the credit side, Benatar adduces the case of a couple who know that any child that they have will suffer badly because of some transmittable genetic defect that they share, and so they would (surely) be said to have a duty not to reproduce. He contrasts this with the case of a couple who have every chance of having a healthy baby and points out that, asymmetrically, they have no duty *to* reproduce. I think he is certainly right about the two cases; but do they show that, asymmetrically, pain counts while pleasure does not? A different explanation – again, building on common intuitions – is that a duty not to harm – without some compelling overriding reason – is universal in scope, while a duty to benefit is subject to considerations of distributive fairness, considerations that will take into account existing relationships.[3] A duty not to harm, understood as a universal duty, applies to anyone, regardless of how they are identified or differentiated, and so is as indifferent to their existence or non-existence as it is to their other identifying features.

This view converges partially with Chris Kaposy's critique (2009). Kaposy argues that we should think in terms of doing harm to potential others, as opposed to simply contemplating potential wrongs. But he believes this makes sense only in the case of what we might term imminent people, as distinct from abstractly possible ones – the duty not to harm should be understood as avoiding harm to a future person who is "part of a ... story that we are aware could come true" (106). The point made here, rather, is that negative duties are not conditioned in this (or any other) way; a duty to benefit, on the other hand, will be profoundly shaped by concrete ties and so will be highly sensitive to questions of existence or non-existence, (prominently) among other questions of how persons are related.

The distinction made here is different from the distinction between negative and positive duties *simpliciter*, as Benatar states it (2006, 32). "It might be suggested," he writes, "that the reason why we have a duty to avoid bringing suffering people into being, but not a duty to bring happy people into existence, is that we have negative duties to avoid harm but no corresponding duties to bring about happiness." He then rightly points out that "even of those who do think we have positive duties only a few also think that among them is a duty to bring happy people into existence" (ibid.). But the distinction that I want to make is not between believers in negative duties and believers in positive duties – I assume that most people think we have some of both kinds – but between the universal reach of the former and the qualified reach of the latter. We have a comprehensive duty not to harm – so the existence or non-existence of subjects is simply not relevant to its scope, its scope being universal – while the fact that, as yet, we have no associative relation to the unborn must, to say the least, qualify what it is that we must do for them.

All this is not to deny that we have positive duties to the unassociated – for example, Good Samaritan duties. But the Good Samaritan parable's moral force, although immense, is limited in what it calls for. As the story stands, it tells us only to respond to suffering that comes our way. It may perhaps sometimes, by extension, even call on us to *put ourselves in a position* to confer benefits, such as learning CPR techniques in case we happen to encounter someone having a heart attack. But it necessarily stops short of calling on us to bring possible beneficiaries into being, as opposed to benefiting them once they are brought into being. The story tells us to be responsive to the needs of proximate (or, by extension, potentially proximate) others, and the conferring of existence cannot be thought of as a response to a need, for it is a precondition of neediness rather than an object of need. Moreover, even if it could somehow be made out to be a response to a need (on some ingenious metaphysical view), the story does not require us to undertake duties of indefinite duration. So on both counts, it is irrelevant to the issue of procreation.

Benatar's second sub-asymmetry is, to my mind, hard to distinguish from the first one. He writes,

> If absent pleasures were bad irrespective of whether they were bad for anybody, then having children for their own sakes would not be odd. And if it were not the case that absent pains are good even where they are not good for anybody, then we could not say that it would be good to avoid bringing suffering children into existence. (ibid., 34)

The argument seems to hinge on the supposed "oddness" of having children for their own sakes, a view he reasserts in footnote 27. I think the oddness must be that since a potential child is yet unborn, she cannot be said to be a being for the sake of whom things could be done. She will be when she is here, but not before. But once again, it is not clear to me that the cases of the potentially suffering child and the potentially happy child are different (for Benatar's reason). The potential parents who carry the dangerous gene could produce any number of potentially suffering children, depending on the hour and day of their conception, so the suffering child must be understood as a class. For the same reason, so must the happy child. And we can imagine conferring benefits on some as yet unindividuated member of that class, just as we ought to imagine inflicting pain on some as yet unindividuated member of the class of suffering children. There is a parallel here with Rahul Kumar's response to Parfit's non-identity problem (Kumar 2009). True, *that* particular human being would not have come into being were it not for our oppressive practices, but our oppressive practices may still generate a remedial obligation to anyone whom they happen to affect, even though they come to be individuated only after (or in the course of) the event that we have brought about.

The third sub-asymmetry, which, among the four, may be the least important to Benatar's position, appeals to our intuition that "we cannot regret, for the sake of somebody who never exists and thus cannot be deprived, a good that this never existent person never experienced" (Benatar 2006, 34). I simply don't think this is true. Imagine a couple who get together not only because they love one another but because they want to have and rear children, who perhaps pick an idyllic spot in the country and build a child-friendly hobby farm with docile animals and rustic swing sets – but then find that they cannot bear children. It would be entirely understandable that they would imagine what it would be like to have beloved children and to imagine, too, sadly, how much they would have enjoyed the paradise prepared for them. It could, of course, be claimed that, in such a case, what would weigh with us would be the disappointed potential parents' suffering, and that may be so; but even if that is what weighs with us, it remains true that the potential parents suffer because they *can* and do regret the fact that an imagined but non-existent being does not experience a good, so that our sympathy for them is second order.

The fourth sub-asymmetry invites us to think about the difference between distant suffering and the absence of pleasure in some distant place. We are distressed by the news that there is suffering in some other land, but "when we hear that some island is unpopulated we are not ... sad for the happy people who, had they existed, would have populated this island" (ibid., 35). The appeal to intuition here is, in my view, successful, but again, its success need not be explained as Benatar proposes and may better be explained along the lines suggested here. We need a felt connection with people if we are to enjoy their pleasure, but not to regret their pain. It is bad that the people in a distant land are suffering because it's bad that anyone should suffer; this, presumably, explains the universal scope of the negative duty not to cause suffering. But we have no felt connection with non-existent people in a faraway place – or in a nearby place either, for that matter – and their lack of pleasure expresses, not an asymmetry between suffering and pleasure, but an issue about *who counts*.

It is not impossible to imagine cases in which we would regret the lack of pleasure on the part of non-existent people. One sort of case that initially comes to mind would be one of regretting that a deceased person was not here to enjoy some event that we know he would have loved – such as an evening playing Monopoly. Now this, of course, could be because, in the case of deceased persons, we have in mind a picture of them to which we attach the sense of loss. So let us imagine another sort of case – much more contrived! – in which a lovely old house, once inhabited by a happy family, had been priced out of the residential market and so had become an accountants' office; noting that the dour, robotic accountants took no pleasure at all in their lovely surroundings, and could just as well be in some soulless high-rise, we might regret that the house was not occupied and appreciated by some purely hypothetical family whose pleasure we could envisage.

Or – much less contrived – what about plays and novels that allow us to share in the joy of non-existent people? The riposte could, of course, be that we empathize because for a time we imagine that they exist – they exist in the fictional field; it is not the illusion that they exist, however, that does the work, but the imagination of felt ties of association with a character. We may suspend disbelief in incidental characters too – the jeweller who, in a story, sells someone an engagement ring, for example – without caring whether the book ends without telling us that *they* found happiness for themselves.

So, to sum up so far, Benatar wants to say that the prospect of pain works against bringing people into existence while the prospect of pleasure does not, attributing this to the asymmetry of pain and pleasure. My view is that what is at work here is an asymmetry between negative and positive duties, the former (because universal) being insensitive to existence or non-existence, the latter (because context-dependent) being sensitive to the nature of connections (and hence to existence and non-existence). I have claimed that this view satisfactorily explains Benatar's asymmetries and better explains other things too.

The asymmetry thesis leads Benatar to reject a view that must be very common in reaction to the claims of his book – namely, that despite the pain that accompanies existence and that non-existence evades, we may count up pains and pleasures in people's lives and find, at least in some cases, that the sum is positive. While his chapter 3 goes on to offer some empirically based objections to this conclusion, chapter 2 offers a logical objection that develops the asymmetry thesis further. The chapter makes ingenious but ultimately unpersuasive use of a series of matrices, two of which, 2.4 and 2.5 (ibid., 46–7) are important here. The former matrix encapsulates the argument outlined above, inviting us to conclude that existence, with its mixture of good (pleasure) and bad (pain), is less desirable than non-existence, with its mixture of absence of pain (good) and absence of pleasure (not bad, for reasons already given). That conclusion would be undermined, ordinary intuition suggests, if it were the case that, in an existing life, at least of a good kind, the good of pleasure would outweigh the bad of pain. The hope that it would is, of course, exactly the hope that normally sustains deliberate procreation. But the second of these matrices is supposed to persuade us that that calculation would be mistaken.

That matrix asks us to evaluate comparatively the case of a person who suffers from illness (bad), but has a capacity for quick recovery (good), and the case of a person who never gets sick (good), but has no capacity for recovery (not bad because she wouldn't miss it). Obviously, we would rate the second person's life above the first person's, in that respect, for it is better never to get sick than to get sick and recover quickly. So a combination of good and not bad trumps a combination of good and bad, a conclusion that we are invited to transfer to the existence/non-existence matrix.

But a reason not to transfer it is that the good of quick recovery is logically connected with the bad of sickness, whereas, in general, the pains and pleasures of life are not. Of course, I would rather not get sick than get sick and recover well; this would be true even if I got sick many times and recovered many times. But the good of recovering would not be a good for me unless I sometimes got sick. (Analogously, owning a suit of armour would be a good for me only if I sometimes engaged in knightly combat.) We cannot conclude from this anything about the general issue on non-logically related goods and bads. It makes sense, at least, to raise questions about these in a way in which it doesn't to ask questions about sickness and recovery. Let's imagine a person who derives enormous pleasure from writing string quartets, but also suffers from a fear of heights; it makes perfect sense to say that the former does, or doesn't, outweigh the latter. And measures of quantity, while crude, are not irrelevant to the case of non-logically related good and bads. A fear of heights could perhaps become so terrible and all-pervasive that it would outweigh a sense of great musical accomplishment. But this still isn't a parallel to saying that quick recovery *cannot* compensate for getting sick in comparison with a life in which one never gets sick at all.

II

Chapter 3 of *Better Never to Have Been* offers reasons for anti-natalism that are said to be independent of the success or failure of the asymmetry argument advanced in chapter 2 (Benatar 2006, 61). Suppose we set out to do what chapter 2 says we shouldn't do – that is, engage in the process of weighing up the goods and bads of life (despite the claim, made, as we have seen, in chapter 2, that only the bads count). We then find, according to Benatar, that the bads outweigh the goods. An apparent obstacle to his view is that, on the whole, people claim to be, on balance, happy and say that they are glad to be alive. There are two responses to this objection. One, already advanced in Benatar's chapter 2, is that the relevant standard for continuing a life is lower than the standard needed to justify beginning a life. The other is the bad-outweighs-the-good case that he initiates in his chapter 3.

I think the first response is good, but for reasons that do not depend at all on accepting the second response. The first response is good for Seana Shiffrin's reasons, which focus mainly on the issue of consent (Shiffrin 1999). That I am content with some state of affairs does not justify my unilaterally creating a person who will have to endure it. It could be that, for any number of possible reasons, my expectations of life are very low. (Perhaps I read and am moved by Philip Larkin's compellingly downbeat poetry.) In the name of realism, I may have made all sorts of accommodations to avoid pointless railing against the world. Since I cannot know what my child's expectations will be, my own resigned contentment cannot be a reason to bring a child into existence. I may have other reasons, of course – *she* won't have to make accommodations, I may say; I'll give her every advantage; she will succeed where I failed – but that just makes the point that my reasons for wanting a child would be entirely unlike my own reasons for pushing on in my own resigned way. Or a different example: my reasons for carrying on could be something to do with not disappointing (or frightening) my parents; then it would be a terrible thing to have a child whose reason to live would be the same as mine. So I have to have some reason to believe that my child's life will be good in her own eyes. That reason could (ideally, perhaps) converge with my own reasons for finding life good in my own eyes, but that would still be a matter of two reasons, meeting different standards, happening to converge with one another.

So Benatar's distinction between what makes a life worth continuing and what justifies beginning a life is valid. But it could be valid because, as Shiffrin argues, even if we have reason to believe that our child's life will be really good, we cannot rightly impose our own judgment of the balance of good and bad on our potential child. One response to this draws on the force of *consent*. In the case of transactions among living people, we cannot simply compel others to accept a pain for the sake of a greater good – I cannot break your arm, against your will, even if, as a result (some insurance thing?), you will be able to pay your way through university. I think a response to this problem will have to depend on distinguishing between situations in which consent is and is not available.[4] To ignore or override consent is certainly objectionable in cases in which consent can be obtained. Where consent cannot be obtained, its relevance seems questionable, to say the least, for acting without consent is objectionable because and to the extent that it overrides someone's will, thus disrespecting their autonomy. Where this is not at issue, "What would they want if they could consent?" seems to be the relevant nearby question (unless doing nothing at all is an available option). And this takes us back to the issues raised by Benatar in chapter 3 of his book: it seems that living people *would* consent, retroactively, to being born – but then, is retroactive "consent" meaningful?

On Benatar's view, no: for, being already in the world, we are subject to psychological mechanisms that skew us in the direction of thinking that life is good; and once we become aware of these distorting mechanisms, we should realize that, without them, we would arrive at a better sense of the balance of good and bad in life and so decline to reproduce. This case is made by considering three measures of well-being and showing that, in each case, there is a serious gap between self-assessment and a true assessment of how good one's life is. That we think it's good doesn't mean that it really is.

On a *hedonist* account, it may seem counter-intuitive, as Benatar points out, to say that while people say their lives are pleasurable, they in fact are not, for one might well think that people are good judges of their own pleasure. They may not be good judges of their beliefs about states of affairs in the world, but if they say they are happy, it would seem odd, at first glance, to substitute our own judgment for theirs and tell them that they are not, really. But Benatar draws a distinction between "(a) how good a person's life actually is and (b) how good it is thought to be" (Benatar 2006, 87). The psychology here could get complicated, for if the subjects record as "good" what the observers code as "bad," then we face an issue about the authority of experience. But Benatar's account shows up best if we read it not in terms of the disputable coding of experiences, but in terms of what we take note of. And his view is that what we take note of is influenced by factors that incline us to downplay the negatives. We note, for example, that we enjoy a good meal, but discount the period of hunger that precedes it.

This sort of example may, however, be open to the charge of making mental states too discrete from one another, so that they can be balanced in an atomistic sort of way. Hunger that, one anticipates, is to be remedied at some dreadful fast-food joint (it's the only one for the next hundred miles) is different, as an experience, from the hunger that one experiences as a master chef slowly prepares a superb meal. Hunger and eating can't be treated as separable mental states, to be weighed against one another in a quantitative way, but are inseparably parts of a single experience in which the quality of one affects the quality of the other. Likewise, the claim that people who got hungry less often than us would be worse off than us because they would have fewer lifetime opportunities to enjoy food (ibid., 79) would seem to neglect the ways in which a very different metabolism would create a very different pattern of life, with different expectations. They wouldn't, after all, spend their lives wishing that they could get hungry more often, and, applying the envy test, it seems unlikely that they would want to change places with differently constituted beings who got hungry ten times a day.

I think we could accept that, on the hedonic measure, lives may be less good than people think they are without coming to the conclusion – even after all the various discounting procedures that Benatar recommends – that lives are very bad. Likewise, on the *desire-satisfaction* measure, we could accept that "adaptive preferences" fool us into believing that we're getting what we want, as opposed to wanting what we get, while simply wondering how often it actually happens to us. I see no way to call the jury back in to deliver a verdict on this; to arrive at a definite view, we would need a detailed psychobiography of every human who has ever lived. But it's the use of the third measure, the *objective-list* approach, that is strikingly bold, offering a logical reason for the imperfection of life that doesn't depend on psychological facts. (Indeed, it is counterfactual.) The point, simply put, is that whatever good we put on our objective list of things that make life good, we could always have more of it than we now do.

One view that obstructs this claim relates to the idea of the golden mean. As an approach to ethics in general, that idea is implausible, but it seems at least approximately right in the case of the social virtues. It seems right to think of modesty, say, as a mean between being cringingly self-lacerating and obnoxiously self-promoting. If we accept that view, then there is, in principle, a stopping point to the attainment of modesty – that is, the correct mid-point, wherever it is, between two vices; so there isn't an indefinitely receding horizon that implies our inevitable imperfection. A mid-point doesn't recede. So it is curious that Benatar should offer that very example, of modesty, as evidence for his view (ibid., 86). Referring to an article by Norvin Richards, he wonders why we should think of modesty as a virtue. He argues that denying that one has some talent (that one has) is a cognitive error, while concealing the fact that one has it is a form of deception, and since neither cognitive error nor deception can be said to be virtues, we should see modesty as a virtue only on the grounds that it contains a recognition that, talented though one is, one could have done still better – and then better again, ad infinitum. Hence our radical imperfection. This is a very implausible way to understand modesty. Modesty about one's achievements is a matter of social skill that has nothing to do with recognizing some superhuman point of view. It's simply a matter of the appropriateness of social norms and, in that sense, is exactly symmetrical with discretion about intimate personal problems, and we wouldn't say that *this* is a social virtue for the symmetrical reason that, however awful one's problems, they could always be worse.

Now of course, not everything lends itself to golden-mean-type analysis, even if (contestably, of course) some things do. But there are other reasons for rejecting the view that more of what we have would always be better. For one thing, there is the issue of compossibility, which is more general in its scope. We could not be compact enough to enter the house through the cat flap *and* tall enough to reach the highest bookshelves unaided. We could not be perpetually happy and still enjoy Billie Holiday's blues songs. We can't have interestingly complicated and also sunny and guileless personalities. These considerations, explored deeply by Isaiah Berlin (1991) and Joseph Raz (1986), also point to the inherent imperfections in human circumstances, not because we could always do better, but because there are necessary, not just empirical, limits to the completeness of individual lives and collective ways of life.

Now there is no room for dogmatism about what is and is not permissibly imaginable in possible worlds. Perhaps we should be allowed to suspend the law of non-contradiction, so that the same person – to borrow Raz's example – could simultaneously have all the virtues of both the nun and the mother (Raz 1986, 395). But there has to be a limit if the possible world is to be usable as a way of throwing light on the real world, for beyond a certain point, one would no longer be talking about people whom we could consider to be human beings.[5] If so, we have to accept that the appropriate measures of achievement are conditioned by human circumstances and that not everything is imperfect just because it could be outdone in a world constructed by unimpeded imagination. Running a mile in four minutes or less is, surely, an achievement, even though if we were differently constructed (e.g., like cheetahs), then we could do very much better; but it is a relevant consideration that we are constructed as we are, so that things that count as achievements are necessarily conditioned in that way. It is, after all, hardly an achievement that (on the other side of the coin) we can effortlessly do what we are biologically programmed to do, such as breathe; if *this* counts against defining something as an achievement, symmetrical reasoning suggests that we should take account of natural limitations when we look at the credit side too.

The contentiousness of the general approach may become particularly clear when Benatar adds the item of "meaningfulness" to the objective list. "It would surely be much better," he writes, "if our lives had meaning independently of our own human perspective – if they mattered from the perspective of the universe" (Benatar 2006, 83). Now first of all, this brings into play an issue raised classically in Plato's *Euthyphro* dialogue and recently strongly reaffirmed in a posthumous book by Ronald Dworkin (2013). Would the universe's (or a divine) perspective matter if it did not coincide with what we, as humans, acknowledge to be good? Could that perspective change our convictions about what is good, or would it be important to us only if it coincided with and reinforced our considered views? Dworkin writes, "The conviction that a god underwrites value ... presupposes a prior commitment to the independent reality of that value" (ibid., 1–2), and "A god's existence or character can figure in the defence of ... values only as a fact that makes some different, independent background value judgment pertinent; it can figure only, that is, as a minor premise" (16).

In support of Dworkin's view, a first reaction to Benatar's claim about meaning is that whether it's true depends entirely on why it is, hypothetically, that we would matter in this way, if we did. Suppose we mattered because, from the perspective of the universe and its controller, we were important merely as the control group for an experiment: the controller had created another world, made up of beings much like us, but containing no suffering, to observe the difference that suffering makes. In such a case, if we somehow found out about the controller's research design (per a cosmic freedom-of-information request), we would, I think, conclude that our lives were really dreadful, quite the worst they could be, in fact, and meaningful only from the point of view of a supreme controller who turns out to be a mad scientist in a bad movie. (Or we would be like the cloned people in Ishiguro's devastatingly sad novel, *Never Let Me Go*.) If this were the case, and we found out, things would not be "much better," but very, very much worse.[6]

A second response would be that the claim here depends on a complicated sort of movement between points of view. Once upon a time, people believed that their lives made sense from a cosmic point of view; now (let's say, with Benatar) we don't believe that, and so we may feel that something has been lost. But either their lives made sense objectively, because they were right and there is indeed a cosmic controller, or we're thinking about the loss of a purely subjective sense of meaning that once added to human happiness. If there is a cosmic controller, then our lives have meaning too. But if we don't believe that there *is* one, then actually nothing has been lost. There is, in fact, a gain in knowledge, and we now see that our ancestors were deluded. If, from our present point of view, we believe that a loss has occurred, it can only mean that, from our point of view, we believe that the loss of illusion is a bad thing. If we regret the loss of certainty, while believing that what people were certain about was false, then we must be attaching value to delusion and the comforts that it brings. But this would be to straightforwardly endorse the hedonic view in its crudest form. As J.S. Mill wrote, "That what is called the consoling nature of an opinion, that is, the pleasure we should have in believing it to be true, can be a ground for believing it, is a doctrine irrational in itself and which would sanction half the mischievous illusions recorded in history or which mislead individual life" (Mill 1874, 204).

A third response to Benatar's claim about meaning recalls a prominent nineteenth-century problem. Would it, in fact, be "better if our lives had meaning independently of our own human perspective"? Some important thinkers disagreed, taking the view that the ages in which people believed there to be a superhuman perspective were not only misguided in their belief, but were mistakenly sacralizing and alienating an essentially human power in a way that impeded both our understanding and our well-being. One famous example is Ludwig Feuerbach (made still more famous because Marx borrowed from him). Another is Auguste Comte, who held that earlier religious beliefs were misrepresentations of the power and dignity of *Humanité* itself and that, in the future, service to *Humanité* would replace the worship of God. Unfortunately, Comte went very far in dressing up the religion of humanity in Catholic trappings, in a way that casts serious doubt on the view that theistic religion was a mere anticipation of the religion of humanity, rather than the model for it. But J.S. Mill, who was very well aware of the manic absurdities of the new Comtean religion – he uses the word "ludicrous" (Mill 1968, 149) – nevertheless wrote the following remarkable passage about its central idea:

> The power which may be acquired over the mind by the idea of the general interest of the human race, both as a source of emotion and as a motive to conduct, many have perceived; but we know not if any one, before M. Comte, realized so fully as he has done, all the majesty of which the idea

> is susceptible. It ascends into the unknown recesses of the past, embraces the manifold present, and descends into the indefinite and unforeseeable future. Forming a collective Existence without assignable beginning or end, it appeals to that feeling of the Infinite, which is deeply rooted in human nature, and which seems necessary to the imposingness of all our highest conceptions. (ibid., 135)

Returning to the topic in *Utilitarianism* itself, Mill writes that Comte's work

> has superabundantly shown the possibility of giving to the service of humanity ... both the physical power and the social efficacy of a religion; making it take hold of human life, and colour all thought, feeling, and action, *in a manner of which the greatest ascendancy ever exercised by any religion may be but a type and foretaste.* (Mill 1972, 34; emphasis added)

Mill's use of the technical term *type* drives home the claim that just as according to Christian theologians the Old Testament contained types, or prefigurings, of the New, so Christian theism is to be valued as the prefiguring of an age in which one's contributions to human well-being are invested with a sense of the sacred. The latter age is to be esteemed more highly, Mill (like Comte) believes because, illusions of personal reward having been abandoned, it expresses more deeply than ever before the idea of altruism that theistic religions have tried to capture for themselves, but have managed to only approximate (Mill 1874, 110).

Now from a later vantage point, the views of both Comte and Mill are connected with a theory of progress that, while not unknown today (Pinker 2011), can hardly be assumed to carry weight. So perhaps a more compelling source, for the relevance of the Victorian views in question, may be the novels of George Eliot. Eliot, like Mill, absorbed Comte's message seriously but selectively, and the idea of a religion of humanity is evident in a refracted way in her work. But whereas Comte and Mill endorse an idea of progress, Eliot's vision is better seen as one of mutual support, patient error correction, and sustaining the values and arrangements that foster our coexistence and bring about our understanding of a shared condition. Eliot's idea of humanity is best interpreted not as some sort of secular project, but as a web of connection that leads individuals to grasp the larger significance, positive or negative, of their smallest actions. While she would have accepted Mill's celebration of "even the smallest help to the right side," it seems unlikely that she could have accepted Mill's prediction of the "not uncertain final victory of Good" (Mill 1874, 256).

The fact that there is nothing outside the human to give human life meaning is not a reason, on views such as Eliot's, to find it meaningless, unless one's view of meaning is still shaped by a theistic mould that one has only nominally abandoned. Here Benatar's position seems to share something with very common forms of sceptical belief, which deny powers to us by way of contrasting what we can do with the powers of some perfect and omnicompetent being. In fact, it can be exactly the imperfection of human powers and circumstances that provides the basis for a compelling idea of life: an idea of improvement[7] or an "ethical project" (Kitcher 2014) understood not as a sort of master plan but as an uncoordinated endeavour by agents who feel the pull of contribution.

Now a view such as Eliot's might have to be described as an aesthetic rather than a morality, even though, as she tries to convey in her novels, it generates a demanding morality, one of sympathetic mutual aid. If someone does not see that the inherently mixed and imperfect character of the human situation, when fully and imaginatively grasped, both offers a challenge and sustains a response to it, then they are simply beyond its persuasive reach. But to demand a straightforwardly moral reason for continuing human life is to make a category mistake. There can be moral ties, reciprocal or unilateral, among beings of various kinds: between existing humans, or between humans and other species, or perhaps natural objects. There can also be moral reasons for making anticipatory arrangements for beings that may come into existence – and those arrangements would, of course, have to figure very prominently in a view of life as necessary imperfection. But the idea of a moral reason to create another person simply falls outside the scope of what morality can do. "Coming into existence," as Benatar nicely understates the matter, "is an unusual case" (Benatar 2006, 53).

What makes it unusual is that we generally operate with a person-affecting view, according to which things are assessed as good or bad only in relation to the felt experience of someone. To say that existence is person-affecting implies that there is a proto-person somewhere for whom coming into existence can be said to be a benefit (or not). The absurdity is obvious. If we still believe that, somehow, ending procreation is wrong, though not a wrong to the non-procreated, then we may be tempted by a view such as Brian Barry's: ending the human race would be a "cosmic impertinence," he says (Barry 1989, 284). That seems to me to be equally unpersuasive. The cosmos, surely, wouldn't care about pertinence. What is at stake has to be human, not cosmic, and as far as I can see, it has to be based on a sense that we are engaged in a process that we didn't choose, but one with a reality that is presupposed by almost all the activities to which humans attach meaning.[8] It is a mistake to suppose that the project itself has to have an assignable meaning in the same way as the activities that presuppose it. It is like trying to stand outside and inside at the same time. Inside the project, we can make judgments that are internal to it, drawing on shared or implicit meanings, and even arriving, sometimes, at conclusions that we should be prepared to impose by compulsion. Standing outside the project, however, there are no such shared or implicit meanings, still less any prospect of arriving at compulsory oughts or ought-nots.

III

It remains, finally, to stress the importance of Benatar's argument even for those who question it. It obstructs unthinking reproduction and compels us to consider whether the creation of new life is something that can be thinkingly done. In making it so starkly clear that creating new life is a momentous act, perhaps the creation of a burden, it stands in the way of any simple-minded idea of a *right* to reproduce derived from the interests of potential parents. As features internal to morality, rights make sense as elements in the relations among existing beings, or among beings who exist and beings who will come to exist, but conferring (or imposing) existence on a being is not something that the idea of rights can accommodate. For reasons stated in the first section of this chapter, it may be doubted that we necessarily do wrong in procreating. It remains true that we may contingently do wrong, and, as noted above, duties of an anticipatory kind may fall to us for that reason. The following chapters turn to these duties.

Chapter 7

Coming to Terms with *Yoder*

Suppose, though, that – as seems overwhelmingly likely – the antinatalists' advice is rejected or (more likely) ignored, and children come to be born: what is owed to them? And, a distinct but strongly related question, who has authority to decide what they are owed? This chapter approaches these questions by way of a famous American case that has provoked far-reaching discussion.

In *Wisconsin v. Yoder et al.* (406 US 205 (1972)), the US Supreme Court ruled in favour of three respondents – two members of the Old Order Amish religious group and one of the Conservative Amish Mennonite Conference – who had been convicted and fined by the Supreme Court of Wisconsin for refusing to enrol their children in school after they had completed Grade 8. The state required attendance until the age of 16. Chief Justice Burger, writing for the court, accepted the respondents' claim that "as a result of their common heritage, Old Order Amish communities today are characterized by a fundamental belief that salvation requires life in a church community separate and apart from the world and worldly influence."[1] The Amish accept the need for elementary education because (they acknowledge) children must be able to read the Bible and must have basic skills for farm management and dealings with the outside world. But they reject high school education because "it tends to emphasize intellectual and scientific accomplishments, self-distinction, competitiveness, worldly life, and social life with other students."[2] Chief Justice Burger accepted the opinion of an expert witness, Dr John Hostetler, that "the modern high school is not equipped ... to impart the values promoted by Amish society" and that "compulsory high school attendance could not only result in great psychological harm to Amish children ... but would also ... ultimately result in the destruction of the Old Order Amish community as it exists in the United States today."[3] The court found, then, that in the specific case of the Old Order Amish, the state's compulsory school attendance law was in conflict with the free exercise of religion guaranteed by the First Amendment to the US Constitution.

This case and the court's judgment have, of course, been very widely discussed ever since because of "the stark and specific manner in which parental and public authority over children clashed" (Arneson and Shapiro 1996, 367); this poses several difficult questions. What does *free exercise* mean once we get beyond the uncontroversial matter of freedom of worship? Should the children concerned have been consulted, as Mr Justice Douglas urged in a written dissent? What weight should be given to a community's common desire to survive, as distinct from individuals' desire to exercise their religion? What interest do states have in the kind of education provided to children? This chapter mainly concerns itself with one (sufficiently large!) question: what right, or authority, or obligation, do parents have to transmit their beliefs or their way of life or culture to their children? If there is such a right (or whatever we are to call it), what justifies it, must it be strongly protected, can it be outweighed by other rights or purposes, and what, if anything, are we to make of the freedom of their children in all this?

I

The *locus classicus* for opposition to *Yoder* is a famous essay by Joel Feinberg (1980), "The Child's Right to an Open Future." Of particular importance to its argument is the class of rights, among those ascribable to children, that we may call *future autonomy* rights. These are rights that have the distinctive feature that although they will become operative only later, when children become mature enough to exercise them, they can be violated now – that is, by acts or omissions that preclude their successful later exercise (126). Conflicts may arise between these rights and parents' present autonomy rights, and courts sometimes resolve the conflict in favour of the children's future autonomy. In particular, respect for children's future autonomy may sometimes require postponing serious commitments until a child is in a position to make them, despite the fact that parents may strongly favour such commitments (129).

The basic value that drives Feinberg's argument is that of self-fulfilment. That value "involves as necessary elements the development of one's chief aptitudes into genuine talents in a life that gives them scope, an unfolding of all basic tendencies and inclinations" (ibid., 143). Autonomy in the sense of self-determination is ancillary to the value of self-fulfilment in that unless an individual's "tendencies and inclinations" have a shaping role in her development, they will be thwarted by it. Feinberg acknowledges that there may be a paradox in the idea of self-determination, in that it seems to imply that there is a self already in existence that acts in determining the self that one comes to have: there would appear to "an infinite series of prior selves, each the product of an earlier self" (147). But this paradox is resolved, Feinberg suggests, if we simply imagine a kind of dialectic in which the self is tentatively formed by a series of responses to inclinations, combined with learning from their results. There is no need for an all-or-nothing binary view that the self either exists or does not. We should think in terms of an "emerging identity," to quote another writer (Morgan 2005).

This is a sensible and realistic idea that recognizes that self-determination is not a matter of radical choosing that makes the agent wholly self-created, but a process in which unchosen dispositions and aptitudes play a role. It is their presence, in fact, that rescues self-formation from being a process that can be wholly controlled by an outside force – such as a parent – with the capacity to manipulate choices by exercising control over incentives. Although he does not himself make the parallel, Feinberg here echoes Locke's *Thoughts on Education*, which notes the crucial role played by a child's "temper" in the process of development; while Locke's much more famous "blank slate" metaphor suggests that external determination is all powerful, his other notion of temper (or temperament) gives full weight to the internal tendencies, however initially unformed, that govern eventual personality (Locke 1823, 204).

Sensible though this idea is, I do not think it justifies Feinberg's claim, earlier in his essay, that "children be permitted to reach maturity with as many open options, opportunities, and advantages as possible" (Feinberg 1980, 130). All the dialectical model calls for is that, in the process of maturing, a child needs those options that are necessary to the eliciting of his particular set of dispositions; and once he has matured, the model says nothing about the number of options that he should then have. Perhaps we should note here, though, that the qualification "as possible" offers interpretative room, and it may significantly lessen the distance between Feinberg and some critics whose objections to his view are described below: does it mean "as theoretically possible," or "as many as surrounding circumstances allow," or "as many as the parents can cope with," or "as many as the child can absorb," or "as many as engage the child's talents"? If, as suggested above, we adopt the last of these possible readings, perhaps we come as close as possible to an idea of reciprocity, modified as it must be in a context of unequal power and experience.

A different line is taken, however, in another critique of *Yoder*, by Richard Arneson and Ian Shapiro (1996); they reject the maximum-options view, in part because it skews the issue between defenders and critics of the case. For critics, the wider world offers many options (chartered accountant, beautician, Formula One driver), while the Amish lifestyle offers only one; however, for the Amish and their defenders, the wider world's supposed options are merely variants of worldliness (accountant? beautician? race-car driver? Who cares?) and so comprise one bad option rather than many attractive ones – an important point that we shall return to later. Arneson and Shapiro advance a view of autonomy according to which critical reflective capacity, rather than merely a variety of options, is essential. "The autonomous person is ... one who is capable of standing back from her values and engaging in critical reflection about them and altering her values to align them with the results of that critical reflection" (ibid., 393).

Not all their discussion is relevant here, for its main thrust concerns the importance of secondary education for democracy; it is a matter of the requirements of a certain kind of political society, or perhaps of the rights of its other citizens, rather than of the rights of the children themselves. (The Amish do not take part in democratic politics, of course, but Arneson and Shapiro point out that numbers of Amish children leave the community [20 per cent is often cited], and all potentially might, so that the larger society still has some stake in the kind of education that they receive. The authors' point is certainly reinforced if one shares Brian Barry's worried demographic projections [Barry 2001, 178].) But the reflective critical capacity that they stress is also important, they claim, for children themselves, not just for the wider society. Here they distinguish between a view of autonomy that regards it as intrinsically important, in the sense that the fact of something's being chosen adds to its value, and an instrumental view. They reject the intrinsic account on the grounds that it amounts to a sectarian view that simply challenges the rival view – held, for example, by the Amish, among others – that the right way to live is not right (or somehow more right) because it is chosen, but because it is, simply, right. What, though, of the instrumental justification of autonomy?

"The idea is simply that what we now regard as good might not be good in fact, and that to improve the quality of our beliefs we must think for ourselves" (Arneson and Shapiro 1996, 399). For people do not simply want a good life that expresses ideas that they currently have, "they want to lead a life that truly is valuable and worthy" (ibid.) and so must have the means to assess whether it is. Arneson and Shapiro regard this view as less prejudicial to the Amish case than a view that celebrates choice as part of the good life or even sees being chosen as something that adds to the goodness of a life. Autonomy becomes no more than a means of increasing the likelihood that the life chosen – worldly or traditional – is good for the person in question.

While this is, as claimed, less prejudicial to the Amish case than other possible views, it falls far short of recognizing its full force. For one thing, it seems excessively cognitive in its focus. Suppose the way to the good is not through assessing reasons, but through habituation to a way of life that embodies piety and deference? Suppose there are no reasons for the good life that speak to or persuade the person who has not been habituated, so that once we accept the sovereignty of reason, the game is over? Perhaps, as Pascal argued, the way to come to believe in God is to go to church, so that belief comes after practice, not before. For another thing, the argument appears to suppose that the critical mind can be contained, as it were, so that it speaks to us only occasionally, perhaps only once in a lifetime, even, at a crucial point of commitment. "At maturity the individual will choose a way of life autonomously or nonautonomously" (ibid., 401), so that in permitting children to acquire critical reflective skills, parents would simply be enabling them to choose the favoured way of life in an autonomous manner. But suppose it is believed, not implausibly, that once the genie is out of the bottle, it is not easily put back in? That, having learned to be critical, one remains critical?

It is, I think, more difficult to accept the limitations of a way of life, especially a strict one, the more completely one has absorbed the lesson that one could be doing something else – something else, moreover, for which good reasons could be given. Suppose, moreover, the deep sense that there is one right way to live is not just something that could lead people to adopt it in the first place, but actually a *part* of what makes it good? Suppose the idea of choice, as one witness testified at trial, "makes you restless, wanting to leap and jump and not knowing where you will land" (quoted in ibid., 394)? The Amish parents would rightly, from their point of view, see no significant difference between the intrinsic and the instrumental valuing of autonomy.

Yoder also has its supporters, who side with the respondents without always accepting the court's specific line of reasoning. One line of support rests on a case for *parental deference*. It is not contentious that states should exercise restraint in proposing to intervene in family life, coercion being a blunt instrument, but the issue is about where the line needs to be drawn. One kind of view asserts that parents have authority over their children on the basis of their own needs or interests, which, of course, sets up potential conflicts between parents' interests and children's. The court's reliance on the *Yoder* parents' free-exercise rights is clearly open to this objection, to the extent that it would seem to make the children's own rights, whatever we take them to be, simply subordinate to the exercise of a constitutional right enjoyed by their parents. But a principle of state deference to parental decisions need not be based on parental rights: it can be based, rather, on the needs of children themselves.

The key here is the claim that "the effort to provide a consistent moral and religious environment for a child represents an important way of building the psychological and cognitive resources which the child will need to choose and live a good life as an adult" (Burtt 1996, 425). Children need "a moral and sentimental education" (428) as a basis for developing their powers of appreciation and evaluation. This would be disrupted – at least before a certain age is reached – if a child received radically conflicting messages from different sources; and the social and psychological reality is that the education is best provided by "small social units distinguished by intense emotional attachments: families" (ibid.). The open future view, in demanding that children be exposed to an array of alternatives, ignores the basic facts about moral development.

Another critic, Claudia Mills (2003), questions the very coherence of the open future thesis as well as the desirability of trying to adopt it. It is impossible, first, to count up the number of options available without specifying a point of view from which options can be assessed as meaningful or not – a point that was acknowledged by Arneson and Shapiro. Told that they are closing off career options for their children by withdrawing them from school, the Amish parents could reply that the supposed options are all, from their point of view, simply variants of one way of life – worldliness – and that they *are* offering their children options – "to be a corn farmer, or a soybean farmer, or a fruit farmer, or to work in various support occupations, such as blacksmith or leather worker" (ibid., 500–1). Second, even if we could somehow quantify options, "the inescapable finitude of life … means that it is simply impossible to keep our options open: they close every day, as we make choices to spend our time this way rather than that, to pursue *x* rather than *y*" (499–500).

As for the desirability of exposing children to multiple options, it is a recipe for superficiality, conveying a smorgasbord view of life. A young child who is exposed in an utterly open-minded way to every type of religion will grow up to have no religion at all, and so the program of exposure hardly qualifies as "neutral" (502).[4] One can understand a religion not by learning and judging its creeds, but by experiencing it as embedded in a community (503). So Mills's view would come to the aid of the "too cognitive" complaint made above: we can't see religions (or any deep commitments) simply as propositions that can be discursively advanced and then accepted or rejected on their own merits; they have to be understood and respected in terms of belonging.[5]

II

Assessing this debate depends in part on which of the two readings of Feinberg we adopt – the maximum-options reading that his words permit or the relevant-options reading that common sense suggests. In this debate, there are also some issues that while far from being easy to resolve, are empirical in nature. One is about whether two years of high school really do make a (positive) difference to a child's capacity to be part of the larger society (Burtt 1996, 430). The *Yoder* parents clearly believed that they *would* make a (negative) difference in their children's aptness to be part of Amish society, a claim that, as far as I know, was not challenged. But it is certainly open to question whether missing two years of school either makes a decisive difference or cannot more or less readily be made up at a later date, as is quite often done. Related to this is Claudia Mills's point that doors are only rarely closed forever, they are simply made more or less difficult to open; and all upbringings whatsoever, real or imaginable, make doors more or less difficult to open.

Another issue is the question of the appropriate age for children to be made aware that there are alternatives to their own parents' beliefs or way of life, for one could well believe that this was essential for teenagers, but confusing for preschoolers (Morgan 2005, 384–5; Mills 2003,

504), a point that has been well made in relation to the comparative religions course made compulsory in 2012 in Quebec (Braley 2011). These sorts of issues point to a middle ground that could very usefully be explored. But there is a core conceptual issue that is not easily resolved, an issue about measuring the significance of choice. It is raised particularly well by Mills's paper, which, as we have seen, emphatically states that there is no context-independent standpoint from which we can say that the meaningful opportunities offered by the wider society are greater than the opportunities offered by Amish society itself.

An interestingly parallel claim is made by Robert Sparrow (2005) in a provocative paper on the concerns of (some) deaf people about the steps that need to be taken to preserve their own culture (generally capitalized [*Deaf*] when referred to by its advocates). Here the issue is not that of withdrawing children from school, but denying them treatment that if provided at a very young age, could enable them to hear and so to participate fully in hearing society. The issue is complicated by the imperfections of current technology, which create a risk that a child could end up in a limbo between hearing and Deaf society, an outcome that no one would desire. Setting that aside, and assuming a (not inconceivable) near-perfect technology, the issue is, once again, about evaluating ranges of opportunities. Hearing people naturally assume that deafness is a loss, and they can point to many things that hearing people can do that deaf people cannot. But advocates of Deaf culture point out, in reply, that deaf people can do and experience things that hearing people cannot. To describe deafness as a disability is therefore to be ignorant of its benefits – the enhanced power of other senses, the ability to work undistractedly in noisy environments, and (perhaps above all) the experience of using a language that communicates in ideographic rather than alphabetic ways. It is also to neglect the affirmative importance, to a community, of a history of achievements that is strongly parallel to the achievements of other oppressed groups, such as women and racial minorities.

Sparrow contrasts liberal and communitarian views of the matter. On the former view, he maintains, "We should seek to ensure that the child grows up in the culture that offers the most opportunities," and clearly Deaf culture, "because of its smaller size … is unlikely to offer the same range of opportunities as the spoken language culture" (Sparrow 2005, 145). But from the point of view of a member of the Deaf community, one "may feel that it is more important to participate in Deaf culture than to communicate with those outside it. More fundamentally, because [the

Deaf] do not identify with the way of life of another culture, they may not value opportunities that exist within it" (146), and indeed, they may believe that "Deaf culture offers a wider range of valuable opportunities than membership of a hearing culture" (147). This calls for several critical comments.

First, it is surely right to insist that we cannot measure real opportunities by the number available, for anyone would rather have two opportunities, both of which they valued, rather than three (or ten) that they were indifferent to. The number of opportunities can, in fact, increase to the point that it becomes inimical to freedom if it passes the number that we can absorb and evaluate (Schwartz 2004). But it is mistaken to attribute to liberalism the view that freedom is measured by the number of choices, the more the better. We may reasonably take the more persuasive of Joel Feinberg's claims as being representative here. As we have seen, it does not advocate multiplying choices, only the availability of those choices that one needs to express and explore one's dispositions and talents. Someone who is fitted by nature to be the world's best sitar player may need only one opportunity (to study with the likes of Ravi Shankar); other people may need more to find themselves. So while it is true that freedom isn't measured by the number of opportunities, one cannot rely on that point to justify restricting their number, for while no one needs every opportunity, we don't know ahead of time which ones we will need.

Second, the opportunities that members of Deaf culture rightly treasure are opportunities that they have come to appreciate because of their personal histories as deaf people forging a cultural place in hearing society. They may reasonably predict that, prospectively, a child who is inducted into their culture will likewise come to appreciate it. But one's own history gives one no authority to plan another person's as yet unwritten future for them because one doesn't know what is as yet unknown – that is, the other person's potential needs and responses to the world. Certain kinds of decisions made for children foreclose the experimental and tentative process that makes parental authority justifiable, the process of offering and persisting or drawing back in light of a child's dispositions and aptitudes. Parents may hopefully enrol a child in violin lessons, thus limiting her free time and definitely steering her in a particular direction, but "constant resistance to practicing, no improvement in performance competence, or even conflict with other important activities or goals" (Morgan 2005, 372) would be compelling reasons for the parents to reconsider. Decisions that are irreversible or, if no decisions are irreversible, tend towards irreversibility may escape this normal model of parental authority. And decisions that are intended to be irreversible certainly do.

Third, if indeed it is true that there is no context-independent way to adjudicate between communitarian claims, one community valuing classical music, the other the distinctively communicative experience of signing, then, of course, we need some other way to decide. We might first think of the economic benefits to the child of being able to hear, a consideration that should weigh with parents who do not discount it altogether – and there is no reason to suppose that they are more willing to discount it than anyone else is. We might think of the greater capacity of a hearing person to adapt to social change. We might think of the cost to the wider society of maintaining accommodations for deaf people. What could be set on the other side of the balance? Two things come to mind: parent-child intimacy and the preservation of a community. Both have indecisive weight.

That one wants to enjoy a unique and uniquely intimate kind of relationship with one's children is among the most important reasons for having children at all (Brighouse and Swift 2006). The standard idea of intimacy, however, implies accepting the other for who he or she is and thereby excludes the very notion of control. "I love you as you are – now change!" is a joke. Outside the parent-child relation, there are no cases in which the desire to be intimate confers a power of control (Hannan and Vernon 2008). Of course, one should be willing to accept that the case of children is different, children being so far somewhat unformed, but surely the differences in this regard indicate that dictation is no better, the unformed potential of children suggesting that imaginative exploration of their needs is what is really called for. This is consistent with the view that parents owe it to their children to provide them with a "consistent moral environment" (Burtt 1996, 425), unless, of course, that environment is one that forbids imagination; and whether such an environment could lead to intimacy rather than conformity is certainly questionable, to say the least.

What weight can be given to parents' desire that their community and its way of life should survive them? Here there is a parting of the ways between an individualist model, which is fully consistent with conferring special rights on members of minority groups as a way of respecting their equality, and a communitarian model, which attaches value directly to the survival of a community as such. In his famous essay on "The Politics of Recognition," Charles Taylor rightly focuses on this as the fault line between liberals, such as Will Kymlicka, who believe that the entitlements of (some) groups can be justified in terms of their members' interests, and more forthrightly communitarian approaches, which present the survival of communities as a good (Taylor 1994, 40–1n16).

The place of children in this disagreement is pivotal and forces a decision. All that can be said here, in the face of such a large and basic question, is that the case for community survival would have to be enormously compelling if it required compromising the right of children to understand the world that they live in. Restricting their linguistic choices (as in the case of Quebec schooling laws) is one thing, for children must, after all, be brought up in one (primary) language or another. But if a community can survive only by deciding in advance not only how its children should view the world but also what resources they should have in arriving at a view of the world, it is essentially surviving by using its children as means.

III

The confrontation between communitarian and certain liberal views often gives the debate an epistemic turn, which may get in the way of an appropriately moral focus. On a strong communitarian view, there is no standing outside a framework of belief: if you are in it, you understand; if not, you can't. The view is much like Church Father Tertullian's claim that Christianity has no critics – if you are not a Christian, you don't know what Christianity is, while if you're a Christian, you don't criticize it. Arneson and Shapiro, however, believe in the possibility of a critical discourse in which the merits of alternatives can be rationally presented and evaluated, and so demand an education that will equip children to take part in it. This disagreement is a very fundamental one. But do we have to resolve it, or even take sides in it, to arrive at a sound view of what equality requires in the case of children?

One way to explore this point is provided by an enlightening discussion by J. Morgan, who addresses the relation and possible tension between parents' religious convictions and the preservation of their children's open future. The solution, Morgan believes, lies in the epistemology of belief. He presents a most useful digest of six views of the basis of religious belief, two of which – antipathy to religion, and pure subjectivism – he sets aside as irrelevant to a question that does not arise for those who despise religion or for those who believe its claims are groundless. That leaves four: (1) exclusivism – one's own faith is the sole means to salvation; (2) inclusivism – other faiths are not false but imperfect and partial; (3) pluralism – various traditions "refract" the truth, as it were, in different ways; (4) henofideism – the view that one should respect other faiths because it is always possible that one is wrong (Morgan 2005, 376–7).

Morgan rejects (1) and (2) as bases for respecting a child's open future. With regard to (1), exclusivism, "One cannot hold one's own religious beliefs are the single acceptable approach to the divine, but also hold that other faiths are candidates for belief" (ibid., 377). The view takes no account of the fact that how we perceive the real is mediated by our conceptual starting points. As for (2), inclusivism, it is "softer" (379), but it admits others only demeaningly, as second-class citizens. "This offers the inclusivist believer the opportunity for a sense of superiority regarding members of other faiths" (379). What of (3), pluralism, which Morgan takes more seriously, referring to the work of the theologian John Hick? Pluralism, in this context, is the view that "the diverse religions are historically and socially constructed frameworks in which people conceptualize, understand and appreciate their relation to the divine" (ibid., 380). Morgan quotes what may seem to be a sufficiently devastating objection – that to know whether pluralism was true, one would have to know already what the divine is – but he places the main weight of his objection on the simple and factually true consideration that many religious believers reject it.

That leaves (4), the less familiar category of henofideism, perhaps close enough to what is generally called fallibilism. The example offered is that of a scientist who says to himself, "I know that theory X is true, even though I also know that I might be wrong about X" (ibid., 382–3). I think this position makes perfect sense as long as we take the first occurrence of the word *know* in that sentence to mean something like "I have so far unrefuted grounds for believing." The upshot is that Morgan maintains that parents may rightfully transmit their beliefs to their children if they do so in this fallibilist spirit and if, in doing so in this spirit, they respect their children's right to an open future.

Now one objection that comes to mind is that the analogy with scientific belief neglects the fact that science, whether its practice is adequately captured by the imperatives of demonstration, is a field in which there are standards of demonstration that are uncontested, in a way for which it is hard to find a parallel in the case of religious belief. The points of departure (for most beliefs) go very far back, and it is hard to know what would count as disconfirmation. What would show that Christ was *not* born of a virgin or that no miracles occurred two thousand years ago? The second and far more important objection is that whatever obscure and remote possibility of disconfirmation there, or whether believers even acknowledge it, has no necessary connection at all with their attitudes to people with other faiths. This point is surely made by the history of the idea of toleration: what we should refrain from doing to those who disagree, toleration theorists argued, arises from our civic relation to them and not from any thought that they might, after all, somehow be shown (how?) to be right.

But the same objection applies even if, as Morgan urges, we go beyond mere toleration to active respect and engagement (ibid., 378). Engagement is "a matter of meeting others as persons, of acknowledging them as individuals with points of view that reflect their diverse cultures, families and experiences" (ibid.). We can accomplish this without any particular epistemic starting point. We need only recognize some very important facts. We need to recognize that "everyone is orthodox in their own eyes," as Locke put it (Locke 2010, 3), and that others – whether right or wrong is beside the point – have experiences of conviction and commitment that are very much like our own. That they arrive at them from mistaken starting points could, in fact, reinforce our sense of what, as fellow humans, they share with us. Even the misguided are our fellows. Like us, they believe that their traditions are rich containers of moral guidance, and, like us, they believe them to be unique.

To revert, for a moment, to Locke and the notion of "tempers": that notion figured, it was briefly noted above, in his discussion of education and in support of his view that children have temperaments that upbringing must take as given. The same notion figures importantly, on a macro-level, in Locke's defence of toleration. The different "tempers" of people enter into their ideas of what worship and godliness require, and they naturally want to associate themselves in worship and in life with people who have the same deeply intuitive ideas of what is fitting. Locke writes, Why should I be persecuted "because I have come to *feel* that some people are not sufficiently serious, while others are just too strait-laced for me to be *happy* to travel in their company?" (Locke 2010, 18; emphasis added).

Feeling, happiness – these terms refer to deeply intuitive ideas about divinity and what kind of deeply personal response it calls for, ideas that were reflected in the profoundly different aesthetics of worship that were advanced (and fought over) in Locke's century. What toleration requires is not that we understand these intuitions when they differ greatly from ours, or even that we find them reasonable, or even that, from our point of view, we can appreciate their significance, but simply that we recognize that others intuit differently. The fact is enough. The fact that others are different doesn't require us to re-evaluate our own preferences, although perhaps it may; it doesn't have to lead us to any sort of relativist or sceptical position; it doesn't require us to stage some sort of contest from which winners and losers will emerge. The underlying value is civic equality. Shared citizenship makes important demands on how we are to adjust our behaviour in relation to others' interests. But it doesn't require us to adjust our beliefs in relation to others' disagreement with them.

So what children have to come to know is a fact: that others have traditions that contain a profound meaning for them. We should leave it at that. At some point, our children will have to arrive at a view about how it is that sincere beliefs conflict, and we have to leave it to them to figure out this deep puzzle. If they arrive at one of the six solutions that Morgan lists, or if (more likely) some arrive at some and others at others, it isn't a result that we should seek to foreclose. If parents try to foreclose it by taking steps to prevent the question from being asked, they become essentially tyrannical. It is not enough to object that all responsible parents take steps to shield children from what they take to be bad choices (Burtt 1996), and that Amish parents simply want to protect their children from exposure to a corrupt world, just as mainstream parents want to protect their children from pornography and recreational drugs. This parallel works, clearly, only for people who are prepared to classify pornography and recreational drugs as essential parts of the good life. Those who worry about the limits imposed by closed, traditional cultures are thinking, rather, of the achievements of scientists and artists, which deepen our understanding of natural and human reality.

Nor is it enough to rely on the unwanted empirical effects of the society around – on the claim that it's all right to deprive people of knowledge because we know they'll learn it in some other way, there being "plenty of opportunity for exposure" (Burtt 1996, 426; also Kukathas 1992, 124–30). How is this different from saying that we don't have to feed our children because, if we don't, the neighbours will do it? If someone has a need, and if we are her provider, we have to provide what she needs or ensure that someone else does so. Moreover, what children will be exposed to by inescapable accidents are not the best but simply the most obtrusive features of the wider culture. One can be accidentally exposed to reality TV, but not to the novels of George Eliot, by walking past a Future Shop window. Perhaps it is true that the Branch Davidians at Waco watched television (Burtt 1996, 426), but what were they watching? Probably not PBS documentaries or Masterpiece Theatre reruns. If it is somehow important that, parental objections notwithstanding, children will get some sense of the world outside their family, then it is all the more important that they should get an accurate sense of what it offers, rather than a sense that is overwhelmingly likely to be governed by commercial imperatives. Traditionally minded parents surely would not want their children's view of their own way of life to be conveyed by way of ignorant mainstream misrepresentations of it; and if they value their children's genuine endorsement of their way of life, then they should not effectively confine their exposure to the mainstream to its most superficial expressions.

IV

A final set of issues concerns the possibility that how parents relate to their children should have an unmediated connection to the ideals of a liberal society: that is, rather than thinking (as was implied by most of the above discussion) that parenting may need only to set the table for a particular ideal of adult life, perhaps it must itself *embody* that ideal. This view is put forward forcefully in a book by Matthew Clayton (2006). The ideal that he takes to define political relations among adults is that of public reason. Briefly stated, this ideal is one that is thought to be required in situations that have certain features, features commonly associated with the state, but that in Clayton's view characterize the family too. Like the political relationship, children's relationship to their parents is non-voluntary (not chosen, hard to leave). Children, like subjects of a state, are subject to coercion. And the family, like the basic institutions of a polity, has a profound influence on its members (ibid., 93). If so, then by parallel argument, it would seem to follow that how parents treat their children should be subject to the same stringent constraints that apply to political relations – those of public reason. What are those constraints? Here he quotes from Rawls's *Political Liberalism* (1993).

> Our exercise of political power is fully proper only when it is exercised in accordance with a constitution the essentials of which all citizens as free

> and equal may reasonably be expected to endorse in light of principles and ideals acceptable to their common human reason. (quoted in Clayton 2006, 93)

Now it is clear from the outset that objections or at least queries are going to arise from the fact that young children do not have adult reason (the very fact that justifies the parental role itself). Clayton's solution is to claim that what parents do to children, in light of their undeveloped reason, must pass the test of future consent: that is, when they reflect on what has been done to them, they must believe that it is consistent with their having been recognized as free and equal persons, even though, at the time when it was done, their freedom and equality were temporarily though necessarily limited by their capacity.

To this claim, an initial objection is that the basic reasons for the public-reason constraint that apply in the case of adults have less force, or perhaps even no force, in the case of children. The constraint has compelling force in light, especially, of the coercion condition. If we think of political society as an arrangement among equals, then its coercive element is inherently problematic: for A to coerce B is surely to deny B's equal status in a very practical way. We can approximate equality only if A can justify the requirements coercively imposed on B in light of B's own exercise of reasoning powers. If the requirements can't be justified in that way, then they amount to a kind of insult to B. Behind that view stands a very long tradition, according to which it isn't the extent of restriction on one's freedom that matters, but the reasons that can be given for it. Locke's examples, in the *Letter Concerning Toleration*, are still as good as any. To forbid some group to carry out its rites on the grounds that the state or the public finds it offensive is objectionable and insulting to the group in question; to forbid the same rites on the basis of some important public interest is not. And the distinction rests on the fact that the group in question is itself part of the public, so that its own interests are included in the public interest and so can reasonably be held to be included in what this interest requires, so that the requirements are not, as it were, merely external to them.

But does this argument come to bear only in cases in which some person or persons have already formed some relevant view, so that we have to exercise a public-reason constraint when we propose to set their view aside? Does it apply in the case of young children, when they have as yet arrived at no view about the matter at hand?[6] When they have not as yet arrived at the view that the nature of God is triune, for example, or that the sacrament brings about the transubstantiation of bread into flesh or wine into blood? Where is the insult, of the kind that occurs when someone's already formed belief is publicly condemned and stigmatized? Locke believed that strong constraints applied to those who proposed to use state power to "work a change" in people's opinions, on the grounds that such a proposal is an affront to civic equality; but his position has little, if anything, to say about producing beliefs in the first place, as opposed to changing beliefs that have already been formed and endorsed.

Exactly this question has been raised in response to the public-reason view: how can it be an affront to autonomy to impose something on beings that (as yet) have no autonomy? In reply, Clayton (2012) adduces examples of cases involving (hypothetical) surgery on adults who, being anaesthetized at the time, cannot exercise autonomy, and he points out that we would consider them affronted: as in the case, for example, of someone undergoing a skin graft and whose surgeon takes the opportunity, unbidden, to carry out cosmetic surgery too. Such examples, one might feel, carry weight because the patient's suspension of autonomy is only temporary and there would be no difficulty consulting them and securing consent before conducting a second, cosmetic operation. It would just cost more. In the case of children, of course, the issue arises just because parents necessarily make some decisions in advance of autonomous consent being possible: so the objection is not fully met. But the important requirement, in the public-reason view, is that parents must be constrained by considerations about what could win a child's future consent, when mature.

Here, though, I am not sure which of two possible lines of reasoning to apply. On one view – arising from the fact that liberal societies contain many possible and reasonable ways of life – there is a risk that the way of life inculcated by a parent may not be the one that a child eventually endorses. The parent might, as it were, get it wrong, by failing to predict the child's eventual psychological and intellectual development. On that view, as it stands, it would seem to be a good outcome in those cases in which parents happened through luck or judgment to get it right. But there is a second and much more demanding idea in play, that of the value of independence itself, and on that view, it is an affront to impose beliefs on a child even if he comes eventually to endorse them.

Of these two views, the former seems too weak. Does it, as it would seem – being outcome-based – contain the worrying implication that the inculcation of belief ceases to be objectionable if it is so thorough and relentless that a child eventually has no option but to endorse it? An alternative reading, however, is that even in cases in which the parents get it right, they do wrong by imposing a risk, since obviously they cannot know in advance whether they have got it right or not, and that imposing a risk is wrong even if it happens to pay off. (By analogy, on this view, even if the involuntary cosmetic-surgery patient is, as it happens, happy with his new nose, the surgery wronged him.) Interpreted in this way, the view converges with the much stronger independence argument, which would tell us that even in cases in which children come to endorse their parents' way of life wholeheartedly, their parents have still done wrong by adopting a policy of inherently illegitimate domination.

If the two arguments converge in this way, it is not important here to decide between them. What is important is to arrive at a view of what parents may do in advance of their children's autonomously given consent – for obviously, they must do some things. They make their children aware, or don't make them aware, that religion is thought to have a place in life; they introduce them, or don't introduce them, to the idea that eating other animals is a possible option; they convey, or don't convey, that material comfort is a value; and so on. The negative option is no less potentially influential, in all such cases, than the positive one. No one is unaware of these obvious facts, and Clayton's argument offers at least two important responses. One is that there must be no parental *intention* to pre-empt future autonomous choices. This view is supported by a parallel with the history of political thought, in which it is a familiar claim that the intention to disadvantage is illegitimate, even though equivalent but unintentional disadvantages may have to be borne as a regrettable cost of coexistence (Clayton 2006, 110).

Another response is that there are ways for parents to convey their views to children that, while powerfully influential, avoid being coercive. An attractive picture is offered of parents who convey their beliefs to their children in an unthreatening and (in the cultural sense) liberal way (ibid., 210–1). This is important to Clayton's argument because it enables him to meet an objection drawn from within the idea of public reason itself: we would want children to be acculturated, not because of an interest that their parents may have in transmitting their beliefs, but because receiving some initial set of values is a necessary condition of becoming a person who is eventually capable of independent evaluation. Children can indeed receive such a set of values, is Clayton's response; but there are constraints on their mode of imposition.

The best way to make sense of these two requirements, I believe, is on the basis of a commitment to preserve the future independence of children, rather than on the basis of respecting an autonomy that they do not yet enjoy. The three grounds for the public-reason constraint (non-voluntariness, coercion, pervasive influence) could be taken to apply, it has been pointed out, to the case of pets (Cameron 2012). If they apply to children but not to pets, then surely it is, for the most part, because children have autonomous futures that pets don't have; or perhaps it would be more precise to say that it is because their present limited autonomy is decisive, not for its relative present magnitude, but as both a basis and a token of future potential; or at least in good part for the latter reason. And to the extent that this is so, then autonomy as an eventual achievement – a goal to be aimed at – may tend to overshadow respect for autonomy in the parental here and now.

The practical conclusions arising from this line of thinking – if it is persuasive – may seem unexcitingly pacific: if the strong public-reason argument can accommodate constrained socialization, and communitarians can accept constraints of reasonableness (see above), then we may seem to have reached a bland plateau. But there is an important fault line sitting only a little below the surface, a fault line between two conceptions of family life and its importance. We can conceive of the family as an entity that produces future citizens and as being important for that reason: we want children to learn the right lessons about equality and justice. This is basically the focus of Rawls's concern, and naturally, it focuses on the issue of gender and the way in which the familial division of labour impacts equal opportunity in the larger political sphere (Clayton 2006, 100–1). But this (Clayton complains) "fails to engage" (101) with the important respects in which the family is not (or only) an organ that affects the polity but, in important ways, is itself *like* the polity – and, hence, itself, like the polity, subject to public-reason constraints. So here there is a basically important issue about whether the family should be seen not only as causally but also (and more strongly) as conceptually related to the polity itself.

It is fairly clear from Rawls's own account that the family counts as part of the "basic structure" for causal rather than conceptual reasons: it is "the *basis of* the orderly production and reproduction of society and its culture" (Rawls 1999, 157; emphasis added). If there is a reason why it should be seen in this way, rather than as itself a small polity internally regulated by justice, it must lie in Rawls's view that each part of the basic structure may influence the rest (161), so that causal relations are to be seen as more salient than analogical ones. If that is so, then we need to take account of the fact that the roles assigned in one part of the structure may constrain or modify what may happen in other parts, even at the expense of maintaining congruence among the parts. Justice assigns to citizens rights and powers that have an impact on what happens in private domains – in particular, by protecting their decisions about the values that should shape their lives; and it is inconceivable that those values would not lead to a variety of views about how family life should be conducted. Some of these will cohere with, others will clash with, the public-reason model of political life.

This should not be taken to mean that the parental role is unconstrained. On the contrary, an understanding of the parental role may be *more* constraining, in some ways, than the public-reason model requires, particularly to the extent that that model forbids only the *intentional* induction of children into ways of life, in the same way that (as noted above) it allows state action to have (objectively) differential effects on ways of life, provided only that the policies are not (intentionally) discriminatory. While this may be a good principle of political morality, surely more should be expected of parents, in this regard, in the family context. Parents would fail in their role if, for example, they conveyed to their children – simply by force of example, with no intention of doing so – that only material success counted in life; or if, again with no intention of doing so, they allowed their children to acquire, without challenging it, some wholly false view of members of some other social group, with whom in future their children would have to interact. A view that places such stress on limiting intentional behaviour, while (regretfully) accepting unintended side effects, seems unsuited to the familial context, in which spin-off effects are notoriously endemic. Of course, this criticism rests on there being an available and attractive view of what the parental role is, and that has not been developed here; but perhaps enough has been said above to indicate what its outline would be. Full reciprocity may not be in place, but full responsiveness surely is, if tyranny over the future is to be avoided.

Chapter 8

Only Egalitarians May Have Children

Moral and political philosophers, following J.S. Mill (1972, 173-5), have discussed the issue of parental personal competence, even broaching the idea that parenting, like other profoundly other-regarding acts, should be subject to licensing (LaFollette 1980, 2010). But – apart from the importantly related issue of the appropriate political education to be provided to children (Clayton 2006, chap. 4) – they have not attended to the idea that becoming a parent may require *political* competence. This chapter argues that giving birth to a child requires that one give support to at least minimally egalitarian social policies. Intending parents who do not already support such policies must do so to avoid complicity in contributing to demographic changes that profoundly affect children's lives.

No doubt many people are inclined to think that parents ought to support *maximally* good policies, whatever these are taken to be, on the grounds that doing so would make the world a better place for their children. This, right or wrong, is not the approach taken here, and I believe it is open to criticism on two important counts. First, it is open to the telling criticisms that have been made of the idea of "procreative beneficence," understood as the view that parents wrong their children if they fail to provide them with the best possible life (Overall 2012, chap. 7). That view is generally criticized in the context of transmitting genetic impairments, but the criticisms would also apply in the case of parents' supposed political impairment – that is, their failure to support whatever the best possible kind of political environment is taken to be. Second, the view entails a violation of parents' freedom in the name of values that the parents in question may very well not accept.

The view defended here is objectionable in neither of those ways. First, it does not begin with a political ideal imported from outside the context of parent-child relations. Second, it attributes liability to parents not on the basis of political views that they may or may not hold, but on the basis of the implications of their very own act, that of procreation itself.

The empirical basis for this chapter's argument is provided by readily available facts about the pervasively negative effects of demographic cohort size. By procreating, parents expose their child to these effects, without, of course, being able by their own personal agency to determine the size of the cohort. They have an obligation, then, to exercise political agency in support of policies that fairly distribute the burdens of bad demographic luck by virtue of their contributing to burdens that they cannot avert by their own personal agency.

This discussion obviously assumes that an answer can be found to a critical view recently advanced by anti-natalist moral philosophers, who hold that it is morally impermissible, in general, to impose on children an unasked-for burden, that of existence (Benatar 2006; Shiffrin 1999; see discussion in Overall 2012, chap. 6). This chapter does not engage in this debate but argues, rather, that if it is permissible for anyone at all to have children, it is permissible only for parents who lend their support[1] to a set of policies that promote equality in certain respects; these are set out below.

The first two sections of this chapter will seek to show that the size of a child's age cohort is enormously consequential for her or his well-being. Since parents have a duty to protect their children from an injustice to which they foreseeably contribute, even in unforeseeable ways, they have a duty of a political kind to support measures that even out the burdens of intergenerational disparity, in ways that section III briefly sketches. Sections IV and V entertain and seek to meet objections to the argument of this chapter, objections based on the critiques of luck egalitarianism and procreative beneficence, respectively.

I

Enormous inequalities arise from the fact that age cohorts differ very significantly in size. Suppose there is an age cohort that is much larger than the cohort that preceded or followed it, as is not at all unusual. Call it cohort B. Since it is much more numerous than cohort A, which preceded it, the cost of supporting cohort A in its old age is relatively light, not only because cohort A is small but also because the cost is shared among a relatively large group. For cohort C, however, the position is exactly reversed: not only does it have to support a relatively larger group, but the cost of doing so is allocated to a relatively small one. Let us say that in cohort B's case, each person had to support 0.3 of an elderly person in cohort A, while in cohort C's case, each person has to support 0.6 of an elderly person in cohort B by virtue of the beneficiaries being more numerous and the contributors fewer. The obligation would thus be doubled, an obvious unfairness. We could, of course, remove it by halving the resources made available to the now elderly members of cohort B, but that would also be unfair since they will not unreasonably have assumed that they, in turn, would be supported with the same level of resources that they had provided (albeit at a much lower per-person cost) to cohort A, and it would be wrong to avert the injustice to C at the cost of treating B unjustly.

This situation apparently exists in North America and Western Europe, and doubtless elsewhere, at the present time. A large post-1945 cohort is now passing into its retirement years, and a smaller cohort born in the 1960s (and later) will bear some of the costs of those years – costs greater than the baby-boom generation ever had to cover in support of the generation that preceded it. The demographic figures are not all that far off the notional figures stated in the paragraph above – a small cohort has to support a large cohort to an extent that its own support has never demanded of anyone else. This is clearly an injustice if we conceive of justice in terms of the fair allocation of benefits and burdens. One generation is burdened with charges from which it never benefited; and there is no guarantee that it will benefit from a similar asymmetry in relation to the cohort that follows it. Indeed, if the habitual trends repeat themselves, the small generation will be followed by a larger one, and members of that larger cohort will therefore carry a lighter burden than was borne by the smaller cohort that preceded it. There may well be a causal mechanism (of a Malthusian kind) that makes this demographic ebb and flow very likely to occur.

Now in some countries, as it happens, national pension plans seek to smooth out these intergenerational disparities, and I will come to those later as an example of the kind of response that the issue raised in this chapter would require. But let us for the moment suppose, as a simplifying assumption, that all or most of the costs of a relatively large preceding cohort are borne from general revenue raised from a relatively small succeeding cohort – as in the case, for example, of health care costs when these are publicly covered in whole or in part; then the intergenerational injustice is manifest. Having been supported, throughout their lives, by a large tax base requiring relatively small per capita contributions, the small cohort is faced with a larger burden, which is magnified by a larger per capita incidence.

But that is not all. A relatively small young cohort is also vulnerable to injustice at the hands of relatively large older cohorts. This is, of course, exacerbated by two other factors, that (1) for the first 18 years, the young have no vote, while older people, asymmetrically, keep it until the end of their lives (Lau 2012); and (2) the voting turnout among the elderly is higher than that of the young, even when the young reach voting age. (The eligible young could, of course, take it upon themselves to vote at a higher rate, and this would mitigate the cohort-size effect, although we do not normally hold people responsible for correcting injustices that are due to others.) The higher the relative size of the older cohort, the more vulnerable to political domination the younger cohort is. Two American economists report that "in 2009 and 2010 nominal spending on primary and secondary education fell while spending on social security and Medicare continued to rise," and they take this to be a paradigm case of "rent-seeking" as a factor in economic inequality (Poole and Rosenthal 2011). Evidence from Switzerland – where, thanks to direct demvocracy, citizens have considerable influence on public spending – suggests a "significant and highly negative influence of the elderly on education funding" (Grob and Wolter 2005).

The sorry history of public school funding in California may provide another lesson. Retirees and empty nesters have no interest in supporting property taxes that are high enough to sustain a public school system of good quality, and so its quality rapidly declines. The notion that younger people's interests are somehow subsumed within the interests of older people recalls discredited ideas such as "virtual representation," according to which the interests of the unenfranchised are somehow reflected in the voting decisions of the enfranchised (Schrag 2004) and, perhaps still more exactly, by the idea of "coverture," according to which not only the interests but also the very identity of wives is supposed to be contained within the political status of their husbands.

To be part of a relatively small cohort, then, is to bear the burden of supporting a larger one and also to be politically exposed to the contrary interests of a large and influential older group. Perhaps the clearest case of its exposure is offered by the case of public debt. An age cohort wielding political power is in a position to borrow money whose repayment falls due beyond its own lifetime and the interest on which it falls to younger people to pay. Now there are certainly cases in which this seems legitimate; for example, there are some trans-generationally valuable projects whose cost must be spread between generations – such as, for example, the upkeep or building of infrastructure of various kinds (Holmes 1995, chap. 5). But there are also cases in which we would want to describe the transfer of costs from one cohort to another as exploitative (Bertram 2009, 158) – for example, when the benefits of an investment do not survive the generation that decides on it, while deferring payment to a future in which the benefits have expired. Theorists of intergenerational justice have rightly paid a good deal of attention to this topic: fluctuating cohort size significantly magnifies its importance.

II

But if we turn to the demographic literature on intergenerational justice issues, we find, most interestingly, a very different story. For here, according to the classic study by Richard Easterlin (1980), it is actually the relatively large cohorts, not the relatively small ones, who suffer injustice. Easterlin's account is thoroughgoing and quite graphic. His main point is conveyed in two passages that he quotes from the economist H. Scott Gordon (in his presidential address to the Western Economic Association, June 1977: "On Being Demographically Lucky: The Optimum Time to Be Born"), passages that are pleasantly hyperbolic but are meant entirely seriously. One passage concerns the lucky small-cohort child.

> When he opens his eyes for the first time it is in a spacious hospital, well-appointed to serve the wave that has preceded him. The staff is generous with their time, since they have little to do while they ride out the brief period of calm until the next wave hits. When he comes to school age, the magnificent buildings are already there to receive him; the ample staff of teachers welcomes him with open arms. (quoted in Easterlin 1980, 31)

This carries on through to the lucky boy's generously pensioned retirement years. The other passage concerns the demographically unlucky large-cohort children.

> These poor souls came into a crowded world – crowded by themselves. There was crowding in the maternity wards when they first saw the light of day; there was crowding in the kindergarten classes. (ibid.)

This too carries on through to the overcrowded funeral parlours and cemeteries (32). (Funeral parlours and cemeteries are not mentioned in the case of the small cohort, which may give the passing impression that they are supposed to be immortal.)

Easterlin examines the effects of large cohort size in several contexts, beginning with the consequences of increased labour market competition at the time of entry to the market. Because the negative consequences of unemployment or delayed employment or underemployment occur at an early stage in life, ripple effects are sustained throughout the life-course, with negative consequences in various domains, including personal and marital stress, family breakdown, crime, suicide, stagflation, and even political alienation.

As one would expect in the case of a bold sociological theory, later research shows the need for shading and nuancing, especially in light of other complicating factors, such as "broader changes in the labor market and other social institutions" (Slack and Jensen 2008, 744). But later research also produces a good deal of less qualified support for Easterlin's claims. However, a later Canadian book replicated many of the theory's findings (Foot 2000), and British research confirmed the prediction regarding cohort size and the earnings of young men (Ermisch 1988). And in relation to the incidence of crime, for example, both British evidence from the 1980s (Maxim 1986) and more recent Australian evidence (Rosevear 2012) point to higher crime rates in larger cohorts, presumably the result, in part, of a shortage of legitimate economic opportunities. Since crime is largely infra-cohort, that also means that the members of a large cohort are more likely to be victims of crime, as well as suffering punitive actions after committing crimes, than are members of smaller cohorts.

III

To clarify what is at stake here, consider a modified version of a thought experiment developed by Joseph Heath (2013) to make a case for intergenerational reciprocity. Heath imagines a circle of eight people, each of whom has a choice between keeping two tokens for herself and passing five tokens to the person on her left. At least once the game is going, everyone will have an interest in passing five tokens to the person on her left, trusting that the person on her right will, in turn, pass five tokens to her. The game is unaffected if, from time to time, one player leaves ("dies") and is replaced by another ("being born").

The circular structure avoids the paradox that a linear structure (e.g., the familiar "unexpected hanging" scenario?) would produce (i.e., that any final termination would roll back through the whole series). The model makes the compelling point that contrary to what has often been claimed, there *is* important reciprocity among generations. But here is the amendment: suppose the number of players fluctuated, and the size of the group had an effect on the value of the tokens available for transfer, so that the five-token rule became unstable (because resources fluctuated with the divisor). Then it could become the case that one received less, or more, from the person on one's right than the person on one's left was required to transfer to *his* left, to avoid defection from the game.[2]

Now it may at first seem odd that one suffers injustice, thanks to such fluctuations, by virtue of being in *either* a large *or* a small cohort, and one may initially be tempted by the thought that somehow the two kinds of injustice must more or less cancel out. (Perhaps there are different kinds of tokens, cashable for different goods?) But first, it's not really odd at all if one bears in mind that societies adjust themselves in all sorts of ways to their present population size, and sharp fluctuations in either direction will cause disruptions and, hence, unfair burdens. Existing population size will strongly tend to set the benchmark for levels of educational, social service, and health provision, and when population size changes significantly, these provisions will be inadequate in various ways. As a parallel, the same is true of migration rates. The doubling of population in the United States, in the late nineteenth and early twentieth centuries, had to be met by the informal expedients that so interested the sociologist Robert Merton (1967, chap. 3) as examples of the way in which officially sanctioned arrangements failed in the face of demographic change. On the other side of the coin, the flight of health care professionals from the developing to the developed world defeats the expectations that governments in developing countries reasonably entertained about the supply of medical services (Millum 2012, 33–6). Fluctuations in the size of age cohorts raise very similar issues and demand similarly careful ethical attention.

What, though, of what we may term the swings-and-roundabouts issue? Being part of a relatively small cohort carries relative disadvantages and advantages, likewise being part of a relatively large cohort. So could we not say to an affected person, first, that your relative disadvantages are accompanied by relative advantages, and second, that the alternative to the disadvantages that you suffer would be to suffer some other (equally bad) disadvantages? So you lose on the swings but gain on the roundabouts?

It is not obviously a relevant consideration, to a young person who lacks any employment opportunities, that she is part of a large cohort that, being large, has a relatively light burden in terms of supporting the old age of the smaller preceding cohort. For given her own values and priorities, she may very well prefer a situation in which she could develop her talents and pursue her goals even at the cost of bearing greater social charges than her parents had to bear. And even if she took the view that having to make disproportionate transfers to another generation was worse than being unemployed, it is still not obvious – ruling out *schadenfreude* – that it would console her. Is it a morally relevant consideration that while I am badly off, people in other generations are worse off still?

But this whole line of argument misses the mark in the context of social arrangements that are subject to modification. We should certainly reconcile ourselves to unmodifiable logical and physical necessity. If one's child is too tall to take the part of one of the Seven Dwarfs in his school play, it is relevantly consoling to point out that if he were shorter, he would be less brilliant at basketball. But the same doesn't apply in the case of conventional arrangements. Suppose your son's complaint is that by taking a course that he wants, in the German language, let's say, he gets a teacher who uses alphabetical order for everything, so that your son, Zack, has to wait until the end of every classroom procedure. There is no necessary connection between having an interest in German and being kept waiting. The teacher, regardless of subject, could surely use reverse order sometimes, after all.

There may be necessary reasons why age cohorts fluctuate in size but the fiscal arrangements made for that fact are a matter of convention, like the German teacher's alphabetical rule, and not ineluctably constraining, as one's basic physique is. So the swings-and-roundabouts defence is unavailable, and the relevant solution is to change the arrangements rather than to console the child. Moreover, the implied analogy with fairground wins and losses misrepresents both the seriousness of the losses at issue here and their individuated character. In the case of both large and small cohorts, the losses entail diffuse negative effects over the whole life-course, rather than resembling one-off disappointments that a later win can compensate for. As for individuation, it is presumptuous to suppose that, from any individual child's point of view, the losses avoided in her circumstances are outweighed by losses that she would suffer were her circumstances different. To pick a non-intergenerational analogy, it was once very frequently argued that the legally "included" status of women was to their advantage because, while closing off some opportunities, it shielded them from the harshness of economic and political competition. It is doubtless true that there were women who saw it as a good deal. But for third parties to make that trade-off on behalf of all women is now regarded as arrogantly demeaning. In an exactly parallel way, for a third-party generation to claim that inter-cohort trade-offs are acceptable, on the swings-and-roundabouts argument, is to abandon any sense of what is owed to the other's perspective.

But let us turn to what can be done about demographic injustice, which is really the heart of the matter. Above I mentioned public pension plans, the structure of which seems, in some cases, to reflect the sort of concerns that are advanced in this chapter. Most public plans are contributory, or "pay as you go," although that term is misleading, for contributory plans are viable only if payments in approximate payments out, which, of course, fails to happen when a small cohort is paying in and a large cohort is receiving payments. Pay-as-you-go plans face "an unpleasant refunding when the process of demographic and economic growth comes to an end or just slows down" (Marchand and Pestieau 1991, 442; see also Bongaarts 2004). The solution is a buffered fund with sufficient reserves to smooth out the contributory costs between cohorts. But fluctuations severely test even this enlightened policy, requiring sharp increases in levels of contribution. (For the especially difficult Japanese case, see Ogawa 2009.) As for the case of "social security" in the United States, a dire prediction made in 2008 was that in the next 15 years, "there is a 50% chance of an aggregate underfunding in excess of $750 billion, a 25% chance of an underfunding of at least $1.74 trillion, and a 10% chance of an underfunding in excess of $2.48 trillion" (Novy-Marx and Rauh 2008, 3). Where should these "unpleasant" charges fall?

In the case of relatively large as opposed to relatively small cohorts, the unfairness arises basically from labour market competition, to which Easterlin ascribes such far-reaching effects. Given the importance of employment to every facet of a person's life, if there is not actually a *right* to work (as nineteenth-century socialists maintained), there is surely a responsibility on governments' part to stimulate the provision of employment opportunities, particularly in the case of younger workers trying to find an initial foothold in the labour market. The only known means at Western governments' disposal is counter-cyclical, or Keynesian: spending directed at job creation. Whatever the theoretical plausibility of pure market solutions that promise recovery "over time," it is plainly unacceptable that entire cohorts of young people should undergo the short-term and long-term effects of high unemployment rates while they wait – for a decade? or more? – for markets to readjust to demographic and other change. To accept such a situation would be to violate the requirement that one (cohort-defined) person not be used for the sole benefit of another.

Once again, though, where should the "unpleasant" cost – of counter-cyclical spending, in this case – fall? Counter-cyclical spending is made possible either by long-term borrowing or by saving in prosperous times. Long-term borrowing, if it exceeds the justifiable intergenerational maintenance costs of a society (Bertram 2009), is obviously objectionable because it transfers one generation's problems to another. Saving in good times is the right answer. But it is politically unavailable if the age cohorts enjoying political dominance demand the tax cuts that good times and high tax revenues make possible. To quote a distinguished Canadian social demographer, "Since health care is largely funded at the societal level, there should have been savings while the baby boom was at prime labour force ages. Instead, we have lowered taxes and increased deficits" (Beaujot 2012, n.p.).

Such "cohortism," to coin a term, is irresponsible. Each cohort, if it has plans to procreate, needs to take account of its place in time and to forgo advantages that are unjustifiable from an intergenerational point of view. Taxation must be at a high enough level to even out the burdens of varying cohort size, whether the burdens are those of supporting a relatively large previous cohort or enhancing the life chances of a relatively large entering cohort. Needless to say, since the overall objective is that of aiding those who suffer demographic bad luck, taxation must be progressive in a way that compels the beneficiaries of good luck to pay at a rate that reflects their good fortune.

IV

It is from the neonate's (potential) point of view a matter of luck that he is born into a cohort that is relatively larger or smaller than the cohorts preceding or following. And so the project of mitigating the consequences of this may seem to fall squarely into the category of *luck egalitarianism* – that is, the body of theory that advances the view that equality requires that people be compensated for unlucky circumstances in their lives. If so, a two-part objection has to be confronted. The first objection arises from the fact that luck egalitarianism is open to important critiques. The other part of the objection arises from the view that if the argument of this chapter is luck egalitarian, it shows not only that parents must take a stand against demographic injustice but also that they must take a stand against unchosen inequalities of all kinds – not only those arising from age-cohort fluctuations. I shall take these two parts of the objection in turn.

Elizabeth Anderson's classic article makes a powerful case for directing egalitarians' concern away from luck and towards oppression, so that they will turn their attention from "supposed cosmic injustice" to "creat[ing] a community in which people stand in relations of equality to others" (Anderson 1999, 288–9). The topic of this discussion, however, falls through the (fairly substantial) gap between "cosmic injustice" and "oppression." Demographic bad luck is not cosmic; it arises from the uncoordinated but causally determining acts of parents. It is not oppression either since no intention to dominate or exploit is involved at all. Without any thought of challenging Anderson's critique of oppression, correcting for demographic bad luck may suggest that the defence of equality may call for more than the critique of tyranny, a classic preoccupation of the liberal tradition, in that inequality of life chances may arise from individuals' failure to take account of the general social processes in which their actions are implicated.

There are two important elements in Anderson's rejection of luck egalitarianism. One is that it cruelly denies help to those whose misfortunes derive from their own agency. The other is that the doctrine demeans the victims of bad luck and places the state in an objectionably paternalistic role in relation to them. A further objection, advanced by Matt Matravers (2002), is that distinguishing between what is and is not traceable to personal responsibility involves metaphysical judgments (about the self) of the sort that much recent political philosophy seeks to avoid.

Now whether the view defended here should be called luck egalitarian (see below for doubts), it is clear that these powerful objections do not apply to the case of cohort luck, as we may call it: for children come into being through the agency of others, not their own, and it is the unplanned collective agency of those who bring them into being that affects their fate. The first objection is simply impossible to apply, there being no children who choose their cohort. The second is possible to apply, but is entirely implausible in this case. Anderson imagines a state sending compensatory cheques to people, together with explanatory letters noting that their misfortune is that of being born unattractive or dim or socially inept, and she rightly points out that there would be something deeply offensive to their self-respect in this, or even in a case in which there were no such demeaning letters, but in which the grounds of the policy were publicly known. But no one could for a moment suspect that bad cohort luck was a sort of personal deficiency – it is a circumstance, not a personal attribute. As for the charge of paternalism, it would seem perfectly acceptable to treat children as though they were children, however objectionable it is to treat adults as though they were.

Matravers's objection is certainly apposite in the case of trying to figure out what is due to personal agency and what is not. It would indeed seem hard, to say the least, to separate what has befallen one from what one has done, given that one has done certain things because of what has befallen one, and there is an onion-like problem here of peeling away layers until nothing is left. I think it is right to say that once we get beyond straightforward cases like compensating for congenital physical disability, we will eventually be faced by issues about personal identity that are metaphysical. But no such problem is posed in the case at hand, for, once again, being part of a particular cohort is not part of one's personal identity, but simply part of one's situation. (Being a baby boomer or a member of Generation X is not, I think, a normal or more than incidental part of anyone's self-description, being typically invoked in the context of comparative advantages or disadvantages, rather than in the context of defining one's life plan.)

Let us turn to the second part of the objection discussed in this section. This is the objection that if parents have an obligation to support policies that protect their children from bad demographic luck, they also and for the same reasons have obligations to protect them from *all* kinds of bad luck, so that there is nothing distinctive about the demographic-bad-luck argument. We could support this objection in many possible ways, but I shall choose the one that I take to be the most compelling and graphic. The horrific violence of the First World War was suffered by boys who were born in the 1890s and so became eligible for conscription during the war period. (Those who directed the war were born in the 1860s or before, and so we may well see the war in terms of violence inflicted on one generation by another.) Now it may seem that, on the argument offered here, parents conceiving children in the 1890s – and so parents conceiving children at any time, since one can never know whether a war is going to break out two decades hence – must support pacifist policies to avoid imposing slaughter on their children in the event that they turn out to be male. (Obviously, this statement would need amendment in the case of countries that also conscript young women.) Does this conclusion follow? (Let us bracket out the case of pacifist parents, who already have the duty in question, as do all pacifists.)

The difference between the two cases is twofold. First, that one decides to have children, or does things that one knows or should know result in children being born, does not foreseeably lead to one's children being born into a generation that will be conscripted for a terrible war (or a generation that will have to live through economic depression or hideous epidemics [see Overall 2012, 142]), even if one knows that wars and economic cycles and epidemics are part (so far) of the human condition. But given the fact that conceptions are interpersonally decided on, while the number of conceptions is unpredictable, in conceiving children one is taking part in a social endeavour that is inherently, not just contingently, risky for one's children, given that the number of conceptions makes such a difference to the life chances of anyone conceived. It is, of course, true that one isn't knowingly imposing a particular kind of handicap, unlike a case in which (e.g.) parents know that their child will have a genetic defect; but this is exactly the point: one doesn't know, one can't avoid the risk by one's own action or inaction, and this is why the duty to mitigate the risk has to involve a political rather than a personal commitment.

Second, as a parent you are by your own voluntary action contributing to the process that entails cohort risk, whereas, unless they were warmongers or intending archduke assassinators, the parents of Great War conscripts did not by their own voluntary action contribute to that war. Potential parents who give birth or do not, who give birth early or late, who give birth to few or many children *are* acted on by those considerations that, in their aggregate effect, determine the size of the next age cohort. The interpersonal decisions or negotiations that lead to no or few or many births are coloured by societal influences, and the interpersonal decisions that are made may be regarded as a form of participation in what was termed above a social endeavour. As a potential parent, you are part of a set of circumstances that will profoundly affect the life chances of a child that you bring into them; you can if you wish decide not to bring a child into them, and if you do, you can properly be called on to consider what those circumstances will entail for him or her and to engage in a politics that improves them.

But is this chapter about luck in the sense in which this term has come to be used? In one sense, of course, yes – from the point of view of a person born into an age cohort of one size or another. It is in this sense that it is a matter of luck, good or bad, that you have or have not been invited to someone's birthday party – it could have been otherwise. But no less obviously, it is not a matter of luck that the party giver invited you (unless the guest list, unusually, is randomized). It is a decision she has made, with consequences for you. This point is fundamental to the argument offered here, an argument about political choices. Parents can take steps, or fail to take steps, to lend their support to policies that mitigate the effects of cohort fluctuation. It is not a matter of luck, but of choice, that they do so or not. Their responsibility is triggered by the fact that their own decision to procreate is one among a number of more or less contemporaneous decisions that collectively exercise a profound effect on the life of each child affected by them. Depending on the success of luck egalitarianism as a moral and political theory, we may or may not have a general duty to correct for the disadvantages that neither we nor their sufferers have chosen. Regardless, we have a duty to correct, as far as we can, the disadvantages that we have exposed another person to.

For this reason, it would be misleading to think of what parents should do as a matter of compensation, like the socially inept person's demeaning cheque, not only for the reasons given above but also because the duty involved is pre-emptive rather than compensatory. If I fail to put up a Wet Paint notice, I (may, depending on various considerations) have a compensatory duty to cover someone's dry-cleaning costs. But putting up a notice of this kind is not compensatory; it is an attempt to prevent the damage from occurring in the first place. The distinction is important; a compensatory view can rightly be objected to because, in many cases, losses may arise as a result of actions that fall within the range of one's legitimate discretion. If my will bequeaths more to X than to Y, my estate cannot have – absurdly – a duty to compensate Y in the amount of the difference. Since procreation is widely regarded as falling within the range of legitimate discretion, a compensatory view is liable to invite criticism on these grounds. But the duty to support certain kinds of intergenerational equalization is better viewed in terms of harm prevention. It is taken for granted here that one has a duty to forestall harm even if one's own contribution to it, taken separately, is negligible, at the very least in cases in which one has a non-negligible duty to a person who will potentially be harmed by it.

V

The second line of critique arises from the idea of procreative beneficence and from objections to that idea, briefly mentioned above. The idea of procreative beneficence, as it has come to be called, is that potential parents may give birth only if they have taken the maximally possible steps towards improving their child's life. Since I have claimed that only parents who support intergenerational equality may have children, I may seem implicitly to have subscribed to this view or to a specific form of it, at least. But the view is open to important criticisms.

Above all, the idea of procreative beneficence is objectionable because it imposes wholly unreasonable duties on potential parents. Christine Overall makes this point strongly. Does it mean, she asks, that parents would have a duty not only to provide the best of every possible service but also to move to a better area, or emigrate to a better country, or even to transfer their children to other parents who would likely do a better job of parenting? "We would need to have a national or international registry of excellent parents to whom children could be transferred once their original parents failed to maximize their well-being" (Overall 2012, 129).

One response to this, although initially tempting, would undermine the thesis offered here. This would be to say that whereas emigrating for one's child's sake or transferring him to better parents is scarcely a requirement of justice, supporting just policies, aimed at more fairly distributing the burdens of cohort effects, is such a requirement. But this would make the support of egalitarian policy a general duty, rather than one arising from parenthood, and we would no longer be able to say, in the case of parents, that the support of egalitarian policy is something distinctively entailed in one's own voluntary acts. We have to be able to say, given the argument of this chapter, that whether the support of egalitarian policies is a general duty, it is one that arises from the act of procreation nonetheless.

A second response is to distinguish between positive duties to give your child the best possible life – duties that Overall rightly questions – and a negative duty not to harm. You harm your child by bringing her to life in a small or large cohort. Does it make a difference that you don't do so intentionally or even (unless you are a gifted, prescient, and very lucky social demographer) knowingly? I don't think so. Consider an analogy with behaviour in traffic. You don't have a (positive) duty to accommodate the desperate lane changer. You do, however, have a duty not to damage the car behind by backing into it in a parking lot, even though your view was obscured by minivans on both sides, and even though, in backing into another car, you are just a statistical instance of many such events.

But the procreative beneficence view sets another and rather different obstacle to the argument developed in this chapter. Suppose potential parents held the procreative beneficence view (whether you and I thought it mistaken or not). They might say, we owe our child the very best, and we can provide it out of our own resources. At whatever cost to ourselves, we will give him a personal gated residence; a personal, privately provided security guard service; and a financial endowment securing the provision of everything he needs in perpetuity. So why should we support the public provision of anything at all? This is a radical objection, for the public provision of anything would seem to depend on the satisfaction of needs, and if all needs can be privately met, then public provision is placed under question.

But the privatization solution does not work, outside the pages of Ayn Rand. First, the proposal is entirely fanciful: the delivery of privately provided services depends on the existence of a public infrastructure – how otherwise would the private security guards get to work? How would the financial institutions carrying the endowment be regulated? Second, we presume illegitimately on the preferences of future people if we suppose that – almost uniquely among previous generations known to us – they desire a completely sequestered life, without contact with those whose life chances are different from their own. Rapunzel went to great lengths (so to speak) to escape from her tower. It is entirely possible that one's child will not want to be shut up in luxury but will want something resembling a normal social existence. So the objection in this case is based not on equality, but on freedom.

VI

Another important point needs to be clarified before concluding. Above it was claimed that the duty proposed here is triggered by procreation. Acts other than procreation alter population size, of course: not procreating affects future population size, while emigrating or immigrating affects present population size. These acts, however, do not bring into being another person whose life is going to be profoundly affected, in remediable ways, by the number of other people who are brought into being at more or less the same time. Since a person's parents have no control over the number of persons conceived at more or less the same time, their agency is limited to mitigating the predictable effects of many or few persons being conceived and born. But I do not think it can be said to be a right of the child that they should do so. It is indeed the child's (future) existence that triggers the duty; but if the duty were to arise from the child's right, it would have to be grounded in that child's interest, and that is implausible. It is certainly in the child's interest that various arrangements be made to equalize inter-cohort opportunities, but no one child's interest can oblige anyone to create arrangements of this kind.

To borrow an example from a classic essay by Joseph Raz (1984), it would be like supposing that because I have an interest in living in a beautiful city, I would be entitled to have one created for me. Nor can *that* child's interest alone oblige the parents to give political support to the arrangements. If it were a matter of promoting *that* child's interest alone, the obligation would be to make provisions to shield her from the effects of cohort fluctuation by (e.g.) taking steps to provide her with a private source of income. It would not be to give political support to arrangements that, if not already in existence, are more than likely to meet with opposition and may not see the light of day, or that may not see it in time for one's own child to benefit from them, or which, if already in existence, are vulnerable to being dismantled by those who are too old to benefit from them.

The duty in question arises not from a child's right[3] but from the parents' participation in a social event that will have enormous consequences for a determinate person, while lacking direct agency with respect to determining those consequences. In situations of this kind, one's choice is between passivity and throwing what weight one has behind just solutions. Given the number of injustices in the world today, we surely have discretion as to what we put our weight behind. But parenting is commonly and rightly thought to diminish discretion and focus our sense of responsibility. We are meant to think about what we are doing to a person's life chances, and among the things that we are doing is something that is remediable, if it is, only by politics.

One critic of intergenerational justice maintains, indeed, that providing for one's offspring is an individual responsibility, becoming a public one only in the case of parental failure (Wissenburg 2011). The idea that it is in the first instance a collective concern, requiring distributive transfers, arises from the illusion that successive generations are related as one entity to another, rather in the manner of distinct countries whose respective welfare is subject to considerations of justice. In reality, this critic points out, it is not inevitable that a future generation should come into being; people of one generation emerge from the voluntary action of earlier people, so that "there are individuals who are responsible and accountable for that choice and its consequences" (ibid., 557). While those individuals are indeed responsible for their choices, the argument of this chapter has been that the consequences of their procreative choices are necessarily a joint product, given the unforeseeability of others' contemporaneous actions, hence the political nature of the obligation that arises.

VII

I hope it will go without saying that this chapter offers moral rather than legal recommendations. It does not propose the compulsory sterilization of right-wing voters. But we can consider what is justifiable without immediately supposing that our conclusions must be made legally obligatory. We can, as a parallel, think about whether potential parents who may pass on genetic defects should have children without supposing that there should be legal prohibitions against their doing so. Being an inegalitarian is not quite the same as having an inheritable defect because the effects of transmitting one's condition are only diffuse. But once we take diffuseness of effect as something that automatically excuses personal responsibility for those whose lives we affect, we open the door to terrible injustices, and these should be met with moral objections, even if not always – for moral reasons – with legal ones.

Finally, this chapter has adopted the familiar but obviously false convention of treating generations as entities, distinct even if non-separate or overlapping. In fact, of course, as Peter Laslett (1979) pointed out long ago, a generation is an artefact, defined in light of some practical purpose or other, and different practical purposes will divide up a seamless reality in varied ways. The significance of this for the above argument is that duties defined by intergenerational concerns cannot take a distinctly intergenerational form, there being no real entities to sustain such a thing. So they would lead to a continuous, unpunctuated process of redistribution to the benefit of continuous but changing sets of young and elderly people.[4] They would lead, in short, to policies largely identical to the familiar prescriptions of social democracy. And to those who already endorse those prescriptions, the route taken in this chapter will seem circuitous.

As mentioned above, however, the point of the chapter has been to show that social-democratic policies should be endorsed by people who do not already endorse them as a premise, if they have children. There is a strong reason, I believe, why the special case made in this chapter converges with a more general case that doesn't depend at all on one's reproductive decisions. Social-democratic policies are best understood as responses to very basic facts about human vulnerability: to facts about genetic and social endowment, about market effects, about the uncertainties of health and the certainty of aging. To have children is to insert oneself in the most direct possible way into the permanent cycle of human vulnerability, by exposing unconsenting beings to life chances that are only imperfectly subject to one's own control as a parent. That is the kernel of truth in the anti-natalist position discussed in chapter 6. Just because one's own parental contribution is so limited, this chapter has argued, a broader political duty follows. This duty, once again, can be given a broader and non-agent-relative basis, as has often been done, by theorists of equality from Richard Tawney to the present. But parents of all people have a reason to be aware of the facts of vulnerability from which ideas of social and political responsibility ultimately arise, and they are morally alienated from their own action if they fail to acknowledge them.

Chapter 9

If the Future Is a Foreign Country …

If "the past is a foreign country" (Hartley 1953, 9), then the future is too, for if the past is other to us, then we will be other to the future, and so they must also be other to us. And in fact, the future, some point out, will be *more* "other" than the past is, in that we can read and interpret more or less successfully the records that the past has left us and have at least a plausible clue about what it was like, while the future is in at least some ways irredeemably closed from our view. Two important political conclusions have been drawn from this claim. One is that we can do nothing for others that we know nothing about. The other is that we actually wrong them by imposing conditions, such as (especially) constitutional provisions, on them. This chapter is mainly about the second conclusion, but for obvious reasons, it cannot entirely avoid commenting on the first.

That the future must be seen as another country is a view defended in the eighteenth century by Thomas Paine and Thomas Jefferson and, more recently, by Michael Otsuka (2003), who elaborates on and proffers a claim to improve Jefferson's arguments. In a famous 1789 letter to James Madison, Jefferson wrote "that the dead have neither powers nor rights over [the earth]" and "by the law of nature, one generation is to another as one independent nation is to another." In consequence of this view, he arrives at his proposal that constitutional arrangements be assumed or rejected whenever demographic change produces a new electoral majority (every nineteen years, given the voting age and average life expectancy at the time). "If [a provision] is to be enforced longer, it is an act of force and not of right."

Shortly afterwards, Thomas Paine, in *The Rights of Man* (1791), his great polemic against Edmund Burke's *Reflections on the Revolution in*

France, took issue with the politics of tradition. "Every age and generation must be ... free to act for itself," he wrote, the rule of the dead over the living is "the most ridiculous and insolent of all tyrannies," and "Those who have quitted the world and those who are not yet arrived in it, are as remote from each other, as the utmost stretch of moral imagination can conceive. What possible obligation can exist between them?" (quoted in Ball 2000, 73). As Terence Ball pointed out (73–4), Paine actually goes further than Jefferson – and, some will think, incurs a loss of plausibility in doing so – in denying that one generation not only must not control, but also has no obligation to, another; for Jefferson, each generation enjoys the world's resources only "in usufruct" and so has a duty to pass them on undiminished to the future (ibid.). (Even without that view, one may note in passing, Paine's "as the utmost stretch of moral imagination can conceive" seems – well, a bit of a stretch – unless we suppose not even a shred of significance to attach to shared species membership.)

Otsuka makes (part of) Jefferson's and Paine's point by way of a vividly effective example. Imagine, he says, that a British Parliament were to enact a Bill of Rights – a very good one – and declare it to apply not only to Britain but also to the United States. To the objection that, however fine it might be from any evaluative point of view, the bill had not been democratically adopted by the people of the United States, the British reply, "Your own Bill of Rights is no more democratic in its origins than our new one. No living American ever cast a vote in favour of the old Bill of Rights" (and in fact, they could add, rather few Americans did so even at the time), so "Why should you be any less outraged by the profoundly undemocratic origins of the old Bill of Rights than by the new?" (Otsuka 2003, 132–3). With regard to living generations, then, an inherited constitutional provision has no more legitimacy than a provision arrogantly imposed by a foreign country. But whereas imposing a constitution on another country requires military force and is generally achieved only in the face of opposition, one generation gets to impose its will on another peacefully and as a matter of course: a moral inconsistency amounting to absurdity?

There is a line of argument, which we might call ontological, that casts basic doubt on this claim, recalling somewhat (but without the political conservatism) the Burkean view that Paine assailed: there are not discrete generations; there is a single subsisting community. The first section of this chapter considers this and suggests that it is attractive but inconclusive. It goes on to consider what would follow if we took seriously, as it therefore seems we should, the view that the future is a foreign country. In recent years, after all, political theorists have given a great deal of close attention to what members of one country owe to foreign ones – we have a very substantial body of literature on the topic of global justice. The view that we take on that topic may well have something to do, then, with how we decide about duties to the future. As Brian Barry wrote, "Access to the earth's resources can be unfairly distributed over time as well as over space" (Barry 1989, 492). And as Christopher Bertram writes, "If mere spatial difference should make no difference to our obligations it is hard to see that temporal difference should make a difference either" (Bertram 2009, 160). The chapter adopts a view on the topic, draws out what it might mean for intergenerational justice, and concludes that there are reasons to reject Paine's and Jefferson's arguments, as well as the libertarian conclusions that Otsuka's reworked version arrives at.

I

The ontological objection that must be considered first is that "a polity *is* an intergenerational community" (Thompson 2009, 1; emphasis added), not something to be defined on a current time-slice basis. Implicitly rejecting Jefferson's view that "we the people" are to be thought of as an age cohort, Janna Thompson writes, "'We the people' is a historical continuum that reaches into the indefinite future" (ibid.). While the theories of reciprocity that are so common in modern political theory have trouble dealing with the deceased and the unborn, an approach that focuses, rather, on identity is much less problematic in this regard, for members of political society see themselves as located in a common history and as having a common destiny (4). There are strong reasons for their doing so. On the one hand, the polity to which they belong is a transtemporal entity that accumulates lasting responsibility for its past actions (5). And on the other hand, as members of a polity, we develop "lifetime-transcending interests" in projects and institutions that outlast our lifetimes. To understand all the ways in which our membership connects us to the past and future is essentially to dissolve the Paine-Jefferson problem at the ground level; we simply *are* not (purely) synchronic beings to whom the future is like a foreign land.

I think there are two main reasons to resist this dissolution of the problem. The first is that the picture we are offered is morally attractive to many people, but optional. It would be wrong, as Thompson herself points out, to put too much emphasis on purely subjective identification by members, for doing so would raise the objection that members vary greatly in the strength of their identification with the polity and, moreover, generally have other identifications too, such as ethnic or religious or professional ones, that may outweigh what identification they may have with the polity (ibid., 34–5). It is more convincing to place the stress on objective ongoing institutions and projects in which, as a matter of fact, one is involved by one's social existence. There certainly are such things. It may not be quite clear, though, that we can get from these to the idea of the polity itself as a transgenerational commitment maker on the world stage. If people are to make transgenerational commitments on their own account, as Thompson convincingly shows that they do and must, then their polity must provide a framework in which those commitments can be made. Does it follow, however, that the polity itself must be able to make intergenerational commitments on its own account – that is, in terms of its (or its managers') decisions about its common interest? Can we get from the need for legal guarantees of personal commitments to, for example, an idea (attributed to Lincoln) of "the polity itself [as] an intergenerational project that citizens have an obligation to maintain" (ibid., 86)?

It would certainly seem true that if citizens' commitments are to have binding force, then there must be some legal vehicle to give them effect. But in the first place, this consideration supports only a very minimal view of the polity, as a legal guarantor rather than something that is readily seen as itself a "project." In the second place, a successor polity may assume its predecessor's legal commitments, as when, for example, a former colony assumes commitments made by its colonizer, or a post-revolutionary state assumes debts incurred by its predecessor, while ceasing to be, in some important sense, "the same."

But even if we grant the point, the same initial problem may recur, in a more attenuated form. Future-encumbering institutions and projects may *be* only matters of fact – that is, they may be normatively empty or even burdensome. Looking to past events, we need more than the fact of membership to implicate us in past actions of the polity – the facts of history may be acknowledged by people who draw very different normative conclusions about what they imply. The phrase "taking responsibility for the past" (Thompson 2002) seems more apt in this case than "bearing responsibility for the past," for what the idea of redress calls for is an act of positively assuming a connection, for moral reasons that one takes to be currently binding. And looking, symmetrically, to the future, we do not know whether the projects that we transmit to the unborn will be welcome or burdensome or simply meaningless to them or how they will figure in their own identity.

The latter problem may, however, sometimes be exaggerated by intergenerational-justice sceptics. Surely it is going too far to say that future people will be "beings quite unlike ourselves" (Ball 1985, 326; see also Beckerman 2006). History suggests that they will in some ways be quite like us. As Brian Barry wrote, "It is true that we do not know what the precise tastes of our remote descendants will be, but they are unlikely to include a desire for skin cancer, soil erosion, or the inundation of all low-lying areas as a result of the melting of the ice-caps" (Barry 1989, 500). We can, anyway, avoid or at least greatly limit any possible relativistic problems by focusing on fungible goods, such as many kinds of capital, that we can transmit to future generations to use for their own purposes.

An exceptionally convincing intergenerational ontology is provided by pension plans, discussed in chapter 8, which work because each cohort pays in with the confidence that succeeding cohorts will pay in turn and which would collapse without the assurance of indefinite continuation (Heath 2013). The example can even be generalized as a model of the larger money economy, which can function only because cohorts are made thoroughly interdependent by intertemporal trust. But this works because the good in question is usable for different purposes; and to the extent that we model intertemporal relations on such a good, we weaken the requirement of continuity among generations. At the limit, later generations may see no moral or cultural continuity and feel no ties of sympathy for ancestors or descendants, and the idea of intergenerational community becomes attenuated, to say the least, if viewed in terms of a stock of assets to the use of which quite different meanings are successively attached.

The second issue is that the model may be *too* diachronic to be attractive. If we want intertemporal justice to complement global justice, we may be worried about a model that places such an emphasis on particular communities as the source and object of loyalty. As a matter of fact, it seems right to point out – implicitly rejecting Otsuka's global-temporal analogy – that people generally feel stronger "solidarity" with past and future members of their own society than with contemporaries in distant societies (Heyd 2009, 187), and a theory of community that celebrates strong continuities within borders may not be congenial to strong obligations beyond. To address this problem, one could, of course, introduce an idea of a future or emerging world in which bordered nation-states give way to multi-levelled forms of organization; but then, ironically, one would certainly be betraying the strenuous nation-building work of ancestors who saw the creation and defence of borders as their priority – so much the worse, might one say, for a strong notion of intergenerational continuity?

Alternatively, or in addition, one could build in a requirement that each particular intergenerational community must respect and aid each other particular intergenerational community. But it is not clear that such an iterative principle can be derived from the idea of intergenerational community itself or that, to sustain it, we do not have to move to some more abstract level, one that requires us to universalize our commitments. Moreover, if we adopt such a requirement, it would seem that we risk losing any *basic* associative connection with our own society, for if understood as a universal principle, it should lead us to prioritize aid to intergenerational projects that most need it, or perhaps the ones that are most worthy by some standard, rather than those of our own society. Peter Singer offers a sharply relevant critique here. Suppose it were the case that associative connections made it especially important to worry about inequalities among associates, rather than among strangers; it would follow – from a strictly universalist point of view – that we would have a reason to reduce inequalities among associates in any and every association, not just in our own (Singer 2002, 174–5). Singer's point is made in the context of global justice, without reference to intergenerational matters, but plainly, it would also apply in the case of any intergenerational obligations that distinct political societies have. And if so, it works strongly against the idea that membership in any particular political association is morally basic.

These brief remarks do not, of course, dispose of the powerful idea of intergenerational community. They are simply meant to suggest that the case for it is not clear enough to dispense with the questions of discontinuity that the "foreign country" thesis raises. Despite important links, generations may lay claim to interests and identities that set them apart from other generations, and to subsume successive generations within an overarching community may be implicitly to deny their distinctive claims. And even discounting that problem, the approach may court an insularity that can be avoided in a way that is not obviously consistent with the premises of the approach.

II

If we suppose that generations' interests are separable to some extent, then we should consider what would follow if each generation made its own social contract. The relevant nearby analogy would be with Rawls's view of what justice requires of nations governed by spatially particularized contracts. Rawls draws out that view in his *Law of Peoples*, resisting his critics' claim that he should adopt the standpoint of a fully global contract. The full requirements of egalitarian justice, he says, apply only in national societies: the "difference principle," or the requirement that inequalities are justified only to the extent that they raise the floor for the worst off, does not apply across national borders. But some things do: "burdened societies" – societies that face such crushing problems that they cannot escape from them by their own efforts – must be given aid by more successful societies. "Outlaw societies" are subject to military sanctions if and to the extent that they threaten the stability of the international order. But societies whose political arrangements fall short of liberal-democratic standards are to benefit from a globally extended principle of liberal toleration – liberal toleration requiring that they not be compelled to become liberal or even to suffer official censure because of their illiberalism. Diversity among peoples is a parallel to pluralism in liberal society and so demands respect, just as diversity of belief and lifestyle in liberal societies calls for toleration (Rawls 1999, 11).

If we transfer these conclusions from the spatial to the temporal sphere, what follows? Interestingly, with respect to aiding burdened societies, Rawls actually inverts this order of thought and draws on the view that he had already developed regarding duties to future generations – the just savings principle, to which we turn in the next section. Assuming the validity of that much-discussed view, Rawls models what we owe to burdened societies on the duty to save for future generations of our own society – that is, a duty to preserve for them a level of well-being that is sufficient to sustain just social and political institutions. "After [that] is achieved, further assistance is not required, even though the now-well-ordered society may still be relatively poor" (ibid., 110–11). When we provide aid, Rawls says rather tentatively, we may attach advice, or even conditions, based on what we know to be the prerequisites for its effective use. He particularly mentions requiring the participation of women in the local use and distribution of aid (ibid.).

But with regard to the global toleration principle that Rawls offers, the intergenerational implications would seem to be highly permissive. If each political society is to be seen as self-determining, then imposing liberal constitutions on future societies would indeed be as objectionable as imposing them by force on other contemporaneous countries. It violates their "equal standing" as members of the community of peoples. To the objection that non-liberal societies should not benefit from the principle of equality since they do not themselves observe the principle of equality in their internal practices, Rawls replies that equality must be understood in terms "appropriate for the case at hand" (ibid., 69), pointing out that churches, for example, or universities, can be given equal status even though they are internally inegalitarian. This line of thinking rests on a deep presumption that the self-determining capacity of associations of all kinds, sub-national and national, demands respect.

To be sure, this principle of respect applies only to decent societies that meet non-liberal but nevertheless non-negligible standards in their internal arrangements. Only decent societies benefit from the free and equal status conferred by membership in the community of peoples. It is only decent societies that "should have the opportunity to decide their future for themselves" (ibid., 85). The outlaw societies remain, and they are potentially more interesting from the present point of view. They are subject to sanctions. Only in "grave cases" (81) can these sanctions be applied out of respect, solely, for the rights of their own citizens – there is, it seems, a liberal interventionist principle that applies only in extremis: perhaps in cases of genocide, for example. In other cases, sanctions are motivated by concern for the interests of decent peoples and the stability of the international order. Here Rawls appears to have been deeply influenced by the example of Nazi Germany. When governments attack their own people, he maintains, it is a prelude to their attacking other peoples, and so outlaw states are a matter of legitimate global concern. But future potential outlaw states pose a problem. It is a fair bet, based on what we know of human history, that some future states will become outlaws, and we could announce that when they do, they will become subject to sanctions; but what, if anything, could we now do, pre-emptively, to prevent their "going outlaw?"

If our concern is with international stability, then the one thing we can rely on, according to Rawls, is democratic peace theory. According to that body of theory, which Rawls endorses, democracies do not attack one another, and so a secure world would be one made up of democracies. Existing democracies, then, would have a strong interest in promoting democratic constitutions around the (future) world. But it seems that they would be prevented by the non-intervention principle, even prevented from advocating democracy out of respect for the sovereign choices of other societies. The one option that they would seem to have would be to establish a system of international criminal law that would punish the leaders of outlaw states in the case of future offences. This would be consistent with what Rawls says about the need to mirror in a general way the major trend in post–Second World War international law, a trend towards limiting the powers assigned to sovereignty (ibid., 27), and also with what he says about holding leaders accountable rather than practising collective punishment (95).

So we achieve a rather mixed result. The bar against "disseminating" liberal principles beyond the borders of liberal states implicitly places at least a question mark over the attempt to impose liberal institutions on future generations. On the other hand, the resources that we save for and transfer to future generations can, it seems, be tied to at least one "condition" – that of gender equality in institutions. Moreover, provisions can be put in place ahead of time to punish and deter aggressive war and domestic genocide. But if we take the future to be another country, the general priority would seem to be to respect its freedom – a broadly Jeffersonian conclusion that the future/foreign analogy does not greatly modify.

III

The natural alternative approach, it would seem, would be to somehow represent future generations directly in the constitution-making contract – a parallel, of course, to the global contract that is urged upon Rawls by critics who, rejecting the modest internationalism of *The Law of Peoples*, want distributive justice to have universal scope. If we could convincingly do so, then future societies would no longer be merely residual beneficiaries of local domestic contracts, but would be on the same footing as our contemporaries. As briefly mentioned above, Rawls attempts to move in this direction in connection with the question of saving for the future. It is obviously unacceptable to him, in that regard, that generations should think of justice only for themselves. But Rawls's one effort to "go intergenerational" turns out to be quite problematic.

Famously, Rawls's device of the original position models fairness on what rational and self-interested people would agree to under conditions that deprived them of particularized knowledge. While this approach, if successful, will model fairness among contemporaries, it obviously leaves open the possibility, as it stands, that a rational and self-interested age cohort could eat the seed corn and leave future people to starve. To deal with this, Rawls, in *A Theory of Justice*, introduced the "motivational assumption" that people in the original position would care for their immediate descendants (Rawls 1971, 128–9). This proposal has (rightly) been subjected to a great weight of criticism. To cite one early and especially comprehensive critique, the motivational assumption disturbs the fiction of rational self-interest on which the whole device rests, it introduces indeterminacy because we do not know how to weight benevolence against other imperatives, and in presupposing an important moral principle, it runs against the avowed project of employing the weakest possible assumptions (English 1977, 93).

Rawls himself had noted, but rejected, an alternative to the motivational assumption – that is, to imagine an original position comprising members of every generation, so that the interests of all generations would be taken into account in arriving at just terms of association. He rejected it on the rather slender grounds that it was "fantasy" (Rawls 1971, 329). But David Heyd offered a further and stronger objection, that "a general assembly of representatives of all generations, which is expected to decide intergenerational principles of justice, is logically absurd" because members of earlier generations decide unilaterally how many future people exist. He continues, "How can an assembly of all *possible* people decide who is to be born? ... Even if we can imagine ourselves belonging to another sex or another social status, we cannot imagine ourselves unborn" (Heyd 2009, 173).

I think this problem is amenable to a solution that has shown its value in another, related context – that is, to focus on general types rather than on persons individuated by their genetic history (Kumar 2009). One can be a representative of an age cohort without being particularized in any way but one – that is, by the fact of being born into it. (This, needless to say, dispenses with the need to imagine oneself unborn.) An assumption has to be made – that is, that some future generations will exist – but this is not in itself more problematic than assuming that the present generation will live out its natural span without being exterminated by a large asteroid. It is true that the size of future generations – unlike the arrival of large asteroids – depends on the choices made by earlier generations. But population policies depend very much on ideas of the good that members of the original position cannot take account of because they are precluded from knowing them. Whether it is better, for example, to have a small population with ample resources or a somewhat larger one less generously provided for is exactly the sort of question that we cannot answer without knowing what ethical and metaphysical principles to bring to bear on it. So it may be that the objection does not apply.

Be that as it may, Rawls himself came to adopt a third alternative, neither the multigenerational model nor the motivational assumption. In *Political Liberalism*, he proposed what has been termed a "strict compliance" model – that is, he required participants in the original position to adopt rules of intergenerational saving that they would want to be adopted by all generations, regardless of which generation they themselves happened to be in (Rawls 1993, 274). Since we would want earlier generations to have saved adequately for us, we will be under an obligation to save adequately for future ones. At first glance, this seems a promising move, one that denies participants knowledge of their generation, just as the veil of ignorance hides from them other features that might unfairly affect their choices. But the problem, I think, is made evident by the locution *would want*. It entails a sort of sovereignty over others' choices, which departs from "What would *you* want?" as the guiding question: it refers no longer to decisions that one would make, but to one's hopes about what other people's choices will have been. Heyd's critique is compelling: here the argument is no longer basically contractualist, although the contractualist form is retained – it has become a variety of impartialism, and the contractual apparatus no longer plays a significant role.

IV

Of course, impartialism could simply be the right answer – we should figure out what justice requires without going through the business of thinking about what reasonable people would agree to in reflecting on the terms of their association. Impartialists face their own problems, though: unless they are willing to turn their backs on the claims of partial associations altogether, they will have to find a way to determine what is owed to others on the basis of partial associations and how this fits in with the larger demands of impartiality itself. This is no small difficulty: no plausible political theory could deny that what we owe to co-citizens is in some way distinctive, or that nothing is owed to outsiders, and so an issue of moral allocation is posed. Before abandoning the contractualist approach, then, let us consider whether it contains the resources for dealing with that allocative issue.

So far, we have considered exclusive social contracts and inclusive social contracts, and we have encountered difficulties with both. But there is another version, one that may be termed *iterative contractualism.* I shall briefly set out what it amounts to in the global case and then consider what conclusions may be drawn for the intergenerational case. The general conclusion is that we should think of contractualism as more demanding, in relation to outsiders, than is generally supposed.

If a transtemporal or atemporal contract poses problems, are we not back to the intergenerational contract? And would that not essentially reinforce Jefferson's position: our contract can have no force for others, and they must be free to make their own, and so imposing a constitution on them would be a violation of their freedom? This would be so, however, only if social contracts had no implications with regard to other contracting or potentially contracting societies; it would not be so, however, if the contractualist approach contained within it a principle of iteration that imposes constraints on the contracting parties' arrangements, so that social contracts are not to be seen as self-enclosed or monadic, so to speak, but as windowed.

Now at first glance, a social contract may appear purely self-referential, even selfishly so. On this ground, Samuel Scheffler (2001) has made a powerful case for the unfairness of social contracts from a cosmopolitan point of view. It is, in fact, a double unfairness; for, first, our social contract excludes outsiders from our direct concern, while, second, leading to the formation of complex social and political ties from which outsiders do not benefit. In response to this powerful point, however, it does not seem that the burden has to be irrevocable. There are ways to make up for unfairness, and we might ask what it is that would relieve contractors of the moral burden in this case. It would be relieved if they accepted two requirements as a condition of their contracting: a duty not to impede others in seeking the same advantages for themselves and a duty to aid others when their own political projects had manifestly failed.[1] Given these two conditions, a social contract would cease to be monadic.

The source of this view is that contractualism is not and cannot be a moral starting point, for it implies a moral background. That background can be interpreted in various ways – for example, in terms of

H.L.A. Hart's natural right to freedom (Hart 1955) – but without one, it would be possible neither to make agreements nor to charge them with unfairness. It would not be justifiable, for example, to make a warrior contract whereby we swore a pact to commit violent aggression against all outsiders, for this would contradict the background values that make things like social and political agreements possible. We need not take such an extreme example; it would likewise be unjustifiable to pursue advantages that prevented other societies from pursuing like advantages for themselves – for example, to adopt protectionist policies while blocking other countries from protecting their own economies. Moreover, the freedom to form and pursue collective social projects cannot be merely formal. It would be hypocritical to claim that others can iterate one's own success when their institutions have collapsed beyond repair or when internal repression removes all hope of political progress or collective self-definition. A duty to aid or even to intervene then comes into play, for the background purposes that support the value of political independence have ceased to apply.

Turning to the intergenerational context, the parallel to the duty not to harm is straightforward and uncontentious. No particular moral starting point is necessary to grasp that one generation should not plant time bombs in the forest at the expense of future generations of hikers, or poison baby food at the expense of future generations of infants, or destroy the natural environment so that future people's survival is placed in question. A social contract that did not implicitly forbid such things would resemble the violent "warrior contract" mentioned above – that is, something most closely resembling a criminal conspiracy. It is the aid requirement, rather than the no-harm requirement, that is more distinctive and interesting. In the global context, the idea of intervention is hedged about with many concerns and qualifications that reflect both the limits of the intervener's capacity and the independence of the subject state. The threshold is therefore quite high, rightly so, given all the considerations of prudence and international law and ethics that have to be surmounted.

But in the intergenerational context, we do not have an option to be weighed and balanced against an anti-interventionist case. We are already and inevitably "intervening" in the course of developing institutions and practices that will be the matrix in which future generations come to be. The question is not whether to contribute, but how; and the global context suggests an answer by way of parallel. The possibility of intervention is triggered by state failure and tyranny. By analogy, what we owe to future generations is (not intervention, but the provision of) a set of robust institutions with the capacity to withstand both ordinary political stress and extraordinary tyrannical abuse.

V

Michael Otsuka, as was briefly noted above, offers to improve on Jefferson's "nineteen-year" proposal. It is, he complains, insufficiently libertarian, for during all those years in which individuals are waiting for their cohort to become a majority, they are subject to a constitutional regime to which they haven't consented. Otsuka's solution is to return to the Lockean expedient of tacit consent, although, of course, he does so with full awareness of the criticisms to which it has been exposed. What Otsuka proposes is that, under certain stringent conditions, the non-resistance of future people to arrangements made by their predecessors amounts to a valid form of consent. We can, then, create constitutions that survive us, but we can do so only if those "stringent conditions" are in place.

The objections to "tacit consent" are originally due, of course, to Hume's essay "Of the Original Contract," which demonstrates the implausibility of Locke's claims in the *Second Treatise*. A labourer living on the margin of existence cannot reasonably be said to have alternatives, Hume objects, that justify imputing anything at all to the fact that he stays where he is, and so we cannot derive *consent*, in any meaningful sense, from, for example, his travelling on the country's roads (Hume 19647, 156). That is so, however, Otsuka contends, only because the labourer has no real alternatives, and that, in turn, arises from the non-enforcement of another Lockean doctrine, the famous "proviso." If the labourer has no alternatives, it is because "enough and as good" has not been left to him, and so he does not have his fair share of the world's resources. If he did have his fair share, then his tacit consent would count for something; and so one generation could legitimately create arrangements that outlast its own life, knowing that the next generation could signify its own consent by tacitly accepting them.

But having the resources to opt out is not enough to ensure that consent is not forced or reluctant. There must also be available options, and these are secured by allowing individuals, with sovereign control over their share of resources, to form any number of associations according to their members' shared beliefs or tastes, thus offering to any individual a rich array of options. They would thus be very much like the "churches" in Locke's *Letter Concerning Toleration*, as Otsuka points out – voluntary associations with powers of discipline tempered by a right of exit (Otsuka 2003, 125). Their powers would also be very significantly limited – unlike the powers of churches in *this* regard – by a requirement that their members' children be given an education in critical thinking that will enable them to make their own choices eventually (120) – so that, for example, the Amish claims discussed in chapter 7 would get very short shrift on the left-libertarian view. Finally, there would need to be an "interpolitical" governing body – one not based on every individual's personal consent – to adjudicate disputes (108–9).

There is a literature defending and evaluating the general merits of the left-libertarian view (Vallentyne and Steiner 2000). Here, however, setting aside its general merits or shortcomings, we need consider only one question: that of presumptuousness. Constitutions, even liberal ones, are said to be objectionable because they involve one generation presuming what it is that another generation will want: the libertarian view just sketched is held to avoid this objection. But does it? There are technical issues, Otsuka acknowledges, about the metric of equality, for some general metric must be assumed for the purpose of allocating resources equally; here, though, one need only claim that when no perfect neutrality is possible, the "more neutral" option is preferable (Otsuka 2003, 109–12). A metric based on a commonplace list of widely desired goods is more neutral than a metric based on some contested claim to have discovered, say, the true meaning of life. So we may regard the adoption of such a metric as minimally presumptuous, given the fact that "when conceptions of the good conflict," we cannot "measure everyone else's welfare by each individual's own lights" (112).

I think we can accept this argument, but I also wonder why we can presume that this version of minimal presumptuousness should be accepted and sustained by citizens themselves. For while it is necessarily true that we cannot "measure everyone else's welfare by each individual's own lights," it is a political fact that people seek to advance policies that reflect their own conceptions of welfare, and they can do so only by compelling others' compliance. While there are all sorts of reasons (some set out by Locke) for confining *churches'* powers of control to their own members, these reasons are ineffective in relation to institutions to which those very powers are essential to their function. As Locke says, states are to be valued only to the extent that they can accomplish things that their members could not do if they were politically unassociated with one another (Locke 2010, 141) and so are basically very unlike churches in that important respect.

Of course, this is to invoke an idea of the state that, departing sharply here from Locke, the left-libertarian view seeks to overturn in analogizing states and voluntary associations such as churches, rather than categorically separating them. But in rejecting it, that view forecloses options no less effectively than, say, liberal egalitarianism (or republicanism), and while it can, of course, conduct its own argument against rival political theories, it cannot do so on the basis of being less presumptuous. It denies important powers to future citizens. Here the defect of the "other country" view, as Jeffersonians and neo-Jeffersonians interpret it, becomes clear. As noted above, we can avoid imposing our views on other countries, if we choose to, while we cannot in the same way avoid imposing on the future because we necessarily leave them something that is profoundly formative, and we do so no less even if we aim for minimalism, simply because minimalism is profoundly formative, too, in setting the institutional and normative context in which the realization of goals comes to be conceivable or inconceivable.

VI

If the future is at all like another country, what kind of country could it be? I want to conclude by suggesting that if it is like anything, it is like a colony. Of course, one major disanalogy leaps to mind at once – that colonies, it is now generally agreed, should not have been acquired in the first place – while the view that we should not have created/should not now create future people is hardly a mainstream one, and chapter 6 offered some reasons for resisting it. But let us set that issue aside by supposing that we are second- or third-generation colonizers, not personally guilty of colonizing, but currently in the position of exercising control over another society. What should we do about it? Well, first of all, of course, we should set about establishing its freedom if we believe that the domination of one country by another is wrong. But we cannot just wash our hands of it, for it is not, as it were, just as we found it, but has been deeply moulded by the system of control that we have exercised. So we owe[2] it the means to recover from domination and to develop self-governing capacity. But it would be pointless to do so if its process of self-government were simply to reproduce our domination in an internalized form.

The argument here can draw on thoughtful accounts of what it is that makes colonialism wrong. One account, by Christopher Morris, notes that if a colonist's extractions from a colony's resources were merely to be replaced by extractive local elites, its replacement by local exploitation would hardly be an improvement (Morris 2006). Another (even more relevant) account, by Lea Ypi (2013), challenges a common view that the wrong was territorial in nature: that the colonized lost control of some territory, to which they were somehow entitled, to the colonizer. That would be a wrong if we supposed that there is some morally weighty link between a group of people and the space that they occupy, a link more morally weighty than their understandable interest in maintaining the status quo against intruders. If there were such a link, then the remedy for colonialism would be, simply, to return control of territory to the group.

But the idea that groups of people have some sort of basic claim to pieces of the earth is far from obviously true, and the wrong of colonialism may lie, rather, in the fact that the colonized were denied the opportunity to negotiate their terms of association with the Europeans. The wrong would then be that of political oppression. It would not be remedied, Ypi points out, if territory were to be returned to formally independent local control while informal domination continued, as is often the case. But I believe that this argument may be taken a stage further. If, having subjected people to oppression, it is the wrong of having done so that motivates lifting oppression, then the very same consideration must motivate concern for what happens to them next: we cannot remedy our placing someone in some objectionable state by replacing it (or allowing its replacement) with some equally objectionable one. If the wrong were simply that we were not the right geographically designated oppressors, then we would remedy it by merely vacating the oppressive role, but if vacating the role is driven by the rejection of oppression, then it necessarily has a forward-looking component. In broad terms, this component would amount to an obligation to create institutions of self-government, permitting the society to substitute collective self-determination for external control and to create defences for the population against potentially oppressive local power.

The analogy with our relation and our duties to the future is not bad. We exercise essentially unilateral control – tempered, in the case of adjacent generations, by their resistance, or our fear of it – but cannot responsibly simply wash our hands of it. We have left our mark on the future even more deeply, probably, than colonists leave their mark on the colonized, and we owe it the means to evaluate and, if necessary, disengage from what we have done to it. Institutions of self-government, whether modelled on the colonists' own preferred political system, are the first prerequisite, and limitations on the unilateral exercise of power are the second. Without these, we are in no sense respecting the freedom of the future society; we are simply depriving it of freedom in the sense of collective self-determination and also of freedom in the sense of security against the tyrannical exercise of power. Just as our colonialism enhances whatever it is that we owe to any distant society regardless of our history, so too our inescapable control over the future creates demanding positive obligations. So even if it *is* another country, the kind of country that it is imposes positive duties that go far beyond any negative duty to leave it alone. What we have done, and what we are doing, counts for a lot in terms of what we should do next.

The apparently overriding worry, it seems, is that in imposing institutions based on our conception of the just, we are being presumptuous – the essential point of Jefferson's equation of the future with a sovereign country. This worry would be quite in place if we took a purely voluntarist view of democratic politics, a view on which majorities were unconstrained by anything at all, just as a country's sovereignty is supposed to protect it from any external dictation. But this is not a view to which we should see Jefferson's generation as being committed, nor even a view that can be given plausible defence. Had the Founding Fathers said, in justifying the Revolutionary War, that they could throw off colonial government just because it was their bare, untrammelled will to do so, then they would indeed face the problem that some future generation could, by strictly equivalent reasoning, throw off the Constitution by a similar act of will, just as they liked – which would, of course, make constitutions pointless. But the Declaration of Independence is very far indeed from making any such claim. Far from using the language of voluntarism, it speaks of moral "necessity," setting out "the causes which *impel* [NB]" separation, and invoking the dispassionate opinions of "mankind" as setting standards that must be met. It appeals to truths that, being "self-evident," are beyond the control of will, and it limits resistance to cases of governments' becoming "destructive" of the rights that they are meant to serve, systematically destructive, moreover – there must be (as Locke too had written) a "long train of abuses" before people acquire the right or duty to rebel – a condition that any sort of pure voluntarism (such as Paine's) would make redundant.

There is nothing in this foundational document to suggest that future generations would do anything but wrong in throwing off a just constitution, and the "foreign country" view of the future, given the revolutionaries' own avowed aims, and their respect for constitutional principle, must be seen as misleading hyperbole. The revolutionaries' appeal was not a self-referential appeal to what *we* decide or believe, an appeal that would indeed close generations (and countries) off from one another, but was directed to a regulative ideal of decent opinion, which, in their view, political claims were obliged to meet.

Chapter 10

The Rights of Past and Future Persons

Some theories of justice rely on an idea of a reciprocity in a strict form – that is, a model of *do ut des*, "I give so that you will give," or "I act justly so that you will too." Others rely on a more mediated or less strictly bilateral model: I benefit from a scheme of relations to which you contribute, and so I should contribute to it as a condition of expecting you to do so. Either way, as noted above at several points, intergenerational issues fit poorly. On the strictly bilateral model, I cannot change the actions of either past or future people, and so the idea that I can derive a reciprocal advantage from what I do in relation to them is a non-starter. The more diffuse model may seem to offer a bit more of a toehold for the idea of reciprocity, in that we can imagine that receiving something from a previous generation might at least incline us to pass on some equivalent to future generations out of considerations of simple fairness.

But Brian Barry has pointed out several damaging objections to understanding reciprocity in this way. For one thing, there is no identifiable general principle that tells us that any good received obliges us to distribute or reproduce it for the benefit of others (Barry 1989, 484–5). To vary Barry's own (receipt-of-a-toffee-apple) example, we may have received, from previous generations, the great benefit of twice-a-day postal delivery, six days a week; but all sorts of factors may make that good unsustainable in the present and future, given opportunity costs. Or it may not even be valued by generations that rely much less on the mail than earlier generations did. For another thing, there is an enforcement problem (see also Heyd 2009, 180). We, generation B, having inherited a good from generation A, may earnestly want to hand it on to the *n*th generation (in light of fairness considerations), but we cannot know that generation C will not selfishly absorb it for its own purposes. So the sacrifice that we make to pass on the good to *n* may be in vain. We cannot, as in the case of reciprocity among living people, effectively prohibit or punish defection from mutually beneficial practices.

Now it is true, as noted above, that there is a particular kind of reciprocity between contiguous age cohorts: that generations overlap with one another is a feature that removes any supposed asymmetry, it has been claimed (McCormick 2009). Overlapping is exemplified, above all, in such things as pension plans, as Heath (2013) has argued. In the context of such plans, cohort B pays in, thus supporting preceding cohort A, trusting that succeeding cohort C will pay in support of it, following the same practical logic. I don't think it's essential to this model that the cohorts overlap (although, of course, contacts and resulting mutual sympathies between overlapping cohorts may well support the availability of trust). But it *is* essential that they are contiguous (otherwise, B would be unsupported if C did not arrive for a while, causing a gap in the series of exchanges). This consideration can be met, it is ingeniously claimed, by the need for indefiniteness. If generation C knew that generation D would be unable or unwilling to contribute, its motivation would disappear, and it could figure out that D's motivation would likewise disappear if, further down the road, E were to be unable or unwilling … And so on. There must be no anticipated last contributing generation, for if there were, then the motivational problem would unwind from the penultimate generation to the present. If there were no generation D to rely on, generation C would have no reason to support generation B, who in turn …

Barry's seminal paper did not anticipate this highly original contribution. But his "sleeper" objection (his term: Barry 1989, 494) still applies – that is, the model works only in the case of transfers between contiguous generations, not of costs such as (notoriously) the disposal of nuclear waste, which can be deferred to a distant or unknown future. I believe there is another issue too. The model requires only that there be anticipated future generations. Whether they actually come to be, or whether they suffer some catastrophe that reduces them to a bare subsistence level or below, is not important to a model that rests on self-interested motivation. All we need to do is imagine future people, and this is, on the face of it, an odd basis on which we and future people could stand in a relation of justice. It isn't important that they should actually experience some good; it's only important that we should believe in them for our own rational sake.

But even if we back away from the idea of reciprocity, we still face an awkwardness posed by justice more broadly conceived. As noted in the Introduction, justice, according to David Hume – and to Rawls, who adopts Hume's view – has an application only in certain "Circumstances." These include the circumstance that the parties' "capabilities are comparable in that no one among them can dominate the rest" (Rawls 1971, 127). But of course, being alive gives one the capacity to impose decisions unilaterally on any interests that those who are not alive may have. Even if we think that deceased people have an interest in being remembered, we can rewrite history so that their achievements are obliterated. We can do things that are destructive to the interests of future generations by using up resources that they could enjoy or imposing on them the debt for paying for our enjoyment of them.

So one might think that the whole issue of intergenerational obligations falls out of the domain of established ideas of justice, reciprocity-based or otherwise. But even at the worst, I see nothing in the issue of intergenerational obligations that would compel us to abandon one available and important normative resource: the idea of rights. To have a right, at least on one dominant understanding, is to have an interest that imposes an obligation on at least one other agent (Raz 1984), whether that agent has an interest that symmetrically imposes an obligation on the right-bearer in question. This peremptoriness of rights is not, of course – or not in most cases – absolute, if only because rights come into conflict with one another, and so reflective adjustments necessarily have to be made: your right to prompt medical treatment conflicting with my property right if the fastest route to hospital is through my land. But at first they seem at least peremptory enough for the purpose at hand. They at least pose serious obstacles – a very high threshold – to policies that would damage the right-bearers' interests. And they impose requirements that are not conditional on any response from their beneficiaries. So may we suppose, then, that justice for past and future people can be understood as their having rights that compel the respect of living people – thus neutralizing the reciprocity problem?

I

The first objection to be addressed is that some have argued that the requirement of reciprocity applies in the case of rights too – A can have no right against B, they claim, unless B has the same right against A. Roger Scruton (2000), for example, in arguing the case against non-human animal rights, contends that only creatures capable of understanding the rights of other creatures can be said to have rights or to be part of the "moral community" in which rights are shared among members and so have application in their conduct. On this view, ascribing rights to creatures that cannot have the idea of respect for duty leads to absurd results. He writes, "A creature with rights is duty-bound to respect the rights of others. The fox would be duty-bound to respect the right to life of the chicken, and whole species would be condemned out of hand as criminal by nature" (ibid., 210). This would seem to be a purely arbitrary stipulation, however. We can simply respond by saying that, as a definitional matter, some being may have rights, given the definition of what a right is, only against potential duty-bearers, so that chickens, for example, may have rights against humans, who can have duties, but not against foxes, who for obvious reasons cannot. A refinement is that humans who put animals in harm's way may well have a further duty to protect them by warding off predators, perhaps even by killing them; but killing foxes is not to be understood, absurdly, as a punishment for their violating the rights of their prey – as Scruton suggests – but as the enforcement of a human duty to protect domestic animals whom we have caused to be vulnerable by gathering them in predator-convenient pens.

Excluding animals from the protection of rights on the grounds that they cannot reciprocate is no more convincing than excluding from the protection of rights human beings who, for one reason or another, are incapable, temporarily or permanently, of exercising the reciprocal duties. Both sets of issues pose questions about the legitimacy of exclusion that are sometimes challenged together. Sue Donaldson and Will Kymlicka (2011), for example, draw in part on the literature on disability for their defence of including (some) non-human animals in (some modes of) citizenship, and Martha Nussbaum, in her book *Frontiers of Justice* (2006), presents both disability and species difference as two of the "frontiers" that theories of justice have yet to convincingly cross.

Scruton's thesis may, however, still draw some plausibility from the indisputable fact that the idea of rights came into being, as a matter of historical fact, in moral communities. Much the same consideration, one may note, is sometimes urged against the idea of *human* rights too – there being no all-embracing human community in which a shared understanding of rights is effectively enforced (Brown 1999), the idea of a human right is said to make no sense. So an argument deployed to privilege humans is also available for undermining the claim to have rights on a merely human basis, for the idea of community contains no inherent defence against further contraction. Be that as it may, moral communities also expand, and the engine that typically drives their expansion is the appeal to the rights of the currently excluded. The reason is not hard to discern. Moral communities do as a matter of historical fact come to be expanded, and they come to be expanded, clearly, on the basis of what is thought to be wrongly done to the excluded, not on the basis of what the excluded are failing to do. Abolitionists were moved, after all, by what slaves were suffering, not by their non-service on juries; advocates of property rights for married women were worried about what propertylessness did for their relative status, not by their non-payment of property taxes.

If rights can drive the expansion of moral community in this way, it must be that demands for liberation can arise from a sufficiently strong sense of what is owed *to* people, operating quite independently of what might be thought to be owed *by* them, and so presupposes no already existing community of reciprocity as its necessary ground. This particular communitarian claim, then, is open to the important complaint that it makes moral change impossible to explain; and moral change happens, so that a view that obstructs its possibility is on the face of things false.

The idea of shared moral community also figures prominently in some of the earliest modern discussions of intergenerational justice. M.P. Golding (1972), for example, also maintained that rights are claims that people have on us by virtue of belonging to our community. In the case of future people, he argued, the community cannot be a contractual one, or one based on shared practices, nor is it a sentimental one. So the claims of future people on us must arise from their being people who ought to count "because, and insofar as, our social ideal is relevant to them, given what they are and their conditions of life" (ibid., 95). If, for, example, future people were to be re-engineered so that we would view them as humanoid rather than human, their good would not count as a good that we should respect or promote (99). Very provocatively, this claim has been implicitly challenged on the grounds that what we need for our life to have meaning is not that there should be continuity of value but that the activity of *valuing* should persist, whether by beings of our species or by beings of another kind, capable of taking up an evaluative stand on the world inherited from us (Shiffrin 2013).

Along lines somewhat similar to Golding's, Terence Ball drew on the facts of *conceptual change* to make the claim that since ideas of justice have changed and will change again, the very idea of intergenerational justice suffers from "incoherence." We cannot know what *they*, future people, will regard as just. There seems to be an ambiguity here, however, in the term *intergenerational justice*. It is, I think, generally taken to mean justice towards future generations, rather than (as Ball apparently assumes) an idea of justice shared with future generations. As far as the former and perhaps more standard idea is concerned, Ball is willing to embrace the view that we should make provisions for the future on the basis of our "present standards," on the grounds that we must act "by the only lights available to us, viz., our lights" (Ball 1985, 334). So an idea of justice would count as intergenerational not by virtue of being shared – something that could only be assumed – but by virtue of the personhood of those to whom it applied.

This "presentist" move, as we may call it, echoing chapter 1, would seem to concede a lot of ground to the theorist of intergenerational justice in what I am calling the standard sense – perhaps as much ground as she wants or needs. And it seems like the right conclusion. It is supported by conclusions that one should reach in other somewhat parallel contexts. One is that of judging the actions of past generations. It was argued above that we are not bound to accept that previous generations' beliefs about slavery or witchcraft are the standards relevant to appraising their actions, and parallel argument surely suggests that, similarly, we have no reason to make provision for future generations' potentially odious beliefs. Another is that of global justice: there would be no incoherence in (e.g.) refusing to trade with countries whose production practices violated what we regard as the standards of justice – even if *they* maintained that it was perfectly all right to exact unpaid labour from political prisoners.[1] In general, the proposition that people must always be appraised or treated according to their own standards, and that accommodation or provision must be made on that basis, seems quite simply unpersuasive as a moral view and so unavailable in the particular case of future generations unless there are special reasons to apply it there.

But the case of future others may *be* special in that it is different from those of past others or global others in one important respect. We cannot change the ways of past others. Our capacity to change the ways of global others, while by no means insignificant, is limited both by norms of sovereignty and by serious practical considerations. But our potential control over future others is real, even frighteningly so. Both Golding and Ball raise worries about the potential restrictions on future people's freedom that imposing our own standards may cause. Golding went so far as to say that respect for future people's freedom may require us "not to plan for them" (Golding 1972, 97–8) – although why, on his own argument, they can be said to have a right to our respect for their freedom may not be clear; for their right to respect would have to flow, surely, from some transgenerational principle of the sort that Golding's argument makes problematic.

Ball, for his part, introduces a cautionary tale, inviting us to think about how we would view a *past* generation's effort to impose its view of justice on *us*. The antebellum South, he argues, regarded slavery "as a normal, natural and eminently just institution" (Ball 1985, 328).[2] Suppose the slave owners had had available to them, and had used, techniques of genetic engineering that ensured the docility of all African Americans in perpetuity; we would, Ball says, "curse" them (329–30).[3] And so how can we consistently will that our own ideas of justice be legitimately transferred to future generations?

Here we have an example of an issue raised in chapter 1: must we take everything called by the same word to be the same thing? If, from our point of view, the idea of justice is connected inseparably with human equality, then a racially stratified society doesn't embody a different idea of justice; it is simply unjust, whatever it happened to call its own arrangements. All sorts of things have wrongly been called *just*. It would be an error to suppose that different "conceptions of justice" – if this means all things called *justice* at various times – must have "a universal conceptual core" (ibid., 335). But another error is to suppose that all the things called *justice* are rival alternatives when they may have nothing to do with what, from our point of view, is just. We would regard the attempted perpetuation of slavery as wrong, not because imposing justice is wrong, but because slavery is unjust.[4] In all this, there is a sort of perspectival play that may remind one of Thrasymachus's dramatic intervention into the dialogue of Plato's *Republic*. Thrasymachus wants to make much of the variousness of justice in the inverted-commas sense (i.e., what is called "just"), while also invoking justice in a non-inverted-commas sense (i.e., what it is right to do), so that what is merely thought to be right is invested with (actual) rightness, becoming normative. Such a view depends on grasping with one hand what is relinquished by the other.

Moreover, if no decisions should follow from what I believe to be the case, on the grounds that what I believe is relative to my circumstances, then how can it be that anything at all should follow from my belief that everything is relative to circumstances? Why should meta-ethical beliefs (i.e., beliefs about the status of ethical beliefs) be less open to relativizing doubt than ethical beliefs are thought to be? In fact, if we are worried about transmitting some ethical view to future generations, why would we not be *more* worried about transmitting to them a meta-ethical view – such as relativism or any other such view – that, if received, will effectively control their ethical choices in a uniquely dominating and pervasive way?

"Imposing (actual) justice" is best understood in terms of creating political institutions that diminish the possibility of domination.[5] It is trivially true that doing so tends to foreclose certain options – i.e., opportunities to dominate. It would also foreclose options if we were to transmit systems of domination, or no systems at all, thereby effectively imposing a state of nature. The unilateral nature of our connection with the future makes neutrality impossible, and the nearby alternative to neutrality is to transmit arrangements that, to the greatest extent possible, make it hard for unilateral impositions to be the way of political life in the future. Perhaps there is a paradox here in that our relation of power over future generations could itself be taken as a model of the very arrangement that we should aid them in avoiding. Its worryingly unilateral nature is mitigated only if what could justify our power is the project of safeguarding future people's freedoms.

II

The most hard-edged objection to ascribing rights to non-existent persons derives from the use of the verb to have. To *have* anything, it is argued, presupposes existence (Beckerman 2006). It makes sense to say that my house has a red door only if my house exists. "My yacht has white sails" makes sense only if I have a yacht. So to say "X has rights" makes sense only if X, likewise, has being. One's first thought about this may be that existence rests quite a lot – with important moral consequences – on a (supposed) fact about language: a dubious move, intuition may initially suggest. One's second thought may be that the claim about language isn't even true. The sentence "Unicorns have one horn" makes sense even if there are no unicorns and never have been. "That's not a unicorn" is an appropriate comment on a picture that purports to be of a unicorn but is in fact of a horse. "The English sentence has a subject, verb, and predicate" makes sense in relation to an infinite number of as yet non-existent English sentences. It would make sense in relation to any sentence yet to be formed and hence (now) non-existent, not only in relation to already formed sentences that someone happens to have uttered.[6]

A slightly less hard-edged and more plausible-seeming objection focuses not on the general capacity to possess things, but on the specific capacity to possess interests. It could be that while the non-existent could possess certain things – such as attributes – there is something about interests the possession of which presupposes existence. And here there are at least two cases that, after consideration, may come to the aid of the sceptic. Both cases involve the (difficult) idea of posthumous interest.

The first case is that of the making and executing of wills. When the topic of posthumous interest arises, for many people the first example to come to mind is –understandably – this. The practice of making wills makes sense only if there is a legal and institutional machinery providing for their execution; and their execution certainly seems to express the idea that, even after death, a person's interest in having this or that done is consequential. So this would seem to count in favour of the idea that interests survive. Against this interpretation, however, is the plausible view that what is valued here is a practice that is important in light of people's ante-mortem interests. While we are alive, we have an interest in seeing our possessions disposed of as we would wish after our death; and obviously, the machinery needed for accomplishing this by making a will would be pointless if, post mortem, our wishes were set aside. So although we could say, if we wished, that a person's interest survives, and even if that might be a perfectly good way of describing things in their legal aspect, it would still be the case, morally speaking, that what matters is the predictability of the machinery from an ante-mortem point of view.

Much the same would apply in the parallel case of deathbed promises. Why, one might ask, should such promises be kept, unless we suppose that the deceased person's interest still counted for something? Here there are probably two complementary answers. From a justificatory point of view, what matters is the integrity of the institution of promising; from a motivational point of view, what matters is some living person's memory of the deceased. Both points are well made, I believe, by a powerful scene in George Eliot's novel *Romola*. Romola's father, a scholar, has died, after making his daughter undertake to keep his valuable library of classical texts together; but Romola's treacherous husband, Tito, makes arrangements for the books to be dispersed and sold. Romola tells him that there can be no good "for cities or the world" if people harden their hearts against the force of promises and thus undermine the conditions of mutual reliance (Eliot 1994, 271). This (rule-utilitarian?) appeal is a (vain) attempt to dissuade her husband, but the context makes it clear that what moves Romola is her loving memory of her father, unmediated by any public rule. From either point of view, however – the justificatory or the motivational – we need not appeal to a posthumous interest of the deceased. It is true, as one account of deathbed promises claims, that the right-associated duty is one that is owed to the deceased (i.e., would not have arisen but for a promise to the deceased), but I believe we give due weight to this fact in acknowledging that the resultant duty is borne by a living person, the promissee (Wenar 2006).

The second case is an ingenious one constructed by Michael Ridge (2003) in the context of slavery reparations. The most common objection to reparations of this kind is that they are too late, the last surviving slave now being deceased. The most common reply is that although there are no longer any living ex-slaves, the slaves' descendants still suffer the long-term effects of slavery. And a common counter-objection is that while this is so, many other groups currently suffer various kinds of deprivation, and the current deprivation of the slaves' descendants gives them no special place in the queue for remedy. Who is really the worst off? Ridge's argument cuts through all this by making a case that *the slaves' own interests subsist* in the present day and can be advanced. The argument works by picking out one interest: the strong interest of the slaves in seeing their descendants do well. The evidence that they, perhaps even more than is commonly the case, had such an interest is incontrovertible. So when societies offer affirmative action programs in employment or professional school admissions, or other forms of benefit to slaves' descendants, they may be seen as advancing one of the slaves' own interests, thus refuting the familiar claim that it is too late to do anything for them. An additional merit of this proposal is that it dispenses with the problem, basic to many arguments for reparations, of establishing a link between past suffering and present responsibilities: on this intriguing view, what calls for a remedy is not past; it is with us still – an interest that survives as long as it remains unsatisfied.

There is no particular difficulty in supposing that an interest survives death; the literature includes many persuasive examples. One is the example of a project that someone began while alive, such as a business enterprise, which could do well or badly after his death. Its doing well could be said to advance the person's interest; its doing badly could be said to defeat it. This consideration could well motivate heirs or successors to do their best for the enterprise. Another common example is that of reputation. We have an interest in being thought well of after we die. We can imagine scenarios in which discoveries subsequent to someone's death change the whole character of her life – some theory that she championed unsuccessfully during her life, for example, is subsequently confirmed, so that she is thought of as a pioneer in her field. Suppose she were asked, ante mortem, if she would like that to happen, post mortem? Surely she would say yes, and her non-indifference to what would happen surely lends some support to the idea that an interest of hers would remain in play.

If we adopt an interest theory of rights, believing that rights impose duties arising from a person's important interest, it may seem that if an interest survives, we can proceed directly to the idea of a corresponding right. But of course, not all interests are the basis of rights. Tests must be passed; standardly, the interest must be of paramount importance – for example, it must be generalizable, it must be compossible (i.e., not prima facie inconsistent with other established or desired rights). Let us suppose that a candidate interest passed all such tests. There would still be another implicit test, one that need not be stated – because obvious – in the case of living people. The interest must *matter* to the bearer of the potential right. Its mattering is all that motivates the advocacy of rights: we advocate them because of concerns about humans' vulnerability to various kinds of preventable suffering or degradation or loss. Of course, we can reasonably stretch the condition to cover potential (not yet experienced) suffering and so on because people are not continuously aware of the ways in which their interests may be damaged, and governments or other third parties may have a duty to anticipate when the persons in question are unaware of them. But if an interest could be defeated without even potential harm to the person whose interest it is, it is hard to see what would motivate protecting it, at least to the extent of converting it into a right, thus giving it a status that would enable it to trump the interests whose defeat *would* cause experienced harm on the part of living persons. This would be to fetishize rights: to suppose that respecting one when the ground of its importance has vanished takes precedence over protecting what it is that grounds rights – that is, a vulnerable interest.

It is here that the cases for ascribing rights to deceased and future persons eventually come apart. For the rights of future people may, of course, protect them against potential harms if and when they come into being. They will be vulnerable to various kinds of damage that are foreseeable and, indeed, to various kinds of damage that we (living people) are in a position to inflict in the course of pursuing our own interests. The obvious moral shabbiness of our doing so is enough to motivate the ascription of rights to future people; it is a way of constraining our own self-regarding interests and making their vital interests salient in our policy making, of recognizing their stake in it. Considered only as interests, they would have to take their chances in the process of weighing and balancing as a result of which there are winners and losers. And those who are not present, given their lack of political standing, are very likely to become losers. There are, however, available constitutional mechanisms that give future people's interests the pre-emptive standing of rights. Some provisions for environmental protection, for example, may be understood in this way, and provisions limiting the extent of public debt are compellingly justified in exactly this fashion.

While it is true that transmitting public debt to the future – in the form of bond redemptions and interest payments – can be justified, the justifications must rest, to some extent, on assumptions whose validity may be only tentative. The most secure assumptions relate to maintaining infrastructure that, on any reasonable view known to us, will be essential to all imaginable future projects – the maintenance of which can justify "running costs," which each generation can be expected to bear its share of, expecting that other generations will bear theirs (Bertram 2009). A future generation's share may take the form of honouring debts that we have incurred for the purpose. Paying for a war of liberation may seem more speculative, but justifiable if we believe that political independence will have benefits that outweigh the burden of future repayments on war bonds.

Beyond this, we can imagine judgment calls at various probabilistic levels. Will future generations appreciate carrying debts incurred to make imperial expansion possible (e.g., by building expensive naval supremacy)? Will they appreciate or reject the sunk costs of a long-term space program? I am not sure that there is a way to escape speculation here. If each generation had to forswear speculation about future persons' values, then some projects would necessarily be taken off the agenda. We couldn't create public parks that would take fifty years to reach maturity, or universities that would take a generation or two or six to establish their intellectual culture, or prizes that would gain eventual prestige only through the sustained merit of their winners. So unless some kinds of good are to be ruled out of court peremptorily, there is simply no alternative to presumptuousness.

III

The possible rights of future people are, of course, to be distinguished from a right to exist. Whatever reasons there are to bring future people into being, they cannot be grounded in the rights of people who do not exist; for the existence of future people is a condition of their having rights, hence not something that they can be said to have a right to. There does not seem to be anything problematic, however, about making rights conditional on existence. People can bequeath their wealth to as yet non-existent grandchildren. Students in my classes next year will have a right to fair assessments, although I don't yet know whether anyone will sign up. In fact, a great many of the rights on the standard list are conditional in an exactly similar way. You have a right to a fair trial if you are arrested, a right to freedom of religion if you believe in anything of a religious sort, a right to free speech if you have something to say, a right to subsistence if you lose the means to support yourself. That none of these conditions happen to apply in your case doesn't mean you don't have the corresponding right, even if they never come to apply. So given this conditionality, it's entirely possible to suppose that people do have rights only on a condition – i.e., in this case, that they come to be.

It's clear that, in at least one important respect, the idea that future people have rights isn't subject to one of the objections to past people having them. If we think of rights as being based on interests, and if (as recommended above) we think of interests as being important only if what happens to them is person-affecting, then future people can have rights because they will be affected if their interests are damaged or promoted.[7] Not only may future people be said to have rights, in that case, but an obvious fact about future people makes the protection of their rights particularly important: once again, their vulnerability to what we do is a fact that should incline us to give at least some of their interests the status of rights so that, in the present, they act as constraints on policy making before it becomes too late to take them into account by acknowledging future persons' stake in what we do.

I now want to suggest, however, building on this consideration, that the ascription of rights to future persons makes up to a significant extent for the invalidity of ascribing rights to past people.[8] If we frame reparations as things that are intended to benefit past people, we face the compelling objection that we are unfairly and pointlessly sacrificing the interests of living people, who can be affected, to the interests of people who cannot be. But there are some significant ways in which the costs of reparative measures can be justified in terms of important future people's interests that can and will be affected.

This argument applies in the case of past injustices that continue to exercise an effect in the present – "enduring" injustices, as some like to call them, to distinguish them from "historical" injustices, which have now run their course (Spinner-Halev 2007). From the standpoint of ordinary theories of justice, these injustices have neither less nor more weight than any other. We should measure and respond to the deprivation that they involve just as we should measure and respond to other contemporary deprivation – for example, the insecurity and poverty of refugees whom we are in a position to aid, even in cases in which what happened to them is no part of our own history. To the consideration that it might be said that *we* caused the deprivation in one case but not the other – that people were enslaved or expropriated by our own state, while refugees are someone else's fault – there is, some would say, a short reply: *we* did not cause it, except on the basis of an implausible idea of a society as a sort of super-person that survives historical change intact.

But whereas *we* didn't enslave or expropriate two centuries ago, we, currently living citizens, are nevertheless complicit in transmitting enduring injustices to the future if we do nothing to remedy them. This, rather than some notion of inherited responsibility, is an idea that is far more consistent with basic ideas of moral agency, which ascribe liability on the basis of what we do rather than who we are said to be: we are liable not because of our identity but because of our response to inherited circumstances, to our agreement to transmit them forward rather than taking steps to terminate them. It remains to be shown, however, that this is something that brings the rights of future persons into play in a way that could be morally decisive. Here I think there are three considerations in favour of this view.

The first and most obvious is, of course, that if the injustice continues to endure, the victims of enduring injustice will be future persons. This point is rescued from mere truism by the consideration that if an injustice has endured over several generations, then there are very likely to be reasons for it. It doesn't mean that the victims of enduring injustice are in a worse plight than, say, autoworkers thrown out of a job by a very recent economic downturn; it simply means that the reasons for their circumstances, being historical, are both less immediate and less open to immediate view, so that the remedy, whatever it is, is likely to call for more far-reaching measures. Here a distinction that has been favoured in recent political theory may be helpful, a distinction between circumstances and choices. As victims of circumstances, the victims of enduring injustice are in the same boat, categorically speaking, as the victims of recent injustice: neither group has chosen to be where it is. But it is characteristic of enduring injustice, in which the experiences of one generation control the outlook of another, that it affects ideas of possibility or horizons of choice and, hence, the very capacity to undertake to change one's circumstances.

Second, we should draw on an important point made by Hannah Arendt (1967): history didn't have to be the way it was, and if for some reason we lost the record of it, there would be no way to reconstruct it *ab ovo*. If all the textbooks were burned, we could eventually reconstruct the truths about geometry; but there is no way that if all the records disappeared, we could, even in principle, reconstruct the causes and history of the First World War. Triangles have to be as they are in every respect, while people don't and so histories don't. Now enduring injustices stem from a history in which political leaders and businesspeople and settlers made decisions and responded to others' decisions in contingent ways, and without the record, future persons would have no way of knowing how things came to be or, hence, how to respond to circumstances. Reparations, and other practices such as apologies and memorial events, are ways of placing a contingent past on the record so that future persons will be in a position even to consider the ways in which its transmission bears on them.

Third – and most speculatively? – may we attribute to future persons an interest in leading a just life? It is a speculative question because it involves making guesses about what people want – and, of course, there is conflicting evidence about this as well as a lack of evidence. But here are two considerations in favour of what may seem an idealistic proposition. One is that faced with situations in which others are deluded about what is real, most people rebel against delusion: they generally resist the temptation of Nozick's experience machine, and they tend to rejoice when Truman discovers that he is an involuntary actor in *The Truman Show*, even though the discovery isn't exactly happiness-promoting. Second, it certainly seems to be important to successful people to believe that they can claim credit for their own success; and even if they are wrong, or exaggerate, their claims may be seen as the homage that self-esteem pays to truth.

The relevance of this is that historical redress is among the principal instruments at a society's disposal for clarifying the account of how things came to be, so that present and future people can form a more accurate picture of how they came to enjoy the advantages that they have. To take these advantages to be natural, or else merited, is to inhabit a mental world that is shielded from the claims of justice. Perhaps there is a sort of presumptuousness in thinking that future people will care about the claims of justice. But starting from the supposition that we care about justice, there is something worse than presumptuousness in supposing that future people won't care about its claims: there is something like contempt in it, in accepting on future generations' behalf a sort of abject cluelessness.

IV

The case made here is actually the reverse of an interesting case made by Annette Baier (1980) in an article, cited in chapter 3, with the same title as this chapter. For Baier, future people have moral standing, in part, because of what we owe to our predecessors. They initiated and sustained important projects from which we benefit: institutions such as universities, for example. If we fail to sustain them so that they can be transmitted forward, we are not only condemnable as free-riders, but we also act unjustly towards our predecessors, who created the institutions not for us (currently living people) alone, but for an indefinite number of future generations. The starting point for the argument, then, is the worth or dignity of our predecessors' intentions, and our successors are the beneficiaries (as distinct from the bearers) of our respect for those intentions. Here, however, it is claimed that a sense of respect for the past, expressed in acts of redress, is driven, above all, by concern for the interests of future people. Past people are (not the bearers, but) the (symbolic) beneficiaries of this. Is this paradoxical?

Leif Wenar (2006) also claims that "reparations are for the future" in an article with that title. There are powerful, "forward-looking" reasons for reparations, particularly reasons connected with the future pursuit of both social peace and distributive justice. As for social peace, a substantial literature sets out the importance of acknowledging and repairing wrongs for the promotion of trust. Apologies, for example, may be seen as "exemplary" demonstrations of the way in which one generation declares its separateness from the ideas and acts of its predecessors so as to put its relations with the previously oppressed on a new footing. "We might rethink state expressions of regret in view of recognizing their … complex role in catalyzing shifts in the public culture of democratic, yet imperfectly just, societies" (Mihai 2013, 220). To this must be added the possible value of apology and other forms of redress for building trust on the part of victims' groups. Reparations are sometime seen as replacing assets that previous generations would have passed down to their descendants but for the injustice that they suffered. However, "It is not so much the inheritance of assets that is relevant for reparations as it is the inheritance of attitudes." Attitudes "cascade down the generations to an alarming extent," preventing groups from trusting people whom they not unreasonably identify with their previous oppressors (Wenar 2006, 404).

As for considerations about distributive justice, a thought experiment suggests the paramount importance of such reasons. Suppose the world were now distributively just (in terms of whatever principle of distributive justice we endorse): would one favour disrupting the just distribution of goods and opportunities to implement reparative policies? "If not," Wenar writes, "then you do not believe that such reparative claims have significant force of their own, separate from their overlap with principles of just distribution" (ibid., 402). By implication, if we do favour reparative policies, it is in large part, in many cases, because such policies *also* further the ends of distributive justice. So reparative ends, he argues, have significant but nevertheless conditional moral force.

But I believe that the future-relevant aspects of reparations extend even further than that. What is at stake is nothing less than the capacity of future generations to exercise suitably informed reason in conducting their common life. Political decisions depend on at least an approximately valid understanding of how and why things happen. But if past injustices are unacknowledged, or not responded to in some way, several deeply corrupting effects on public understanding are very likely to follow. Majorities are likely to overlook the role of unappreciated minorities in the construction of their society. Opinion is likely to overlook the ways in which benefits are won and held at others' cost. The historical role of violence is likely to be hidden from sight. Above all, people may come to feel that, in the historical process, the winners are the virtuous ones and that losers deservedly lose – an illusion that not only sanctifies the present order of things but also blunts the sense that important institutions and principles need to be critically sustained against assault and corruption because their survival is not guaranteed. Without widely shared "knowledge and an understanding of institutions," as Rawls wrote, a society lacks the "human capital" required for justice (Rawls 2001, 140).

So to conclude: future people do have rights, in the sense that they have important interests that may obstruct policies that we (other citizens) might otherwise be entitled to adopt. Past people don't have rights because, although their interests may be said to survive them, they cannot experience setbacks to those interests. Of course, we need to remember what they went through because of "the interests of justice" – that is, the idea of justice needs to be constantly reinforced by memories of the cost of its violation. But the idea of justice itself has no rights, and the rights that come into the matter are those of future people, who have a "need to know" status when it comes to understanding how the interests of some people get to be promoted while others' interests are blocked. And what they need to know cannot but be affected by what people like them, in relevant ways, have experienced.

Conclusion

This book has made a number of claims – many or all of them contestable – and I shall review them briefly (in sections I and II) before discussing (in sections III to VI) what general conclusion should be drawn from the topics discussed.

I

First, looking back: the book began, necessarily, by assessing the view that we are separated impassably, in terms of moral judgments, from earlier historical periods, so that any effort to do justice in relation to the past would violate the self-understanding of previous generations, in rather the same way that foreign interventions violate the sovereignty of other countries – an issue that recurs, as chapter 9 noted, in relation to future generations too. The chapter advanced a number of reasons for questioning that view of the past. But its main claim is that, even in hard cases, the evidence is that those who supported oppression had available to them the moral resources to reach conclusions different from those that they favoured. Those resources were to be found in the very traditions that the oppressors and their ideologists ransacked for support as well as in an open-minded interpretation, using the most ordinary criteria of personal assessment, of what was going on around them. What may get in the way of appreciating this, it was suggested, is an overly impressionable response to the language of paradigms and, hence, a readiness to construct intellectual boundaries where none exist. It may be that the strictly bounded and as it were replicative model of thought neglects its adventurous potential, presenting the mind as something like a role-bound functionary with an officially defined remit – the mind as Eichmann, one might perhaps say.[1]

All of the above is critical in spirit, though. Can we find a positive way to ground the idea of intercultural and intertemporal judgment? Some conclusions of experimental philosophy were briefly noted as a possible route to answering this question. Of course, they invite questioning, as all empirical work and all philosophy do. But they effectively pose a deep challenge to the cultural or temporal anti-presentist. If you believe that the moral beliefs of one society are incompatible with the moral beliefs of another society, how do you know which beliefs to count as moral ones, so that you can begin to make a comparison? One proposal – that we think of the moral domain in terms of certain common sensitivities – is promising; and it raises the question, Would we actually count a belief as a *moral* one if it was entirely indifferent to (say) harm, or unfairness, or disloyalty? Or would we not say, rather, that whatever there might possibly be to be said for it, it didn't count as a moral belief? But just as a folkway, something that people happen to hold with?

There is the further consideration that, for certain purposes, such as compensation and apology, we do not even need to know, for sure, whether present standards converge with older ones: our standards apply well enough to govern what we should do to make what it is after all *our* point to make, for present and future purposes. But only if we accept something like the main conclusion of chapter 1 can we begin to entertain the topic of chapter 2, punishment. If a society were morally sovereign – if, that is, it alone could define the terms on which its conduct was to be evaluated – then the issue of collective guilt would not arise. It would simply judge and vindicate itself in an automatically self-validating fashion.

So when we consider holding societies accountable for what they have done, something else must be going on. What gets in the way here, though, is a basic principle of moral responsibility. We can be held responsible only for what we have *done,* and the events that we are concerned with here – genocides, aggressive wars – are not things that a personal agent can *do*. They are essentially collective in nature, and unless we can capture this aspect, we incur a normative loss in the sense that our attributions of responsibility miss their mark. Their collective nature is captured in a conceptual way by the idea of a "criminal state," a term used by Jaspers, Arendt, and others. But this idea sits very uncomfortably, it was argued, in Jaspers's own normative framework, and to recover it, we need to stand outside his set of well-known categories and also withstand the temptation to hold *nations* collectively responsible – a temptation that we should resist if we recognize that what a nation is, is a subject of protracted internal dissension.

If we focus, then, on states rather than nations, we need to bear down quite heavily on two things. One is the enormously violent potential of states as concentrations of force that are sustained by their insiders' obedience and outsiders' deference to their sovereignty. The other is the complicity that their insiders' deference entails. A state can become criminal, not because all its members are criminal, but because states are structures of power that rest on small increments of obedience. How to connect each of these small increments, in a causal manner, with what is done with the power is an impossibly complex task. But if we take a forward-looking perspective, and focus on moral rather than causal responsibility, then there is much to be said for creating incentives that heighten awareness of what, collectively, we are making possible when we obey. This was termed *obedience responsibility*. The idea rests on the notion that citizenship should be imagined as a kind of role that opens its occupants to liabilities that, considered only as persons, they would not be exposed to. But since the distinction between role and person is conceptual, not material, in nature, the heightening of complicity may need to be matched by caution in punishment, for what is owed to the role, as such, is necessarily experienced by the person, as such.

There is, however, another, distinct (and very common) approach to liability for past wrongs, one that draws neither on Jaspers's classic categories nor on the notion of political complicity. This is the idea of receiving benefits, the topic of chapter 3. The idea has the potentially simplifying merit of shifting the question of continuity from agents to things, which subsist in a less problematic way than agency does (Goodin 2013). Just how presently existing agents are to be connected to past wrongdoers and victims is surely the central question in the discussion of historical responsibility. We can dispense with this difficult question, however, if we say that what links past and present is not a hard-to-prove, subsisting identity but a thing that was once lost and now is possessed by someone. The legal doctrine of *unjust enrichment* provides a compelling model: something that has come to be unjustly possessed carries with it an indelible claim to be returned as long as it continues to be possessed.

But the usefulness of this view, for the (non-legal) purposes of this discussion, is limited in several ways. First, it is misleading to place the moral emphasis on *what* was gained when actually what we want to condemn was *how* it was gained: no doubt people gained a great deal from slavery, but our condemnation of how they sought it surely doesn't depend on their policy's success. Suppose slavery was less productive than other alternatives available to the slave-based economies, so that, on balance, slavery was a bad deal for everyone? Second, suppose that if indeed there were profits, perhaps they have long since been dissipated – and surely we wouldn't want to say that their dissipation removes any cause to redress, in some way, the cruelty of their original extraction? And third, distinctions come into play between receiving and accepting, benefiting and contributing. It isn't obvious that passively receiving some benefit creates the same obligation as actively taking steps to accept it would; nor is it clear that benefiting from some injustice creates the same liability as actually contributing to it would, as we can see in the case of contributing to injustice in a way that, as it happens, did not pay off in terms of benefits.

Finally, the receipt of benefits tends too easily to rest on the idea of gratitude, which is an important moral feeling, but one whose requirements seem rather easily defeasible by considerations of current justice. The idea of receiving benefits seems, in general, either to elide moral wrong with material harm or to function as a proxy for other considerations that need to be distinguished and more precisely stated if they are to be accurately assessed.

Some, though not of course all, benefits are of the sort that can be given back. Prominent among these are valued cultural objects, and much discussion about historical redress has focused, understandably, on their return to their original home. As chapter 4 noted, this issue is sometimes approached through the lenses of two large theories, nationalist and cosmopolitan. But the appeal of both theories tends to wane when we address particular cases, for cultural objects obviously comprise a variegated set. In some cases, what we may call their provenance may be more salient than what we may call their aesthetic reference in deciding where they should end up. In some cases, their provenance, in the context of influences in which they were produced, may not be territorial at all. In other cases, the trumping consideration may be an artefact's best realistic chance at preservation.

But politically, a central question is that of what the object reflects about the relationship between current and original possessors. The cosmopolitan view is uncomfortably close to an imperialist one, given the South-to-North direction in which cultural objects inexorably move. Moreover, one country's possession of an object may be emblematic of a previous history of domination that it becomes important to disavow: continued possession expresses, in concrete form, an insulting absence of reciprocity. This may not always apply. But even where it doesn't, there is a larger category of stakes fairness that should incline us to think about respective gains and losses. While the nationalist and cosmopolitan views are directly distributive in privileging one outcome over the other, the idea of respective stakes points towards deliberative or negotiated solutions, which may reflect a better model for resolving disputes than distributive-justice considerations generally tend to do.

Suppose, though, that – once we have come to set aside the claims of anti-presentism in evaluating the past – what is important is not the punishment of the guilty (or their descendants), or the taint of receiving benefits, or the duty to return those of the benefits that can be returned, but simply the memory of the past, as a large and often moving literature insists? Memory, discussed in chapter 5, may refer to different things: recovering significant facts that some knew about but others didn't, recalling subjective experiences of oppression and pain, and (most ambitiously) the calling-to-account of entire episodes or regimes. The premier vehicle of memory, in all three senses, is the truth commission, an institution that is often contrasted, favourably, with the criminal trial, which was the subject of chapter 2. The truth commission does much better than trials do with the first two kinds of memory. As for the third, we may see it as accomplishing rather the same ambition as a criminal trial if its purpose is to affirm the dignity and equality of victims, but in a context in which violations have been systemic as opposed to exceptional. In this way, injustice is normalized or, as one commentator puts it, "As atrocity becmes more widespread in nature, and more popular, it becomes more difficult to construct participation therein as deviant" (Drumbl 2011, 29), with the state and the criminal changing places, an inversion that calls for redress.

A distinction needs to be made, however, between the affirmation of justice and the construction of public narratives that some may conscientiously – which is not to say rightly – refuse. Such narratives are too highly motivated by overriding political purposes to do justice to individual stories. They claim a sort of finality that is in tension with the provisional victories of democracy. Moreover, public-narrative memories share in many of the all too familiar defects that are characteristic of personal memories and that render them so unreliable, particularly in their aggregating and de-individuating tendencies. In this respect, memory (if uncritical) may ally itself with repression rather than redress, given that aggregating and de-individuating thinking is so often responsible for the events for which redress is sought in the first place.

This book began by noting the shortcomings of reciprocity in intergenerational matters – a problem, it is often alleged, for theories of justice that depend on some form of that notion. But I believe that a reasonable conclusion to be drawn from the first five chapters of this book is that the problem is highly mitigated. In every case that we have discussed, the prime reason for forms of redress derives from present and future needs – the affirmation of standards of justice, the punishment of offences, the return of valued objects, and memorializing the past are all things that are most clearly understood in terms of the needs of people who live or will do so one day. One may make an exception of ideas that justice matters for its own sake, not for person-affecting reasons – as Kant may have believed, as one notorious passage at least suggests[2] – and of ideals of memory that have no instrumental point at all.

But these are unusual views, and, in any event, may be brought to bear, by those who believe in them, on past events in one's own lifetime, not just on what past generations have done or suffered. This greatly diminishes the distinctiveness of the past in terms of what justice requires; and the underlying reason is quite simple. What past generations have done continues to affect the living, and we *are* in some sort of reciprocal relation with those who are currently affected. If they are in our own country, then they are subject to rules and institutions that we sustain, and they have claims in terms of equal respect or the requirements of democratic interaction or both. If they are in other countries, then considerations of mutual global respect apply. The important question of whether any of this should be expressed in terms of *rights* was put off until the second half of this book.

II

To move on, now, to "going forth": if past people are beyond our reach, the issue posed by future people, by way of contrast, is that they are too wholly subject to our decisions to be in reciprocal association with us. Nothing could make this more graphically clear than the fact that their very existence is optional for us. This may seem to be a merely theoretical consideration, given that the options that many people exercise in their lives are going to produce future people anyway. But the consideration needs to be taken seriously if, as some claim, there are compelling reasons *not* to exercise the option of reproducing. Discussion (in chapter 6) of the most fully worked-out version of this radical view suggested reasons to reject its central claim – that is, its proposed asymmetry of pain and pleasure, an asymmetry whereby if people come to be born, their pains will count against existence, while if no one is born, the absence of pleasure will not count, being experienced by no one. That claim should be reformulated in terms of a distinction between negative duties not to cause pain to anyone who exists and positive duties to promote pleasure among those with whom one has a special connection. Neither of those person-affecting views can have anything to say about whether persons should or should not exist. If, indeed, pain generally outweighed pleasure in life, it would be a different matter, but views that it does so are, it was argued, rebuttable. In particular, the pain allegedly arising from cosmic meaninglessness is one that arises only by way of contrast with theological comfort, and if one believes such comfort to be a mirage, then it is inconsistent to mourn its demise.

That brings us to a once-familiar (nineteenth-century) context in which writers (such as George Eliot and Mill) gave earnest attention to what the demise of faith meant for morality. In attaching value to a common project, their response isn't, ultimately, a person-affecting one, but if person-affecting views cannot touch the question of whether persons should exist, then only non-person-affecting views are on point. Unlike person-affecting views such as Do No Harm, they are optional rather than universal in their appeal: but then there is no universal duty to procreate, nor any need for one.

If children do come to be born, however, they are vulnerable to domination by those who have brought them into being, and chapter 7 examined several ideas about the extent to which parents are entitled to include their children in what we may term their ideational projects – a question generally explored in the context of parental religious projects, especially of a sort that are thought to involve limiting children's options and their exposure to them. The view that children ought to have a maximally open future is strongly resisted by some philosophers on the grounds that there simply is no context-independent measure of openness: each culture has its own view of what a significant range of options is. In partial defence of the open future view, the chapter argued that it is one thing to provide children only with those options that are valued and something else to shield children from the fact that different options are valued by others. How it comes about that values differ is a question that evades definitive resolution by sophisticated enquiry and is not a question that should be imposed unasked on children! But unless we attribute implausibly mechanical views of choice to open-future theorists, and atypically totalitarian ambitions to their opponents, the two positions may converge on an ideal of parental responsiveness: responsiveness to a sense that children are neither replicas nor blank slates but distinct centres of personal experience. In this way, something quite parallel to reciprocity may be attainable.

The requirements of parental *political* competence – the topic of chapter 8 – have been generally overshadowed by such considerations of moral competence, or the capacity to provide the conditions for a child's development as a person. A maximal idea of parental political competence will, of course, simply reproduce one's favoured political theory: it would say that one should transmit one's political ideal, just as conservative libertarians believe that parents should be free to transmit their religious views. But is there a minimal idea of parental political competence, one that is implicit in the very idea of procreating? There is, in that procreation is an individual decision with consequences that depend on the nearby decisions of others. One's responsibilities for those consequences must take a political form. Minimally understood, again, those responsibilities must take the form of supporting arrangements that mitigate the effects of fluctuations in cohort size, fluctuations that have an enormous effect on the lives of one's own and others' children – effects that may even be greater, in fact, than effects that would follow from the adoption of one political ideology or another. The arrangements are, approximately, those of social-democratic politics. The conclusion should persuade even those who reject the similar-looking (but different) ideas of luck egalitarianism and procreative beneficence. It is not luck-egalitarian because it is grounded not in what just happens to occur but in what one personally does – i.e., procreate, even though the duty cannot be fulfilled by personal action. It should not be classed as a procreative beneficence thesis either, for it is grounded in negative rather than positive duties to children: on harm avoidance.

Beyond supporting arrangements that mitigate the collective effects of individual actions, can one generation impose constitutional arrangements on another – that is, systems of very hard-to-change rules that constrain their collective decision making? Chapter 9 took up this question. If one generation does this to another, isn't it pretty well identical to a colonialist imposition by a strong country on a weaker one? Or to a domineering parent imposing her world view on a child? These conclusions are obstructed by two considerations. One is the difference between acts that imperiously set aside an already formed will and acts that necessarily require an anticipation of others' as yet unasserted needs. An answer is offered that draws on the parallel models of decolonization and parenting. We have to think about what is called for by the necessary conditions of freedom, individual or collective. Responsible decolonization would call for creating conditions under which a freed society has the possibility of exercising self-determination once other-determination has been withdrawn from it. This possibility cannot be simply a matter of pure abstract freedom, but must take an institutional form, without which the very idea of a collective *self*, of a sort to which decisions can be attributed, is unintelligible. And this consideration applies to the libertarian utopia as forcefully as to any other political ideal in that it, too, will foreclose potentially valuable options. This utopia is deceptive if it inclines us to avoid the inevitable.

Finally, the idea of *rights* was discussed in chapter 10. This idea is brought prominently into play in the whole discussion undertaken here, given worries about whether the conditions for reciprocity hold, for while rights (by definition) involve corresponding duties, no reciprocal duty needs to be held by a bearer of rights. So there is a possibility here, built into the very idea of rights, of unilateral obligations that can survive the fact that the living, the deceased, and the unborn are not in symmetrical relations with one another. That said, the idea of rights does nevertheless have its paradigm in the relation between one living person and another, and whether the deceased and the unborn can be said to have rights is a topic open for discussion. If we persevere with the idea that moral views are essentially person-affecting, then speaking of the rights of the deceased is going to look deeply implausible or else look like an elliptical way of talking about the ante-mortem advantages of post-mortem arrangements. From this angle, the idea of the rights of future people is going to fare much better since they will be profoundly affected by what living people do;[3] and reasons are available, it was argued, for fending off some standard objections to their having rights.

By an apparent paradox, however, the chapter concluded, the rights of future people can provide a way to think about what is due to the past. When the material effects of past injustice are transmitted to the present, the justice to be sought ceases to be intergenerational: the effects are part of an array of current burdens that need to be either remedied or justified. When the material effects have been dissipated, or when what demands attention is not a material loss but a wrong, a residue remains, unattended to. But among the things that future people can plausibly be said to have a right to is an account of the past that allows them to conduct their own political lives in an unmystified way. If this is so, then non-material or symbolic remedies for past injustices cease to be optional and become imperative, as duties responsive to rights. For while future generations will be in a position to re-create some things for themselves if they come to be lost, history is not among them. Things didn't have to be as they were; and knowing how things come to be is a prerequisite to effective action.

III

The overall conclusion of parts I and II, taken together, is that we can make some headway in relation to redress for past injustices if we connect redress with forward-looking considerations of the kind just mentioned. But this, of course, throws more weight, correspondingly, on the case for future justice. On what general basis can we rest the claims advanced in the previous section? The question is a pressing one, for while we can blunt the no-reciprocity objection in the case of historical redress, by pointing to the ways in which unaddressed past injustices may impede fair reciprocity in the present, in the case of future justice the no-reciprocity objection is even more potentially damaging. Brian Barry makes the point strongly. "We can now be quite certain … that people alive in several centuries' time will not be able to do anything that will make us better off or worse off now, although we can to some degree make them better or worse off" (Barry 1989, 495). So even given that we can choose whether to transmit the burdens of the past to future people, any duty to do so, being unilateral, may seem gratuitous.

This objection withstands even enormously interesting attempts to show that living people depend on future people in important ways. One attempt involves a model of intergenerational cooperation whereby each generation's benefit depends on non-defection by later generations. There are real-world examples – such as, notably, pension plans – but the clearest example is the hypothetical one devised by Joseph Heath (2013), discussed briefly in chapter 8. Imagine, Heath says, a circle of eight people passing tokens to the person on their left. Each player can choose to keep a two-dollar token or pass a five-dollar token to the next player. They will all be better off (after one round, when the amount in each player's account is recorded) if all players pass on the five-dollar token, and they will do so if they trust the person on their right to understand how the game works. We can intergenerationalize the game by supposing that, from time to time, a player leaves the circle and is replaced by a new player: the logic of the game still works. But the game would collapse if it were known that some player (established or new) would defect at some future point, for then the consequences would unwind from the person on the future defector's left all the way back around the circle. Relevantly similar schemes, then, depend for their viability on the assumption of indefinite continuation: we pay forward only on condition that future cooperators will play the game. And many important institutions, Heath shows, *are* relevantly similar to the hypothetical game.

Criticism of this model of reciprocity is likely to focus on its range of reference, or completeness, rather than its logic. One kind of question has its source in the continuity of the goods involved. The tokens that are exchanged in the game have a stable, intertemporal quantity and meaning. But changes in either quantity or meaning would seem to disrupt the game. If we suppose the supply of tokens (collective wealth) to be limited, then an increase in the number of players would necessitate a smaller per capita share, so that a player who had contributed a certain sum in a leftward direction would begin to receive a smaller sum from the right. The loss would, of course, be temporary only if the player in question then adjusted his leftward contribution. But changes in meaning are more intractable. It would be irrational to pass valued clamshells to the left if players to one's right began to disvalue clamshells and adopt a currency of pebbles instead.

The problem is solved if we suppose the currency to be completely fungible, as money is sometimes supposed to be. But this, of course, is contentious. Suppose the players, or some of them, perhaps the new players who eventually enter, respond to values that they refuse to see as monetized, such as environmental protection or the treatment of non-human species? To the extent that the game presupposes either a common good or a common measure of goods that permits exchange, it will be undermined by "transvaluations of values" – a problem that will be more serious, of course, the more we imagine future generations to be capable of moral transformations. Will future people value a space program if we devote resources to it or, alternatively, blame us if we don't? Such questions reinforce general doubts about insurance models of political society, models that, despite their obvious usefulness, cannot take up the whole space that political morality needs to occupy (Hibbert 2010).

A second kind of discontinuity is what may be termed *discontinuity of effect*. In the hypothetical game, the consequences of defection travel round the circuit with electric speed. But suppose the consequences of lack of cooperation are significantly delayed? Here, as noted in chapter 10, we encounter "sleeper" problems, as Brian Barry called them. Suppose, for example, that you are an antisocial picnicker and also a gifted statistician with close knowledge of the local terrain and demography. You know that if you leave broken glass in the forest, it will likely be a hundred years before someone cuts their foot on it; then you have no reciprocity-based reason to clean up the glass. Or suppose a current generation can solve its energy problems by going nuclear, creating substantial amounts of radioactive waste; if the problems won't show up for many generations, then again a reciprocity-based approach falls short.

But there is another possible source of mutuality altogether, one derivable from Samuel Scheffler's book, *Death and the Afterlife* (2013). The book brings out brilliantly the ways in which our own activities depend – implicitly, for the most part – on the indefinitely long continuation of our species after our own death. This continuation is a condition of things *mattering* to us, and Scheffler shows, by a series of compelling thought experiments, that we can reconcile ourselves to our own personal death much more readily than we can to the prospect of human extinction, so that, surprisingly, the existence of later generations matters more to us than, as we might say, "life itself." What point would many of our activities have if they had no future? So here is a possible challenge to the claim of Brian Barry's with which we began: future people *will* be able "to make us better off" – that is, by the very fact of existing. Time is indeed unidirectional, but anticipation is unidirectional in the opposite direction, and if the anticipation of future human life were not to be sustained, we would suffer a severe loss. Future people exercise a sort of counter-temporal influence on our lives. Is this a kind of reciprocity? We give them life, they give us meaning?

There are several reasons to doubt this. One is that non-reproducers can evade reciprocity by free-riding on the reproduction of others – future people don't have to be one's own children; they just have to be someone's. Another is that, without a great deal of (highly contestable) further argument, one cannot claim that conferring existence is a benefit, for the claim faces the difficult question: a benefit to whom? There are not, as it were, proto-people in some limbo awaiting the gift of life from us (as a Benatarian would quite correctly point out). So what is the quid that we give in return for the quo provided by a human future? A third reason is prompted by concerns about presumptuousness. We value future people, on this argument, because we assume or hope that they will carry on activities – art, philosophy, classical music – that we value, thus giving us assurance that practising them ourselves is not a vain gesture but something that matters. But of course, we don't know what conclusions future generations will come to about such things, or how to practise them if they do adopt them, or whether the nature of their practice is one that we would recognize as continuous with our own. We just do not know what Rembrandt would have made of Lucian Freud's work, what Kant would have made of Zizek's, Berlioz of John Cage's.

IV

So Barry's scepticism is vindicated, even though there is more reciprocity between generations than his remark suggests and even though implicit anticipations about the future loom larger in our lives than we may have thought before reading Scheffler's deeply provocative book. But another strategy altogether is to rely, rather, on an idea of purely hypothetical reciprocity. Doing so is less drastic a concession than may first appear, for after all, what theorists of reciprocity mainly rely on, even in the case of living persons, is a thought experiment and not a plebiscite designed to uncover the actual state of public opinion. But to go straight to what has become the classic attempt, even *this* idea of a (diagnostic) thought experiment seems troubled when we bring future generations into the picture.

Above we briefly noted some of the standardly detected difficulties arising from Rawls's effort to bring future generations within the scope of a hypothetical contract. Sensing that the inhabitants of a single generation would lack motivation to care about the future, given the constraints of the original position as he had set it up as a test of fairness, he first proposed care for the next generation or two as a remedy – caring for them, we would want a savings principle that would enable them to enjoy primary goods and a level of prosperity sufficient to sustain just institutions. In response to many (merited) critiques, he later came to stipulate instead that each generation would agree to save at the rate at which it would wish any generation to save. This poses problems of a different kind: it seems to introduce an impartiality condition into a choice situation that is meant to be modelled on self-interest, and it raises serious enforcement issues in relation to both past and future. How do we know that we won't be the first generation to save justly, so that a huge unreciprocated burden will fall on us? And how do we know that if we save justly, the next generation, for which we save, will do so too, rather than squandering its inheritance – thus making our own sacrifices pointless (Barry 1989, 276; Heyd 2009, 180–1)?

A large and very sophisticated literature has grown up around these two ideas.[4] They contain perplexing problems. Could the original position include people of any generation, indifferently? Even Rawls himself rejected this idea as "fantasy" (Rawls 1971, 329), but surely it comes closest, among the various proposed solutions, to treating generational membership in the same way as class or taste or talent or gender – that is, by denying one knowledge of it. Why is it that generational membership should *not* follow this general and (in my view) generally productive basic pattern?

One obstacle is Rawls's requirement that, behind the veil that denies each of us knowledge of our particular identity, we still have enough general knowledge to sustain judgments about the kind of social institutions that are possible. This general knowledge is to include knowledge of world history. This poses a problem for supposing that people in the original position can be ignorant of their generation, for if they all have knowledge of world history up to 2016 but no further, then they are all obviously of this generation; while if we suppose generational membership to be randomly assigned, it is impossible to know what stage in world history we are to ascribe knowledge of to any given participant.

Jonathan Wolff may be responding to this problem with a light touch in his introductory book on political philosophy. He imagines that, as a participant, "You do recall some general theories you once learnt in economics and sociology classes, but you cannot remember anything from your history lessons" (Wolff 1996, 159). That is a helpful and convenient (if very informal!) amendment of what *A Theory of Justice* required; but what justifies it? One reason for amending it could be that while some understanding of how social and political change takes place is important to making political choices, it does not seem crucially important that one should know what particular stage of history one is at.

This would be so, however, if some particular stage of history contained lessons that it would be indispensable to know to arrive at a just basic constitutional structure. But we know (e.g.) from *The Law of Peoples* that the events of the Holocaust impressed Rawls deeply, and so one could well imagine that the record of twentieth-century violence could shape one's view of politics in a basic way. It is true that it was an important defence of the proceedings at Nuremberg that while the charges against Nazi leaders involved (in part) retroactive law, it was humanly inconceivable that anyone should not understand before the fact that mass extermination was wrong; and if that defence of the Nuremberg trial is convincing, then there is no reason to suppose that the experience of even great evils is needed to reach the understanding that, for example, basic liberties are to be protected. Lesser evils would do the job, if less vividly, suggesting that Wolff's amendment is not only convenient, but right – knowledge of the course of history up to the present can and should be abandoned as a condition for the original position. But all the same, continuing the back-and-forth here for one final move, this defence would lose its plausibility to the extent that, reasonably, we would want political judgment to be as fully informed as possible and to the extent that we believe that recent history contains irreplaceably informative examples, as some believe it to do.

The second obstacle may be more serious. Obviously, not all conceivable people come into existence, and those that do come into existence as an intended or unintended result of decisions made by other people. So, it has been complained, if representatives of all generations are supposed to meet together, the absurd and paradoxical result is that some of those present would not exist unless others had made certain choices. "It is surely a curious sort of choice if the results of it are already instantiated in the composition of the group of people doing the choosing!" (Barry 1989, 281). Or perhaps representatives of, say, generation 216 could, as it were, withdraw existence from the representatives of generation 217 by declaring that they did not plan to bring them into the world? (This would certainly undermine the standing of the 217 people to contribute.) Can the any-generation view survive this complaint?

We could challenge Barry's use of the word *choice* by pointing out that the rate of reproduction is not a collective decision – i.e., something that people in the original position are called on to make, despite the important general consequences that it has. The people in the original position are called on to settle on a basic structure for the intentional distribution of benefits and burdens. Why, though, could this structure not distribute reproduction – considered either as a benefit or a burden, or a mix of both – in a prescribed way? Knowing the facts of human nature, and quickly arriving (it would seem) at the sense that we would want the freedom to pursue our own plan of life rather than a plan coercively imposed by someone else, we would recognize that having children, or equally not having children, would be important to the kind of life that we wanted to lead, as is often argued in other contexts. The decision to reproduce or not to do so would thus be among the basic liberties – that is, those that we need to express our personhood. But this, if a valid conclusion from the veil-of-ignorance situation, can only be a conclusion of adopting some version of that situation as a test, and so it cannot tell us whose interests should be represented in the situation in the first place.[5]

But what is perhaps the largest problem of all remains. Suppose that, in one way or another, we can smooth out the obstacles to an intergenerational contract: does this mean that the full requirements of Rawlsian justice would apply intergenerationally? And if so, is this conclusion acceptable? It is one thing to say that people of all generations have equal moral standing – something that would win general agreement – and something else to say that the interests of every generation must be given equal weight in our decisions – which may be not only undesirable, but impossible. Let me take these two objections in turn.

Even though I acknowledge the equal moral standing of future people (and on what conceivable moral basis could I do otherwise?), it doesn't follow that, in my own decisions, I have to give their interests equal weight because I may have overriding commitments that prevent me from doing so. Equal respect, as Richard Miller has pointed out in the global context, does not at once translate into equal concern (Miller 2010, 17–18). Here family commitments come into play at once (I would feed my starving child meat from the last surviving passenger pigeons even though this meant that future generations of children would, sadly, never get a chance to see a passenger pigeon); but are family commitments special? They are, but they are not unique. Surely we would feel justified in making an altogether exorbitant claim on the world's remaining stocks of oil and gas if, as a generation, we needed to do so to survive some terrible episode of global cooling. But in this sort of case, we would seem to be stepping outside the realm of justice considerations. The "circumstances of justice," as both Hume and Rawls define them, assume moderate, not absolute, scarcity. If you and I can both survive on the available resources, then there can be a question (based perhaps on equality, or contribution, or merit, or future utility …) about how to allocate the resources between us. But if one of us has to die, justice, on this view of its circumstances, has nothing to say about it.

The impossibility objection may be more serious, given the real prospect of doubt about what we may or may not claim for ourselves – doubt that parallels debates about the scope of legitimate compatriot preference in the context of global ethics. Suppose we simply *cannot* treat future generations equally? This would take the matter out of the realm of legitimate disagreement. Some initial moves in this direction were considered, and rejected, above. Surely we know that there are things that future generations will not want (smallpox epidemics, skin cancer). And surely we know that future people will not be *wholly* unlike us, so that we can have no idea about what they would want. But these are easy cases. A much more difficult case concerns the question of how we could even set about providing for equality between our generation and future ones, given measurement problems.

Here global justice again offers a parallel. David Miller has given reasons to question the coherence of the idea of distributive equality among national polities, reasons based in part on issues of measurement (Miller 2000, chap. 10). It is at least a real complication, and perhaps even an obstacle, that, for cultural and perhaps other reasons, different societies have different ideas about what a good is. Cultures differ in the priority that they give to leisure time, for example, so that if, for that reason, one comes to have less material wealth than another, it is not unjust. Societies may differ greatly in the amount of risk they consider acceptable in a good life. A climate suitable for vineyards is not a valuable resource for a society whose religion forbids alcohol. An infrastructure designed to facilitate exports is not an asset to a former colony engaged in internal economic development. It is easy to see that the problem not only recurs in the intergenerational case but is also potentially even more severe. For not only may future societies have different culturally based values, but even things currently agreed to be valuable resources may cease to be so: uranium deposits, for example, would lose most of their value if nuclear weapons were banned and if the problems of storing waste were to lead to abandoning nuclear power as an energy source.

Two critics, Meyer and Roser, pursue this objection in their discussion of intergenerational egalitarianism (Meyer and Roser 2009). They write, "Our knowledge of the relevant conditions of life of future people is limited and this epistemic situation of ours seems insuperable" (241). We may contrast our situation here with the presentist issue discussed in chapter 1: in the case of past societies, we can at least form some judgment about what we share with them and come to the conclusion that what we share is enough for some purposes of judgment, while in the case of future societies, we cannot know what is yet to be known. This is (at least) because the ways of life of future people will depend in part on their having technological knowledge that we cannot predict and (in part) because their ways of life will depend on future collective decisions, and on the aggregate outcomes of individual decisions, that are as yet necessarily unknown. Their argument is refined in an important footnote (242n64). Even if it is the case, as is likely, that our list of goods overlaps with theirs, even quite extensively, we cannot know that their ranking of them will be the same as ours, and so even in the relatively easier case of shared goods, we will not be in a position to measure their overall well-being in relation to our own.

V

But passing on to the future goods that are measurable, even if only in principle, is only one way, and perhaps among the least plausible ways, to think about equality between present and future people. Rawls's basic proposal remains: that there is an obligation to pass on to future generations the requisites of a just society. This may initially look like a weak requirement, arguably satisfied by passing on no more than a modest economic surplus. Does it simply mean, for example, that we must avoid passing on a level of scarcity so extreme that political conflict over resources becomes too intense to be sustained by democratic politics? If so, nothing much would seem to be left to distinguish his position from that of future-justice sceptics, such as Beckerman, who, as we saw above, maintain that any duty we have is satisfied by preserving the conditions of justice among presently existing people.

Moreover, David Heyd points to two very damaging problems. First, whatever it is that we owe to future people faces competition from the strong demands of *infra*generational distributive justice, grounded in the difference principle; and, second, a duty to promote justice cannot itself be a duty of justice (Heyd 2009, 182). So on both counts, it would seem, we are left with a proposal that has a very fragile status within the structure of the theory. It resembles, Heyd says, the limited duty of aid in Rawls's view of global justice, a duty whose strength has long been a disappointment to global egalitarians who hoped that a theory of justice would do more than *The Law of Peoples* offers (Beitz 1999; Pogge 1989). However, I believe that a contractualist approach can resist these negative conclusions if we turn to another resource that it offers: we may term it *iterative contractualism*, a topic already introduced in chapter 9, but that now needs a fuller account and defence.

To expand, now, on that idea, let us again begin with the global case, where more familiar parallels may apply. In a political society, a contractualist argument leads, of course, to the conclusion that co-members must have obligations to one another that they do not have to outsiders (otherwise, the contract would be pointless). We may suppose that they also have a natural duty of aid to other political societies, a duty falling well short of principles of distributive justice (such as equality) in the demands that it makes. That is a conclusion that Rawls himself insists on in *The Law of Peoples* and that other theorists second or adopt, with somewhat parallel lines of reasoning. But is there only a duty of aid? Or is there a further implicit duty: not to impede or undermine contractual arrangements made or sought by others? Here I shall argue that there is.

There is such a duty in the case of ordinary contracts, in a political society's legal order. We cannot contract with one another to monopolize some good that others have a right to or render impossible others' capacity to associate to pursue like advantages for themselves. Now we might initially suppose that these limits are artefacts of political society itself, which defines and enforces rights, of which freedom of association is only one, and which hence, of course, cannot be absolute because the compossibility of rights requires interpretation or compromise. But this is to take a narrowly positivist view, one that becomes implausible when we return to the case of the social contract itself. For a social contract must obviously presuppose – because it cannot itself create – a right of association. It implies both an initial freedom and a moral capacity to limit this freedom in a binding manner by consenting with others to mutually agreed arrangements. But we can hardly suppose a right to associate to be, implausibly, the *only* right arising from these background conditions. If freedom can be surrendered only by consent, there will also be rights against harms that avoidably diminish one's freedom and impede its exercise. Such rights, needless to say, would be universally attributable; and so they would limit what potential contractors could do in forming political societies and defining their aims. They could not, for example, rightfully create a warrior society dedicated to the destruction or pillaging of its neighbours. Doing so would imply that contracts take place against an amoral background. But they cannot take place against such a background, for reasons stated above.

To remain, for a moment longer, in the global context, these considerations gather weight from the issue of distributive unfairness that Samuel Scheffler has pointed to in the contractual model. Not only do contractors take on a special responsibility to safeguard one another's background rights, but they also develop among themselves additional positive responsibilities from which outsiders do not benefit (Scheffler 2001, 56–64) and which, one might add, have the potential to undermine or erode outsiders' pursuit of their own well-being. (International political economy today offers many clear and disturbing examples of this [see Pogge 2002].) There is, then, a complex of moral considerations that bear on one society's impact on another, not because societies are part of a larger (global) contractual arrangement, but simply because discrete contracts have morally significant external consequences. What does owing more to some mean in terms of what we owe to others?

Strongly parallel considerations come to bear in the intergenerational case. We may attribute to contemporaries a power to rightfully associate for several related purposes: to enable the pursuit of justice in conditions of security, to manage the consequences of their interaction, and to respond to defects in their previous circumstances. The social contract device is a way of formalizing the exercise of this power. But the argument above points to ways in which its exercise must be constrained by the need to respect the exercise of the same power by future people. Just as contractors must not adopt terms of association that deny the equivalent associative ambitions of others, so contemporaries cannot rightfully make arrangements that foreseeably and avoidably prevent future generations from pursuing the same basic objectives that form the justifying aims of their own political society.

One way to formulate what is owed to future people – one that is suggested by the argument of chapter 10 – is in terms of what we may call "equality of political opportunity."[6] Admittedly, future generations may arrive at collective views of themselves that differ from our own distinctive and generationally defined ideas of value. Admittedly, even if their lots of goods overlap significantly with ours, they may rank the items differently, with consequences for both private decision and public policy; and admittedly, those considerations undermine the idea of any simple comparative measure allowing us to say that they are worse or better off than we are. But those same considerations assume that future generations will, first, be able, in fact, to arrive at common decisions; second, to do so in a context that is unburdened by an inheritance of unresolvable dilemmas; third, be in a position to exercise freedom to arrive at determinations, over and above the mere determination to survive, and to execute them with a reasonable chance of success.

The first condition requires that we hand on institutions that permit collective decisions to be legitimately made and that we maintain these institutions with a higher standard of care than our own in-lifetime needs may dictate: that is to say, risks to their integrity must be assessed over a time frame longer than that of our own lifetime and that of our children. This goes for political institutions, in which agents constantly face short-term temptations of a partisan kind, and institutions such as universities, in which temptations to ignore the essential point are manifold – Annette Baier, quoted in chapter 10, is surely right to pick them out as examples of intergenerational projects in which the longer view collides so sharply with the shorter one, to their constant (and currently evident) peril.

The second condition would include, very prominently, well-known and important issues relating to environmental effects and the consumption of natural resources. Practical dilemmas of an obviously severe kind are posed by an economic system whose operation becomes progressively inconsistent with both the existence of a liveable habitat and a finite supply of the materials that it depends on. To hand these dilemmas to future generations is to hand them the equivalent of a ticking bomb of the nuclear variety. The literature on these matters is large and impressive. But for the present purpose, the issue can be simply stated. We have inherited from the past whole systems of production and consumption that are built into our way of life and our physical infrastructure and that it would be enormously costly for future generations to change. They will have to change them, however, when the natural resources on which the systems depend are exhausted, or become prohibitively expensive to acquire, and our historically situated duties include, prominently, a duty to anticipate and respond to that circumstance too, simply as a condition of respecting the capacity of future generations to exercise unburdened choice. This view does not, of course, preclude a different understanding of what environmental concerns entail, but it is the view that is most consistent with the argument developed in this book.[7]

The third condition requires a level of material wealth that permits discretionary judgments to be made, and also – to repeat – an understanding of historical process (social and political) that enables judgments to be practically effective, and not to be derailed by myth.

The argument for demystification was given above. The argument for material adequacy, however, has not yet been defended; and it needs defence because it risks identification with a view that is exposed to an important critique: the sufficientarian view, which seeks to displace equality as the basic distributive value. According to sufficientarianism, one person's position relative to another is not important provided that both persons are above a threshold judged to be adequate. In a fictional society in which all were at least millionaires, to take an easy example, would it matter if some were billionaires (Casal 2007)?

To the extent that we can put our intuition to work in situations of fantasy, we may think of two reasons why it would matter. One is that subjective measures of well-being are comparative, so that what one aspires to is not based on some potentially finite criterion but on a perpetually escalating scale. To use Adam Smith's famous example, a labourer may come to feel that wearing what was once a luxury item (a linen shirt) is essential to respectable appearance; or, updating his example, it is said that, in contemporary Beijing, a minimum requirement of status, among the party elite, is a very good-quality German car. If this is so, then the possibility of a stable sufficiency threshold is, in principle, ruled out: there is a status escalator, as it were. A second objection arises from the connection of wealth with power. I may have quite enough, but if you have a lot more than me, you have a potential for political advantage that you may use to limit my future prospects. If a better-funded campaign tends to win, however much you have is not enough if someone else has more. So again, for different reasons, we have an escalator, not a threshold.

These are good objections, even in a millionaire-majority society. But note that they apply only among contemporaries. To the extent that the status-escalator issue applies, it is driven by concern with what other living people have: it is a possible but unlikely ambition to have as much as the Emperor Nero had, and in fact, given very different metrics of well-being in ancient Rome and in our society, it would be hard for someone to know whether they had come out ahead. (Nero had no iPhone; we don't eat baked dormouse.) As for political power differentials, they too apply only among contemporaries, who are in a position to dominate one another in the sense of defeating the other's projects. So in these respects, sufficientarianism might be less open to objections in the intergenerational context. And some advocate it, indeed, as the right approach in that context.

But all the same, what is suggested here is best understood as an application of the idea of equality, rather than as an example of an alternative basic position. For the threshold notions proposed here are not directly connected with well-being thresholds, but, rather, with the further opportunities that they open up: opportunities to make collective decisions and make reflective choices among priorities that can only be made when a certain material level has been reached. This, it was argued above, is the most plausible understanding of intergenerational equality. And, interestingly, it actually becomes more plausible the more we suppose future generations to *differ* from us – and thus to require autonomy in making collective decisions that express what they value – while the same supposition tends to undermine the very possibility of sufficientarian measures, given the evident lack of common metrics for evaluating the iPhone and the baked dormouse.

VI

In at least two respects, this will seem too thin and abstract a conclusion from a point of view that puts more weight on the historical embeddedness of the relations between one generation and another. For one thing, it substitutes a general and abstract value – equality of opportunity – for the actual substantive content of national and political identity, content that is specific to each nation and polity. For another, it threatens to reduce the past to something that is important only to the extent that it exercises residual effects in the present. In her perceptive treatment of the matter, Janna Thompson contrasts "universalizing approaches" (which would be typified by the argument above) and "historical approaches" of the sort that her book defends. The former, while not dismissive of the past and future as sources of obligation, draw nothing at a basic level from the character of the polity in question, while a historical approach "focuses on a polity as an entity with a particular nature and history and gives citizens duties in relation to the deeds of the past and the traditions, values and projects that are the products of its history" (Thompson 2009, 85). Thus, the historical view recognizes that "citizens of different societies are likely to have different ideas about what is socially valuable and thus will have different intergenerational projects" (92).

In light of the fundamental no-reciprocity objection, this approach points to another kind of response altogether. Reciprocity – real or hypothetical – is a condition that can arise among distinct agents and so is attributable only when agency can be mutually exercised – hence the problem that arises when only one of two parties has agency. But suppose the parties in question are wrongly conceptualized, in the first place, as distinct from one another? Suppose they are better thought of as members of a single, subsisting, community? While some definitions of community may presuppose the simultaneous (or overlapping) coexistence of their members, nothing in the idea of community requires that, and so nothing rules out the idea of a community that spans and includes distinct generations. To identify it, we could refer to shared values, shared projects, and shared traditions: nothing precludes the sharing of such things across generations. But none of the three, I believe, gives us a problem-free picture of what is owed to the future. Let us consider these three elements in turn.

Shared *values*, first, would seem to pose two problems if taken as a feature of intergenerational community that creates moral demands for transmission. The first is easily disposed of, for no advocates of value transmission would take themselves to be committed to the transmission of obnoxious values, whatever their ancestors may happen to have believed. Unless one takes the radical view that inheritance is the source of all moral standards whatsoever, there is no inconsistency in holding both that inherited values have importance and also that they are subject to limits set by some independent standard of morality. The second problem is more severe, however; as Thompson notes, the adoption of values is optional, and a values-based view of community tends to be exclusive of minorities or critics. To this one may add a view stressed in chapter 2: that values, even when shared, are open to contested interpretation, so that one person's view of what Americanness or Germanness entails may be different from or even radically offensive to another.

One response to this issue of subjectivity is to rely, instead, on specific *projects* or practices or organizations in which one is objectively engaged. One is, as a matter of fact, part of arrangements that subsist through time – most of the arrangements that comprise civil society, which differ in this respect from spontaneous gatherings or chance meetings. Moreover, many of these arrangements depend on the subsistence of an institutional or legal order that underwrites them: corporations, professional associations, charities, marriages, universities, personal estates can exist because there is a larger context of law through which their identity is created or guaranteed. So the objective fact of being part of such arrangements may be said to connect one in an important way to the larger order of the state. This seems importantly different, however, from being objectively connected to any state- or nation-level project; for, as noted above, the legal continuities required by civil society can survive basic changes in the state- or nation-level project, as when, for example, a revolutionary state honours the obligations of a previous regime or a newly independent colony acknowledges colonial-era arrangements with indigenous peoples.

Shared *traditions* may seem more robust, however, than either subjective identifications or collective projects. At least since Tocqueville wrote, it has been understood that traditions have a depth that can survive revolutionary change, the Jacobin state inheriting monarchical centralism, for example, or the post-Maoist Chinese state affirming Confucian values. On a smaller scale, the maintenance of a tradition is among the most compelling sources of the idea of a duty to future generations. Annette Baier, as we saw, employs the example of her university, founded by Scottish immigrants to New Zealand who believed passionately in the value of advanced education. Having benefited from it, Baier writes, one is led naturally to the idea of an obligation to pass on the institution intact or improved to later generations, for, after all, the founders didn't intend only one's own generation to benefit from it.

What is open to question here, though, is the work being done by the idea of tradition, as opposed to the underlying value itself. To change the example, women's colleges at universities such as Oxford and Cambridge established a strong tradition of advanced education for women, but at a certain point came to consider whether to maintain the traditional pattern of single-sex institutions or adopt the later co-educational model. Those that opted for the latter may be described as adhering to a value rather than a tradition; but even those that opted for the former would presumably have had to re-evaluate the tradition in light of the value. Appeals to community, then, while far from negligible in their weight, may fall short of the sort of conclusiveness that the idea of reciprocity is often thought to carry: if value-based they may be too optional,[8] if project-based too indeterminate, and if tradition-based not normatively independent enough.

The communitarian objection to abstractness, however, does contain an important consideration that bears on what it means to realize, politically, the abstract value of equal opportunity. Opportunities, as we saw in chapter 7, cannot be measured numerically, but must be assessed in terms of judgments of value. To some extent, one generation can safeguard the opportunities of later generations by passing on general institutional capacity and fungible goods, but only to some extent. Within the limits, obviously, of its own world view, it must also pass on a political and general culture in which a range of desirable goods is embedded. In this respect, the model of child rearing is better than the model of decolonization – to contrast, now, two models that were juxtaposed above. The decolonization model requires the former colonizer to hand over general institutional and economic capacity – the more general the better, in fact, since we can assume the colony to have its own independent cultural heritage to draw on, whatever (if anything) it may also have drawn from its colonial masters. (That Indians learned to play cricket hardly supersedes the role of indigenous traditions.)

The child-rearing model, however, requires a parent to provide an initial framework of culture that, while not totalitarian, is necessarily particular in containing only some of a potentially limitless set of options. A polity can provide a very much larger set than a parent, but the same point applies. There is an obligation to pass on a framework of values as a necessary condition of future people having an idea of what an opportunity is, unless we reduce "opportunity" to an episode of random picking without evaluation. Given that each society can imagine only what it can imagine, neutrality among all possible world views is obviously impossible; but unless we set the bar for neutrality at a godlike level, a society preserves earthling-appropriate neutrality in handing on to the future the network of beliefs that offers the options that, collectively, it values (Dobson 2003, 164–5).

Because of this, Thompson's other concern can be met, at least in part. On the universalist view, it may well seem, at least at first glance, that a bright line has been drawn between past and present and that our forebears cross it only by virtue of the lingering negative effects of their misdeeds: as skeletons in our cupboard, a cupboard that we should be sure to empty before our children find it. One might perhaps arrive at this view on the basis of the claim that injustice demands redress only to the extent that it endures. But there is no reason why this claim, endorsed above, should exhaust our entire view of our connection with the past. We didn't arrive at our beliefs *ab ovo*, and in passing them on, we necessarily form part of an intergenerational chain. This fleshes out, in a valuable way, what the idea of equal opportunity requires one generation to do for another, and it is an important corrective to purely abstract and unembedded political theory. But the province of Ontario in Canada has no obligation to pass on the anti-Catholic bigotry of the

Orange Order, nor does France have an obligation to pass on the hypocrisies of *pétainisme*, nor (to cut a potentially very long list short) does any society have an obligation to pass on values *just because* they were important in its past. Inherited values have to pass a test, and perhaps as good a way to define the test as any other is to say that they must meet it to the extent that we should want to pass them on.

Beyond this, however, is the consideration that what we owe to future people cannot be contained within national borders, given what are by now very familiar facts about the ways in which environmental effects spill over boundaries and the no less familiar and likely irrevocable conditions of a globalized economy. Now there is no reason why an approach that finds its point of departure in the continuities of national societies should be altogether blind to what happens to national societies other than one's own. Nationalism too, after all, can be "iterative" – that is, it can recognize that the considerations that lead to concern about a particular society's future will also apply, simply by virtue of moral consistency, to the case of other societies. But as noted above, this is to take what it is that we owe to our own society to be contained within a theory of undiscriminating justice and so, eventually, to take the universalizing side.

What does the universalizing side owe, finally, to the historicizing side? I think it owes a lot. It owes it an acknowledgment that what we transmit to the future is a mix of what we have inherited and what we choose to select or reject from it. The emphasis falls, on this account, not on an idea of continuous identity, but on an idea of responsibility for freeing future people of the moral burdens that we carry, so that their lives may become less morally clouded than our own. The present is best thought of, in short, as a remedial opportunity.

The idea of remediation, however, should take us well beyond the kinds of restitutive or restorative remedies that are discussed in the literature on historical redress. We do indeed have possessions that should be returned for the sake of affirming the equality of those from whom they were taken, and there are indeed outrages that need to be acknowledged and (when possible) compensated, again for the reason of affirming equality. But we have also inherited institutions whose integrity we need to preserve if we find them valuable and whose defects we should correct if we have experienced them. We have also inherited from the past dilemmas that we compound and become complicit in if we fail to do what we can to find a way out of them. Thinking of the present, then, as a point of both recall and transmission, as this book has suggested, would call for changes across a whole range of current practices. This is not *because* we are part of a community that makes us consubstantial with our past and our future, nor is it *because* a theory of distributive justice can specify a sum that we owe. It is *because*, in the spirit of the social contract tradition, we recognize our common vulnerabilities and so a duty to do less harm to the future than the past has done to us.

Why focus on the negative in this way, though? It would be natural, on a more communitarian view, to place the emphasis on the good things, the identity-constituting values, that we are in a position to transmit to future people. We should not, of course, need much persuasion to agree that we should transmit good things. But we should transmit them because they are good in our view, not because they are our goods; to say that they should be transmitted because they are ours is implicitly, and very contestably, to subsume future people within "us." It is a different kind of argument that should lead us to refuse to transmit wrongs. To transmit wrongs would be to exercise our freedom at the expense of future people's important opportunities, and to do so would be objectionable because, unless we presumptuously include them in us, they are other; and without invoking an unsustainable claim to privilege, a society is not entitled to extend its own freedom in a way that deliberately undermines another's. There is a difference, it was argued above, between a social contract, whereby associates settle on terms of just relations among themselves, and a criminal conspiracy, whereby associates adopt arrangements that are fundamentally destructive of others' basic interests.

But although the focus is negative for this reason, I hope enough has been said above to ward off the fear that the obligations involved, because negative, are minimal. On the contrary, to harm is not merely to perform damaging acts but also to place others in situations in which they bear avoidable costs, face unenviable dilemmas, and lack the resources – material, institutional, cognitive – to conduct their common arrangements in a productive way – not, of course, in a problem-free way, but in a way in which the problems that they face are, as far as possible, of their own making rather than ours.

As argued above, the very idea of a social contract implies a background right on the part of people to do certain things: to establish the conditions in which each can act justly without fears about being the only one to do so, to create institutions that will manage the unsought consequences of interactions, and to respond to whatever is taken to be the common inherited situation in ways that draw on common resources to everyone's benefit. The notional agreement of people to create and support institutions of this kind is binding because (as Hart argued in his famous paper) they can be supposed to be surrendering a background right in doing so and so to be conferring a normative power on the arrangements that they create – just as promises get their normative power from the freedom that is surrendered in making them. But if we – that is, living people – can claim legitimacy for our common arrangements on these grounds, we cannot, without arbitrariness – without claiming, absurdly, that we have a unique stake that others lack – deny that the same grounds should be available for others' claims. Still less can we act in ways that avoidably burden others in their making of arrangements that are designed to do, for them, just what we believe we have a right to do for ourselves and, in light of which, we justify our own institutions and practices.

Notes

Introduction

1 Rawls (1971, 126): the first of the "objective circumstances which make human cooperation both possible and necessary" is that "many individuals coexist together at the same time on a definite geographical territory."
2 For the spatial case, see Vernon (2010).

1. Should We Worry about Presentism?

1 I distinguish between standards (measurements) and criteria (things to be measured). The final section of this chapter suggests reasons for believing that (some) criteria must be stable; otherwise, we would not know that one standard contradicted another.
2 A qualification may be needed in light of Pablo Gilabert's distinction between evaluative and prescriptive judgments, the latter depending on feasibility in a way in which the former do not: see Gilabert (2011). Critics of presentism must have evaluative judgments in their sights.
3 I do not mean to slight the differences between Nussbaum and Cooper here. It appears to be Nussbaum's view that, for Aristotle, a belief is validated by its coherence within the circle of convention, while Cooper maintains that, for Aristotle, conventional beliefs, while subject to coherence tests, were valuable, nevertheless, for their probable truth.
4 The plausibility of this view is questioned in the final section of this chapter.
5 "Aristotle was right; but he mistook the effect for the cause. Anyone born in slavery is born for slavery – nothing is more certain" (Rousseau 1968, 51–2).

6 Kuhn (1962) identifies paradigms with "achievements" and so is hardly to blame for later uses of the term as a synonym for "mindsets," etc. For some further comments, see the Conclusion.
7 In his short book on *Ancient Warfare,* Harry Sidebottom remarks that it is "part of the definition of a culture ... that it allows its members to hold views which are logically incompatible" (Sidebottom 2004, 8). He gives examples of cultural borrowings that tend to undermine the idea that such and such a military practice is "essentially" (say) Greek. I do not know which definition of "culture" he is referring to, but the idea seems exactly right. Cultures grow by accretion and are transmitted by habituation, and neither accretion nor habituation follows the laws of logical consistency. The culture that we get is a grab bag or miscellany, and so it presents us with alternatives to explore if we have any sort of openness to enquiry at all, an openness that (it seems to me) one would need quite special reasons to deny. I am not sure how far back we can push the responsibility to explore the resources of a culture – suppose someone has no openness to enquiry; can he or she be blamed for that? The question arises, as noted above, in connection with Moody-Adams's paper, and I have no answer. But it can hardly be respectful of past people to take this sceptical thought as far as denying their agency outright and in general.
8 Different possible dates are evaluated by Gosseries (2004).
9 The value of Haidt's idea is independent of the claim for which he is notorious, that in moral matters the emotional tail wags the rational dog. See Appiah (2008, esp. chap. 4) for a balanced appraisal.

2. The Question of [Anyone's] Guilt: Collective Liability to Punishment

1 This translation was first published in 1948, the German original in 1947.
2 See Arendt (2003, 147–58) for an extended discussion of Jaspers's use of "guilt."
3 This matches the conditions for complicity (or "complicity simpliciter") set out by Lepora and Goodin (2013, 80–3), who distinguish between "contribution" and the stronger notion of "participation." What is especially relevant to the discussion of citizenship above is that Lepora and Goodin do not confine complicity to cases in which a contributor foresaw a particular outcome; they assign it to cases in which one can or should foresee a range of outcomes (ibid., 95).
4 "The question addressed to those who participated and obeyed orders should never be 'Why did you obey' but 'Why did you support?'"(Arendt 2003, 48). Arendt's preference for "support" expresses her view that

"obedience" is too closely tied to the conscious following of explicit orders. I don't take the meaning to be confined in that way, but Arendt's understanding of the term I call "obedience responsibility" would have to be called "support responsibility."

5 The following paragraphs draw from Vernon (2011).

3. For Benefits Received

1 See Janna Thompson (2009 31, 78) for some critical remarks about the benefits view.

2 See Brighouse and Swift (2014) for discussion.

3 David Lyons (2013, 89) contends that the moral use of the idea "tracks notions of legal liability too closely," particularly in occluding the systemic nature of oppression and its irreducibility to particularized gains and losses.

4 The following four paragraphs summarize an argument presented in Vernon (2012, 56–61).

4. Giving Back: The Case of Stolen Art

1 The classic modern discussion is Waldron (1992).

2 This is distinct from the recently (at the time of writing) renewed efforts to return works of art to their *individual* owners (or their descendants); see Mary M. Lane, "Germany to set up agency to find art looted by Nazis," *Globe and Mail* (Toronto), February 12, 2014, A15. A strong theory of ownership by national origin (see below) would, of course, undermine the private-ownership approach to restitution and, as noted below, would also seem to set limits to any private stake in works of national importance. It would be a possible but, I think, odd response to Edmund de Waal's heart-rending memoir, *The Hare with Amber Eyes* (2010), to wish that the miniature *netsuke* sculptures should be returned, not to descendants of the Ephrussi family from whom they were taken, but to Japan, their place of manufacture. As it happens, the objects are in Japan for a time because the heir of the previous owner lives there; but after his death, the family claim, the author contends, is stronger (de Waal 2010, 348).

3 For this distinction, see Appiah (2005, chap. 3).

4 "What is the relationship between, say, modern Egypt and the antiquities that were part of the land's pharaonic past? The people of modern-day Cairo do not speak the language of the ancient Egyptians, do not practice their religion, do not make their art, wear their dress, eat their food, or play their music, and then do not adhere to the same kinds of laws or form

of government the ancient Egyptians did. All that can be said is that they occupy the same (actually less) stretch of the earth's geography" (Cuno 2011, 9–10).

5 Despite his eventual decision (see note 2 above), de Waal (2010, 305–6) accepts the force of this view: when he sees the netsuke in Japan, his understanding of their deftness and accuracy is deepened. Strictly speaking, of course, this is as much an argument for their admirers to go to Japan as it is for the objects to remain there.

6 For a more extended account, see Vernon (2001 chap. 4).

7 See chapter 7 for a parallel question about parenting.

5. Bad Memories

1 For the "complementary" view, see Drumbl (2007).

2 The following section draws from Chinapen and Vernon (2006). I am grateful to Rhiana Chinapen for allowing me to make use here of ideas that were a joint product.

3 See chapter 9.

4 Margalit himself cites Freud's comparison of the neurotic person to a present-day Londoner who bursts into tears at the sight of the monument commemorating the Great Fire of 1666 (Margalit 2002, 4).

5 The Japanese director Hirokazu Koreeda's brilliant film, *Like Father, Like Son* is an imaginative exploration of the case that Miller's example sets up.

6 See http://www.theguardian.com/world/2011/sep/23/child-argentina-disappeared-adoptive-name, accessed November 4, 2014. I am grateful to Dr Gabriela Welch for drawing my attention to this case.

6. The Prior Question: Assessing the Benatar Thesis

1 As Sarah Hannan has pointed out to me, self-regarding reasons may move even people who hold anti-natalist beliefs since in a non-ideal world in which reproduction is taking place, it may be unreasonable to make a severe personal sacrifice. This is one of many enlightening points that Dr Hannan has made in commenting on a draft of this chapter.

2 I do not know whether Benatar would think that even God could make us all happy all the time: see chapter 3 of his book and comments in section III of this chapter.

3 This distinction is put to effective use in the global context by Thomas Pogge (2002) and in many other writings.

4 Shiffrin accepts that we may harm without consent (when consent is unavailable) to prevent a greater harm, but not to confer a benefit. This

requires another discussion. Surely there are counter-examples? A right-libertarian party proposes to withdraw welfare benefits, thus causing short-term harm to people (without consent) to confer (it believes) the great benefit of enhanced self-worth: wrong for all sorts of reasons, but is it because we must never harm for the sake of benefit?

5 I owe this formulation to Meena Krishnamurthy.

6 Even imagining a benevolent controller may not give our lives meaning. "We are minute cogs in a vast machine whose point exceeds our comprehension. How our condition of alienated labour confers meaning on what we do must remain a mystery" (Kitcher 2014, 115).

7 "The best feature of the present life [is its] improvability by our own efforts" (Mill 1874, 210).

8 As is brilliantly argued by Samuel Scheffler (2013).

7. Coming to Terms with *Yoder*

1 Wisconsin, 406 US at 1.

2 Ibid., 2.

3 Ibid.

4 J.S. Mill himself – no friend of unquestioned authority – could have supported this point. "It is especially characteristic of the impressions of early education, that they possess what it is so much more difficult for later convictions to obtain – command over the feelings … it is only persons of a much higher degree of natural sensibility and intellect combined than it is at all common to meet with, whose feelings entwine themselves with anything like the same force round opinions which they have adopted from their own investigations later in life; and even when they do, we may say with truth that it is because the strong sense of moral duty, the sincerity, courage and self-devotion which enabled them to do so, were themselves the fruits of early impressions" (Mill 1874, 81).

5 Mills's view is a useful corrective to ideas of religious commitment that are purely propositional; see, e.g., Bedi (2007).

6 This is parallel to the remarks about Shiffrin's view of consent in chapter 6.

8. Only Egalitarians May Have Children

1 *Support* embraces both advocacy of policies that are not yet in place and support of policies that are in place already.

2 Axel Gosseries (2009) has carefully investigated such a problem from the standpoint of reciprocity among generations (how can we ensure

that transfers in equal transfers out?), while the topic of this chapter is unilateral (or downstream-only) transfer. This is because the issue is approached here in terms of parental responsibility rather than distributive equality. So it would not be an objection that the argument offered here required any generation of parents to pay in more than they had taken out. The asymmetry here is surely well enough explained, it seems to me, in terms of the basic asymmetry of responsibility between parents and children.

3 The child may have rights to employment opportunities, etc. by virtue of a general theory of social justice, but, again, what is at issue here is a duty specific to parenting.

4 It may not be generally true that intergenerational obligations can be met by promoting justice in the present, as is sometimes maintained (Beckerman 2006) – one thinks, of course, of long-term environmental damage as a counter-example – but here is one case in which it clearly is.

9. If the Future Is a Foreign Country …

1 This is a summary version of an argument developed in Vernon (2010).

2 If we think in terms of an obligation, rather than an entitlement, then we avoid the asymmetry issue raised by Otsuka (2003, 142) – i.e., that it would be absurd to suppose that future generations (if their will could be discovered by time travelling) were entitled to make rules for the present. Temporal precedence can create one-way obligations non-absurdly.

10. The Rights of Past and Future Persons

1 This may be stronger than Ball's view that we must not do what is unjust (Ball 1985, 333) unless we take "doing" to include complicity arising from dealings.

2 Although Ball significantly, if only implicitly, qualifies this on p. 329 as "the Southern theory of justice (*if I may call it that*)" (emphasis added). Perhaps, though, he intended to admit that it was its status as a "theory" that was challengeable? My own view is that the lack of critical reflectiveness that casts doubt on it as a theory also rules it out as an example of justice.

3 We would, I think, rightly curse them because introducing the threat of genetic engineering ups the ante here, for closing off the actual availability of future thoughts is different from guaranteeing a constitution that allows future thoughts to be given expression or prevents some future thoughts from being acted on.

4 So, for example, we would not be deterred from constitutionalizing some value by the thought that another generation might misunderstand the word for it.
5 See Slaughter (2005) and Taylor-Smith (2013) for the view that, in the intergenerational case, the avoidance of domination should replace the search for reciprocity that is appropriate among contemporaries. Mira Bachvarova has pointed out to me that the element of uncertainty that figures in many accounts of domination does not apply intergenerationally, for each generation already knows what previous generations have done to it.
6 Beckerman's claim would appear to rule out the idea that future people could "have" interests (just as it rules out the claim that they can "have" rights), but that conclusion is one that his own argument must, and does, reject: see p. 65, where he argues that future people do have interests that we should take account of, but that these interests do not have the trumping power of rights.
7 "Due to the *direction of causation*, present actions may have an impact on the future. This makes it possible to have a current obligation correlative to a right that *will* exist. The reverse option of an alleged obligation correlative to a right that *did* exist in the past is clearly philosophically much more problematic" (Gosseries 2008, 456). As Gosseries makes clear, the view depends on assuming an interest theory of rights.
8 The following paragraphs develop an idea from Vernon (2012, chap. 5).

Conclusion

1 It is interesting, one might add, that the original idea of the paradigm may lend itself better to this account than to the relativism often derived from it: for what Thomas Kuhn had in mind, in his stimulating but recurrently misunderstood book, was the intellectual power of brilliantly compelling examples, from which conclusions were drawn in unpredictable ways, as distinct from prescriptive mindsets that function as blinkers, permitting us to see one thing rather than another. "The concrete scientific achievement … is prior to the various concepts, laws, theories and points of view that may be abstracted from it" (Kuhn 1962, 11).
2 "Even if a civil society were to be dissolved by the consent of its members …, the last murderer remaining in prison would first have to be executed, so that each has done to him what his deeds deserve" (Kant 1996, 106).
3 See Winter (2010) for the view that rights depend on potential experience.
4 For an excellent summary, see Gardiner (2009).

5 I see absolutely no reason why, though, when the veil is lifted and we move towards more specific arrangements and policies, this should preclude measures to encourage or discourage reproduction on the grounds that high or low levels are at various times a matter of great public interest, for ecological or other reasons. (It would follow, however, that these measures would have to take the form of modifying incentive structures, rather than compulsion, if procreation is among the basic liberties in being connected to important plans of life. For doubts about this, see Hannan, Brennan, and Vernon [2015].)

6 This is not to be confused with the idea of passing on equal opportunity on an individual basis, a proposal that is open to objections, mentioned in the text, based on the unreliability of metrics. See Caney (2001); Moellendorf (2006).

7 See the discussion of the "climate debt" thesis in chapter 10.

8 From a certain attractive point of view, it is not "optional" to locate values within a temporal framework because evaluation is a matter of constant amendment and transmission; see, e.g., Philip Kitcher's (2014) "ethical project." Even so, we have options to contribute to one or more of many processes of amendment and transmission.

References

Abizadeh, Arash. 2004. "Historical Truth, National Myths, and Liberal Democracy: On the Coherence of Liberal Nationalism." *Journal of Political Philosophy* 12 (3): 291–313. http://dx.doi.org/10.1111/j.1467-9760.2004.00201.x.

Allen, Jonathan. 1999. "Balancing Justice and Social Unity: Political Theory and the Idea of a Truth and Reconciliation Commission." *University of Toronto Law Journal* 49 (3): 315–53. http://dx.doi.org/10.2307/826002.

Anderson, Elizabeth. 1999. "What Is the Point of Equality?" *Ethics* 109 (2): 287–337. http://dx.doi.org/10.1086/233897.

Annas, Julia, and Jonathan Barnes. 1985. *The Modes of Scepticism: Ancient Texts and Modern Interpretations*. Cambridge: Cambridge University Press. http://dx.doi.org/10.1017/CBO9780511586187.

Anwander, Norbert. 2005. "Contributing and Benefiting: Two Grounds for Duties to the Victims of Injustice." *Ethics & International Affairs* 19 (1): 39–45. http://dx.doi.org/10.1111/j.1747-7093.2005.tb00488.x.

Appiah, Kwame Anthony. 2005. *The Ethics of Identity*. Princeton, NJ: Princeton University Press.

Appiah, Kwame Anthony. 2008. *Experiments in Ethics*. Cambridge, MA: Harvard University Press.

Archard, David. 1995. "Myths, Lies and Historical Truth: A Defence of Nationalism." *Political Studies* 43 (3): 472–81. http://dx.doi.org/10.1111/j.1467-9248.1995.tb00315.x.

Arendt, Hannah. 1967. "Truth and Politics." In *Philosophy, Politics and Society*, 3rd ser., edited by Peter Laslett and W.G. Runciman, 104–33. Oxford: Blackwell.

Arendt, Hannah. 1977. *Eichmann in Jerusalem: A Report on the Banality of Evil*. London: Penguin.

Arendt, Hannah. 2003. *Responsibility and Judgment*. New York: Schocken.

Aristotle. 1941. *The Basic Works*. New York: Random House.

Arneson, Richard. 1982. "The Principle of Fairness and Free-Rider Problems." *Ethics* 92 (4): 616–33. http://dx.doi.org/10.1086/292379.

Arneson, Richard J., and Ian Shapiro. 1996. "Democratic Autonomy and Religious Freedom: A Critique of *Wisconsin v. Yoder*." In *NOMOS 38: Political Order*, edited by Ian Shapiro and Russell Hardin, 365–411. New York: New York University Press.

Baier, Annette. 1980. "The Rights of Past and Future Persons." In *Responsibilities to Future Generations: Environmental Ethics*, edited by Ernest Partridge, 171–83. Buffalo, NY: Prometheus Books.

Ball, Terence. 1985. "The Incoherence of Intergenerational Justice." *Inquiry* 28 (1–4): 321–37. http://dx.doi.org/10.1080/00201748508602055.

Ball, Terence. 2000. "'The Earth Belongs to the Living': Thomas Jefferson and the Problem of Intergenerational Relations." *Environmental Politics* 9 (2): 61–77. http://dx.doi.org/10.1080/09644010008414524.

Ball, Terence. 2001. "New Ethics for Old? Or, How (Not) to Think about Future Generations." *Environmental Politics* 10 (1): 89–110. http://dx.doi.org/10.1080/714000512.

Barry, Brian. 1989. *Democracy, Power and Justice: Essays in Political Theory*. Oxford: Oxford University Press.

Barry, Brian. 2001. *Culture and Equality*. Cambridge, MA: Harvard University Press.

Beaujot, Roderic. 2012. "Aging in Canada, 2011 – The Aging of the Past Will Be Different from the Aging of the Future." *Population Change and Lifecourse Strategic Knowledge Cluster* (blog). http://pclc-cppv.typepad.com/changes-in-patterns-and-t/.

Beckerman, Wilfred. 2006. "The Impossibility of a Theory of Intergenerational Justice." In *Handbook of Intergenerational Justice*, edited by Joerg Chet Tremmel, 53–70. Cheltenham, UK: Edward Elgar.

Bedi, Sonu. 2007. "What Is So Special about Religion? The Dilemma of the Religious Exemption." *Journal of Political Philosophy* 15 (2): 235–49. http://dx.doi.org/10.1111/j.1467-9760.2006.00269.x.

Beitz, Charles R. 1999. *Political Theory and International Relations*. 2nd ed. Princeton, NJ: Princeton University Press. http://dx.doi.org/10.2307/1288081.

Benatar, David. 2006. *Better Never to Have Been: The Harm of Coming into Existence*. Oxford: Oxford University Press. http://dx.doi.org/10.1093/acprof:oso/9780199296422.001.0001.

Berlin, Isaiah. 1991. *The Crooked Timber of Humanity*. New York: Knopf.

Bertram, Christopher. 2009. "Exploitation and Intergenerational Justice." In *Intergenerational Justice*, edited by Axel Gosseries and Lukas H. Meyer, 146–66. Oxford: Oxford University Press.

Blustein, Jeffrey. 2008. *The Moral Demands of Memory*. New York: Cambridge University Press. http://dx.doi.org/10.1017/CBO9780511818615.

Bongaarts, J. 2004. "Population Aging and the Rising Costs of Public Pensions." *Population and Development Review* 30 (1): 1–23. http://dx.doi.org/10.1111/j.1728-4457.2004.00001.x.

Booth, William James. 2008. "The Work of Memory: Time, Identity, and Justice." *Social Research* 75 (1): 237–62.

Boraine, Alex. 2000. "Truth and Reconciliation in South Africa: The Third Way." In *Truth v. Justice: The Morality of Truth Commissions*, edited by Robert I. Rotberg and Dennis Thompson, 141–57. University Center for Human Values Series. Princeton, NJ: Princeton University Press. http://dx.doi.org/10.1515/9781400832033-008.

Braley, Alison. 2011. "Religious Rights and Québec's Ethics and Religious Culture Course." *Canadian Journal of Political Science* 44 (3): 613–33. http://dx.doi.org/10.1017/S0008423911000515.

Brams, Steven J., and Alan D. Taylor. 1996. *Fair Division: From Cake-Cutting to Dispute Resolution*. Cambridge: Cambridge University Press. http://dx.doi.org/10.1017/CBO9780511598975.

Brighouse, Harry, and Marc Fleurbaey. 2010. "Democracy and Proportionality." *Journal of Political Philosophy* 18 (2): 137–55. http://dx.doi.org/10.1111/j.1467-9760.2008.00316.x.

Brighouse, Harry, and Adam Swift. 2006. "Parents' Rights and the Value of the Family." *Ethics* 117 (1): 80–108. http://dx.doi.org/10.1086/508034.

Brighouse, Harry, and Adam Swift. 2014. *Family Values: The Ethics of Parent-Child Relationships*. Princeton, NJ: Princeton University Press. http://dx.doi.org/10.1515/9781400852543.

Brown, Chris. 1999. "Universal Human Rights: A Critique." In *Human Rights in Global Politics*, edited by Tim Dunne and Nicholas J. Wheeler, 103–27. Cambridge: Cambridge University Press. http://dx.doi.org/10.1017/CBO9781139171298.005.

Burtt, Shelley. 1996. "In Defense of *Yoder*: Parental Authority and the Public Schools." In *NOMOS 38: Political Order*, edited by Ian Shapiro and Russell Hardin, 412–37. New York: New York University Press.

Butt, Daniel. 2009. *Rectifying International Injustice: Principles of Compensation and Restitution between Nations*. Oxford: Oxford University Press.

Butt, Daniel. 2014. "'A Doctrine Quite New and Altogether Untenable': Defending the Beneficiary Pays Principle." *Journal of Applied Philosophy* 31 (4): 336–48. http://dx.doi.org/10.1111/japp.12073.

Cambiano, Giuseppe. 1987. "Aristotle and the Anonymous Opponents of Slavery." In *Classical Slavery*, edited by Moses I. Finley, 21–41. London: Cass. http://dx.doi.org/10.1080/01440398708574925.

Cameron, Christina. 2012. "Clayton on Comprehensive Enrolment." *Journal of Political Philosophy* 20 (3): 341–52. http://dx.doi.org/10.1111/j.1467-9760.2011.00396.x.

Caney, Simon. 2001. "Cosmopolitan Justice and Equalizing Opportunities." *Metaphilosophy* 32 (1–2): 113–34. http://dx.doi.org/10.1111/1467-9973.00178.

Caney, Simon. 2010. "Cosmopolitan Justice, Responsibility and Global Climate Change." In *Climate Ethics: Essential Readings*, edited by Stephen M. Gardiner, Simon Caney, Dale Jamieson, and Henry Shue, 122–45. Oxford: Oxford University Press.

Casal, Paula. 2007. "Why Sufficiency Is Not Enough." *Ethics* 117 (2): 296–326. http://dx.doi.org/10.1086/510692.

Chinapen, Rhiana, and Richard Vernon. 2006. "Justice in Transition." *Canadian Journal of Political Science* 39 (1): 117–34. http://dx.doi.org/10.1017/S0008423906060070.

Clayton, Matthew. 2006. *Justice and Legitimacy in Upbringing*. Oxford: Oxford University Press. http://dx.doi.org/10.1093/0199268940.001.0001.

Clayton, Matthew. 2012. "The Case against the Comprehensive Enrolment of Children." *Journal of Political Philosophy* 20 (3): 353–64. http://dx.doi.org/10.1111/j.1467-9760.2011.00397.x.

Cooper, David. 2001. "Collective Responsibility, 'Moral Luck,' and Reconciliation." In *War Crimes and Collective Wrongdoing*, edited by Aleksandar Jokic, 205–15. Oxford: Blackwell.

Cooper, John M. 1999. *Reason and Emotion: Essays on Ancient Moral Psychology and Moral Theory*. Princeton, NJ: Princeton University Press.

Cuno, James. 2011. *Who Owns Antiquity? Museums and the Battle over Our Ancient Heritage*. Princeton, NJ: Princeton University Press.

Dagger, Richard. 1997. *Civic Virtues: Rights, Citizenship, and Republican Liberalism*. Oxford: Oxford University Press.

De Waal, Edmund. 2010. *The Hare with Amber Eyes*. London: Chatto and Windus.

Dobson, Andrew. 2003. *Citizenship and the Environment*. Oxford: Oxford University Press. http://dx.doi.org/10.1093/0199258449.001.0001.

Donaldson, Sue, and Will Kymlicka. 2011. *Zoopolis: A Political Theory of Animal Rights*. Oxford: Oxford University Press.

Drumbl, Mark. 2007. *Atrocity, Punishment and International Law*. New York: Cambridge University Press. http://dx.doi.org/10.1017/CBO9780511611100.

Drumbl, Mark. 2011. "Collective Responsibility and Post-Conflict Justice." In *Accountability for Collective Wrongdoing*, edited by Tracy Isaacs and Richard Vernon, 23–60. New York: Cambridge University Press. http://dx.doi.org/10.1017/CBO9780511976780.002.

Dworkin, Ronald. 1978. "Liberalism." In *Public and Private Morality*, edited by Stuart Hampshire, 60–79. Cambridge: Cambridge University Press. http://dx.doi.org/10.1017/CBO9780511625329.007.

Dworkin, Ronald. 2013. *Religion without God*. Cambridge, MA: Harvard University Press.

Dyzenhaus, David. 2000. "Justifying the Truth and Reconciliation Commission." *Journal of Political Philosophy* 8 (4): 470–96. http://dx.doi.org/10.1111/1467-9760.00113.

Easterlin, Richard A. 1980. *Birth and Fortune: The Impact of Numbers on Personal Welfare*. New York: Basic Books.

Eliot, George. 1994. *Romola*. Oxford: Oxford University Press.

English, Jane. 1977. "Justice between Generations." *Philosophical Studies* 31 (2): 91–104. http://dx.doi.org/10.1007/BF01857179.

English, Jane. 1991. "What Do Grown Children Owe Their Parents?" In *Aging and Ethics: Philosophical Problems in Gerontology*, edited by Nancy S. Jecker, 147–70. Clifton, NJ: Humana Press.

Ermisch, John. 1988. "Fortunes of Birth: The Impact of Generation Size on the Relative Earnings of Young Men." *Scottish Journal of Political Economy* 35 (3): 266–82. http://dx.doi.org/10.1111/j.1467-9485.1988.tb01051.x.

Evans, Richard. 2011. "Art in the Time of War." *National Interest* (May–June): 16–26.

Evarts, Jeremiah, ed. 1973. *Speeches on the Passage of the Bill for the Removal of the Indians: Delivered in the Congress of the United States, April and May, 1830.* Millwood, NY: Kraus Reprint Co. First published 1830 by Perkins and Marvin.

Feinberg, Joel. 1980. "The Child's Right to an Open Future." In *Whose Child? Children's Rights, Parental Authority, and State Power*, edited by William Aiken and Hugh LaFollette, 124–53. Totowa, NJ: Rowman and Littlefield.

Finley, Moses I. 1998. *Ancient Slavery and Modern Ideology*. Princeton, NJ: Markus Wiener.

Fleming, Eleanor Bright. 2008. "When Sorry Is Enough: The Possibility of a National Apology for Slavery." In *The Age of Apology: Facing Up to the Past*. edited by Mark Gibney, Rhoda E. Howard-Hassmann, Jean-Marc Coicaud, and Niklaus Steiner, 95–108. Philadelphia: University of Pennsylvania Press.

Foot, David K. 2000. *Boom, Bust & Echo 2000: Profiting from the Demographic Shift in the New Millennium*. With Daniel Stoffman. Toronto: Stoddart.

Francis, Richard. 2005. *Judge Sewall's Apology*. New York: Harper-Collins.

Gardiner, Stephen. 2009. "A Contract on Future Generations?" In *Intergenerational Justice*, edited by Axel Gosseries and Lukas H. Meyer,

77–118. Oxford: Oxford University Press. http://dx.doi.org/10.1093/acprof:oso/9780199282951.003.0004.

Garnsey, Peter. 1996. *Ideas of Slavery from Aristotle to Augustine*. Cambridge: Cambridge University Press.

Garvey, James. 2008. *The Ethics of Climate Change: Right and Wrong in a Warming World*. London: Continuum.

Gilabert, Pablo. 2011. "Feasibility and Socialism." *Journal of Political Philosophy* 19 (1): 52–63. http://dx.doi.org/10.1111/j.1467-9760.2010.00383.x.

Glover, Jonathan. 2001. *Humanity: A Moral History of the Twentieth Century*. London: Pimlico.

Golding, M.P. 1972. "Obligations to Future Generations." *Monist* 56 (1): 85–99. http://dx.doi.org/10.5840/monist197256118.

Goodin, Robert E. 2013. "Disgorging the Fruits of Historical Wrongdoing." *American Political Science Review* 107 (3): 478–91. http://dx.doi.org/10.1017/S0003055413000233.

Goodin, Robert E., and Christian Barry. 2014. "Benefiting from the Wrongdoing of Others." *Journal of Applied Philosophy* 31 (4): 363–76. http://dx.doi.org/10.1111/japp.12077.

Gosseries, Axel. 2004. "Historical Emissions and Free-Riding." *Ethical Perspectives* 11 (1): 36–60. http://dx.doi.org/10.2143/EP.11.1.504779.

Gosseries, Axel. 2008. "On Future Generations' Future Rights." *Journal of Political Philosophy* 16 (4): 446–74. http://dx.doi.org/10.1111/j.1467-9760.2008.00323.x.

Gosseries, Axel. 2009. "Three Models of Intergenerational Reciprocity." In *Intergenerational Justice*, edited by Axel Gosseries and Lukas H. Meyer, 119–46. Oxford: Oxford University Press. http://dx.doi.org/10.1093/acprof:oso/9780199282951.003.0005.

Grob, Ueli, and Stefan C. Wolter. 2005. "Demographic Change and Public Education Spending: A Conflict between Young and Old?" CESifo Working Paper No. 1555. http://ssrn.com/abstract=843326.

Gutmann, Amy, and Dennis Thompson. 2000. "The Moral Foundations of Truth Commissions." In *Truth v. Justice: The Morality of Truth Commissions*, edited by Robert I. Rotberg and Dennis Thompson, 22–44. University Center for Human Values Series. Princeton, NJ: Princeton University Press. http://dx.doi.org/10.1515/9781400832033-003.

Haidt, Jonathan. 2012. *The Righteous Mind: Why Good People Are Divided by Politics and Religion*. New York: Pantheon.

Hannan, Sarah, Samantha Brennan, and Richard Vernon, eds. 2015. *Permissible Progeny? The Morality of Procreation and Parenting*. New York: Oxford University Press. http://dx.doi.org/10.1093/acprof:oso/9780199378111.001.0001.

Hannan, Sarah, and Richard Vernon. 2008. "Parental Rights: A Role-Based Approach." *Theory and Research in Education* 6 (2): 173–89. http://dx.doi.org/10.1177/1477878508091110.

Hart, H.L.A. 1955. "Are There Any Natural Rights?" *Philosophical Review* 64 (2): 175–91. http://dx.doi.org/10.2307/2182586.

Hartley, L.P. 1953. *The Go-Between*. London: Hamish Hamilton.

Heath, Joseph. 2013. "The Structure of Intergenerational Cooperation." *Philosophy & Public Affairs* 41 (1): 31–66. http://dx.doi.org/10.1111/papa.12009.

Heyd, David. 2009. "A Value or an Obligation? Rawls on Justice to Future Generations." In *Intergenerational Justice*, edited by Axel Gosseries and Lukas H. Meyer, 167–88. Oxford: Oxford University Press. http://dx.doi.org/10.1093/acprof:oso/9780199282951.003.0007.

Hibbert, Neil. 2010. "Exchange and Social Justice." *Theoria* 57 (122): 26–50. http://dx.doi.org/10.3167/th.2010.5712204.

Hillerman, Tony. 1989. *Talking God*. New York: Harper.

Hitchens, Christopher. 1987. *The Elgin Marbles: Should They Be Returned to Greece?* London: Chatto and Windus.

Holmes, Stephen. 1995. *Passions and Constraint: On the Theory of Liberal Democracy*. Chicago: University of Chicago Press.

Howard-Hassmann, Rhoda. 2008. *Reparations to Africa*. Philadelphia: University of Pennsylvania Press.

Hume, David. 1947. "Of the Original Contract." In *Social Contract: Essays by Locke, Hume, and Rousseau*, edited by Ernest Barker, 145–66. London: Oxford University Press.

Isaacs, Tracy. 2011. *Moral Responsibility in Collective Contexts*. New York: Oxford University Press. http://dx.doi.org/10.1093/acprof:oso/9780199782963.001.0001.

Jaspers, Karl. 2000. *The Question of German Guilt*. Translated by E.B. Ashton. New York: Fordham University Press.

Kant, Immanuel. 1996. *The Metaphysics of Morals*, edited by Mary J. Gregor. Cambridge: Cambridge University Press. http://dx.doi.org/10.1017/CBO9780511809644.

Kaposy, Chris. 2009. "Coming into Existence: The Good, the Bad, and the Indifferent." *Human Studies* 32 (1): 101–8. http://dx.doi.org/10.1007/s10746-009-9106-4.

Kelly, Erin. 2003. "The Burdens of Collective Liability." In *Ethics and Foreign Intervention*, edited by Deen K. Chatterjee and Don E. Scheid, 118–39. Cambridge: Cambridge University Press.

Kitcher, Philip. 2014. *Life after Faith: The Case for Secular Humanism*. New Haven, CT: Yale University Press.

Klimchuk, Dennis. 2004. "Unjust Enrichment and Reparations for Slavery." *Boston University Law Review* 84 (5): 1257–75.

Kuhn, Thomas. 1962. *The Structure of Scientific Revolutions*. Chicago: Chicago University Press.

Kukathas, Chandran. 1992. "Are There Any Cultural Rights?" *Political Theory* 20 (1): 105–39. http://dx.doi.org/10.1177/0090591792020001006.

Kukathas, Chandran. 2003. "Responsibility for Past Injustice: How to Shift the Burden." *Politics, Philosophy & Economics* 2 (2): 165–90. http://dx.doi.org/10.1177/1470594X03002002002.

Kumar, Rahul. 2009. "Wronging Future People: A Contractualist Proposal." In *Intergenerational Justice*, edited by Axel Gosseries and Lukas H. Meyer, 252–72. Oxford: Oxford University Press. http://dx.doi.org/10.1093/acprof:oso/9780199282951.003.0010.

Kundera, Milan. 1980. *The Book of Laughter and Forgetting*. London: Penguin.

LaFollette, Hugh. 1980. "Licensing Parents." *Philosophy & Public Affairs* 9: 182–97.

LaFollette, Hugh. 2010. "Licensing Parents Revisited." *Journal of Applied Philosophy* 27 (4): 327–43. http://dx.doi.org/10.1111/j.1468-5930.2010.00497.x.

Las Casas, Bartolomé de. 1974. *In Defense of the Indians*. Edited and translated by Stafford Poole. DeKalb: Northern Illinois University Press.

Laslett, Peter. 1979. "The Conversation between the Generations." In *Philosophy, Politics and Society*, 5th ser., edited by Peter Laslett and James Fishkin, 36–56. New Haven, CT: Yale University Press.

Lau, Joanne C. 2012. "Two Arguments for Child Enfranchisement." *Political Studies* 60 (4): 860–76. http://dx.doi.org/10.1111/j.1467-9248.2011.00940.x.

Lepora, Chiara, and Robert Goodin. 2013. *On Complicity and Compromise*. Oxford: Oxford University Press. http://dx.doi.org/10.1093/acprof:oso/9780199677900.001.0001.

Lévi-Strauss, Claude. 1966. *The Savage Mind*. London: Weidenfeld and Nicolson.

Locke, John. 1823. *The Works of John Locke*. Vol. 10. London: Thomas Tegg.

Locke, John. 1975. *An Essay Concerning Human Understanding*. Vol. 1 of *The Works of John Locke*. Oxford: Clarendon. First published 1689.

Locke, John. 2010. *Locke on Toleration*. Cambridge: Cambridge University Press.

Lu, Catherine. 2011. "Colonialism as Structural Injustice: Historical Responsibility and Contemporary Redress." *Journal of Political Philosophy* 19 (3): 261–81. http://dx.doi.org/10.1111/j.1467-9760.2011.00403.x.

Luban, David. 2011. "State Criminality and the Ambition of International Criminal Law." In *Accountability for Collective Wrongdoing*, edited by Tracy

Isaacs and Richard Vernon, 61–91. New York: Cambridge University Press. http://dx.doi.org/10.1017/CBO9780511976780.003.

Lumpkin, Wilson. 1971. *The Removal of the Cherokee Indians from Georgia.* New York: Arno Press. Reprint of the 1907 edition.

Lyons, David. 2013. *Confronting Injustice: Moral History and Political Theory.* Oxford: Oxford University Press. http://dx.doi.org/10.1093/acprof:oso/9780199662555.001.0001.

MacIntyre, Alasdair. 1971. *Against the Self-Images of the Age.* London: Duckworth.

MacIntyre, Alasdair. 1995. "Is Patriotism a Virtue?" In *Theorizing Citizenship,* edited by Ronald Beiner, 209–28. Albany: SUNY Press.

Maier, Charles. 2000. "Doing History, Doing Justice: The Narrative of the Historian and of the Truth Commission." In *Truth v. Justice: The Morality of Truth Commissions,* edited by Robert I. Rotberg and Dennis Thompson, 261–78. University Center for Human Values Series. Princeton, NJ: Princeton University Press. http://dx.doi.org/10.1515/9781400832033-014.

Marchand, M., and P. Pestieau. 1991. "Public Pensions: Choices for the Future." *European Economic Review* 35 (2–3): 441–53. http://dx.doi.org/10.1016/0014-2921(91)90145-9.

Margalit, Avishai. 2002. *The Ethics of Memory.* Cambridge, MA: Harvard University Press.

Marx, Karl. 1977. *Capital.* Vol. 1, *A Critique of Political Economy.* New York: Vintage.

Matravers, Matt. 2002. "Responsibility, Luck, and the 'Equality of What?' Debate." *Political Studies* 50 (3): 558–72. http://dx.doi.org/10.1111/1467-9248.00385.

Maxim, Paul S. 1986. "Cohort Size and Juvenile Delinquency in England and Wales." *Journal of Criminal Justice* 14 (6): 491–9. http://dx.doi.org/10.1016/0047-2352(86)90092-9.

May, Larry. 2005. *Crimes against Humanity: A Normative Account.* Cambridge: Cambridge University Press.

McCormick, Hugh. 2009. "Intergenerational Justice and the Non-reciprocity Problem." *Political Studies* 57 (2): 451–8. http://dx.doi.org/10.1111/j.1467-9248.2009.00786.x.

McDonald, Lynn. 2013. "Wonderful Adventures: How Did Mary Seacole Come to Be Viewed as a Pioneer of Modern Nursing?" *Times Literary Supplement,* December 6, 14–15.

Mercouri, Melina. 1986. Address to the Oxford Union. www.greece.org/parthenon/marbles/speech.htm.

Merryman, John Henry. 1985. "Thinking about the Elgin Marbles." *Michigan Law Review* 83 (8): 1880–923. http://dx.doi.org/10.2307/1288954.

Merryman, John Henry. 1986. "Two Ways of Thinking about Cultural Property." *American Journal of International Law* 80 (4): 831–53. http://dx.doi.org/10.2307/2202065.

Merton, Robert K. 1967. *On Theoretical Sociology*. New York: Free Press.

Meyer, Lukas H., and Dominic Roser. 2009. "Enough for the Future." In *Intergenerational Justice*, edited by Axel Gosseries and Lukas H. Meyer, 219–48. Oxford: Oxford University Press. http://dx.doi.org/10.1093/acprof:oso/9780199282951.003.0009.

Mihai, Mihaela. 2013. "When the State Says 'Sorry': State Apologies as Exemplary Political Judgments." *Journal of Political Philosophy* 21 (2): 200–20. http://dx.doi.org/10.1111/j.1467-9760.2012.00418.x.

Miles, Margaret M. 2008. *Art as Plunder: The Ancient Origins of Debate about Cultural Property*. New York: Cambridge University Press.

Mill, John Stuart. 1874. *Three Essays on Religion*. New York: Henry Holt.

Mill, John Stuart. 1968. *Auguste Comte and Positivism*. Ann Arbor: University of Michigan Press.

Mill, John Stuart. 1972. *Utilitarianism, On Liberty, and Considerations on Representative Government*. London: Dent.

Miller, David. 1988. "The Ethical Significance of Nationality." *Ethics* 98 (4): 647–62. http://dx.doi.org/10.1086/292997.

Miller, David. 2000. *Citizenship and National Identity*. Cambridge: Polity Press.

Miller, Richard. 2010. *Globalizing Justice*. Oxford: Oxford University Press. http://dx.doi.org/10.1093/acprof:oso/9780199581986.001.0001.

Mills, Claudia. 2003. "The Child's Right to an Open Future?" *Journal of Social Philosophy* 34 (4): 499–509. http://dx.doi.org/10.1111/1467-9833.00197.

Millum, Joseph. 2012. "Global Bioethics and Political Theory." In *Global Justice and Bioethics*, edited by Joseph Millum and Ezekiel J. Emanuel, 17–42. Oxford: Oxford University Press. http://dx.doi.org/10.1093/acprof:osobl/9780195379907.003.0002.

Minow, Martha. 2000. "The Hope for Healing: What Can Truth Commissions Do?" In *Truth v. Justice: The Morality of Truth Commissions*, edited by Robert I. Rotberg and Dennis Thompson, 235–60. University Center for Human Values Series. Princeton, NJ: Princeton University Press.

Moellendorf, Darrel. 2006. "Equality of Opportunity Globalized." *Canadian Journal of Law and Jurisprudence* 19 (2): 301–18.

Moody-Adams, Michele. 1994. "Culture, Responsibility, and Affected Ignorance." *Ethics* 104 (2): 291–309. http://dx.doi.org/10.1086/293601.

Morgan, J. 2005. "Religious Upbringing, Religious Diversity and the Child's Right to an Open Future." *Studies in Philosophy and Education* 24 (5): 367–87. http://dx.doi.org/10.1007/s11217-005-0257-0.

Morris, Christopher W. 2006. "What's Wrong with Imperialism?" *Social Philosophy and Policy* 23 (1): 153–66. http://dx.doi.org/10.1017/S0265052506060067.

Mulgan, R.G. 1977. *Aristotle's Political Theory.* Oxford: Clarendon Press.

Novy-Marx, Robert, and Joshua D. Rauh. 2008. "The Intergenerational Transfer of Public Pension Promises." NBER Working Paper No. 14343. Cambridge, MA: National Bureau of Economic Research. www.nber.org/papers/w14343. Accessed July 21, 2012. http://dx.doi.org/10.2139/ssrn.1156477.

Nozick, Robert. 1974. *Anarchy, State and Utopia.* Oxford: Blackwell.

Nussbaum, Martha. 1986. *The Fragility of Goodness: Luck and Ethics in Greek Tragedy and Philosophy.* New York: Cambridge University Press.

Nussbaum, Martha. 2006. *Frontiers of Justice: Disability, Nationality, Species Membership.* Cambridge, MA: Harvard University Press.

Ogawa, Naohiro. 2009. "Changing Intergenerational Transfers and Rapid Population Aging in Japan." Paper prepared for the United Nations Expert Group Meeting on Family Policy in a Changing World, April 14–16, 2009, Doha. http://dx.doi.org/10.1007/978-1-4020-8356-3_7.

Oldenquist, Andrew. 1982. "Loyalties." *Journal of Philosophy* 79 (4): 173–93.

Otsuka, Michael. 2003. *Libertarianism without Inequality.* Oxford: Oxford University Press. http://dx.doi.org/10.1093/0199243956.001.0001.

Overall, Christine. 2012. *Why Have Children? The Ethical Debate.* Cambridge, MA: MIT Press.

Parlevliet, Michelle. 1998. "Considering Truth: Dealing with a Legacy of Gross Human Rights Violations." *Netherlands Quarterly of Human Rights* 16 (2): 141–74.

Pasternak, Avia. 2011. "The Distributive Effect of Collective Punishment." In *Accountability for Collective Wrongdoing,* edited by Tracy Isaacs and Richard Vernon, 210–30. New York: Cambridge University Press. http://dx.doi.org/10.1017/CBO9780511976780.009.

Pauer-Studer, Herlinde, and J. David Velleman. 2015. *Konrad Morgen: The Conscience of a Nazi Judge.* New York: Palgrave-Macmillan. http://dx.doi.org/10.1057/9781137496959.

Perez, Nahshon. 2012. *Freedom from Past Injustices: A Critical Evaluation of Claims for Intergenerational Reparations.* Edinburgh: Edinburgh University Press.

Pickering, Jonathan, and Christian Barry. 2012. "On the Concept of Climate Debt: Its Moral and Political Value." *Critical Review of International Social and Political Philosophy* 15 (5): 667–85. http://dx.doi.org/10.1080/13698230.2012.727311.

Pinker, Steven. 2011. *The Better Angels of Our Nature: Why Violence Has Declined*. New York: Viking.

Plato. 1961. *Collected Dialogues*. Edited by Edith Hamilton and Huntington Cairns. Princeton, NJ: Princeton University Press.

Pogge, Thomas. 1989. *Realizing Rawls*. Ithaca, NY: Cornell University Press.

Pogge, Thomas. 2002. *World Poverty and Human Rights*. Cambridge: Polity Press.

Poole, Keith T., and Howard Rosenthal. 2011. "The Political Economy of American Economic Inequality." http://voteview.com/blog/?p=7. Accessed July 20, 2012.

Rachels, James. 1997. "Punishment and Desert." In *Ethics in Practice*, edited by Hugh LaFollette, 470–79. Oxford: Basil Blackwell.

Rawls, John. 1971. *A Theory of Justice*. Cambridge, MA: Harvard University Press.

Rawls, John. 1993. *Political Liberalism*. New York: Columbia University Press.

Rawls, John. 1999. *The Law of Peoples, with "The Idea of Public Reason Revisited."* Cambridge, MA: Harvard University Press.

Rawls, John. 2001. *Justice as Fairness: A Restatement*. Cambridge, MA: Harvard University Press.

Raz, Joseph. 1984. "Rights-Based Moralities." In *Theories of Rights*, edited by Jeremy Waldron, 182–200. Oxford: Oxford University Press.

Raz, Joseph. 1986. *The Morality of Freedom*. Oxford: Oxford University Press.

Raz, Joseph. 1988. "Autonomy, Toleration, and the Harm Principle." In *Justifying Toleration: Conceptual and Historical Perspectives*, edited by Susan Mendus, 155–76. Cambridge: Cambridge University Press. http://dx.doi.org/10.1017/CBO9780511735295.009.

Ridge, Michael. 2003. "Giving the Dead Their Due." *Ethics* 114 (1): 38–59. http://dx.doi.org/10.1086/376717.

Rosevear, Lisa. 2012. "The Association between Birth Cohort Size and Fluctuating Crime Levels: A Western Australian Case Study." Canberra: Australian Institute of Criminology. http://apo.org.au/node/28404. Accessed July 18, 2012.

Rotberg, Robert I., and Dennis Thompson, eds. 2000. *Truth v. Justice: The Morality of Truth Commissions*. University Center for Human Values Series. Princeton, NJ: Princeton University Press.

Rousseau, Jean-Jacques. 1968. *The Social Contract*. Harmondsworth: Penguin. First published 1762.

Rummel, R.J. 1994. *Death by Government*. New Brunswick, NJ: Transaction Books.

Sartre, Jean-Paul. 1948. *Existentialism and Humanism*. London: Methuen. First published 1946.
Schacter, Daniel. 2001. *The Seven Sins of Memory: How the Mind Forgets and Remembers*. Boston: Houghton Mifflin.
Scheffler, Samuel. 2001. *Boundaries and Allegiances: Problems of Justice and Responsibility in Liberal Thought*. Oxford: Oxford University Press.
Scheffler, Samuel. 2013. *Death and the Afterlife*. New York: Oxford University Press. http://dx.doi.org/10.1093/acprof:oso/9780199982509.001.0001.
Schlink, Bernhard. 2009. *Guilt about the Past*. Toronto: House of Anansi Press.
Schmitt, Carl. 1996. *The Concept of the Political*. Chicago: University of Chicago Press.
Schrag, Francis. 2004. "Children and Democracy: Theory and Policy." *Politics, Philosophy & Economics* 3 (3): 365–79. http://dx.doi.org/10.1177/1470594X04046248.
Schwartz, Barry. 2004. *The Paradox of Choice: Why More Is Less*. New York: Harper.
Scruton, Roger. 2000. "The Moral Status of Animals." In *Ethics, Humans and Other Animals: An Introduction with Readings*, edited by Rosalind Hursthouse, 209–28. New York: Routledge.
Sebok, A.J. 2000. "Should Claims Based on African-American Slavery Be Litigated in the Courts?" http://writ.news.findlaw.com/sebok/20001204.html.
Shaw, Rosalind. 2005. "Rethinking Truth and Reconciliation Commissions: Lessons from Sierra Leone." Washington, DC: United States Institute for Peace. www.usip.org/pubs/specialreports/sv130.html.
Shiffrin, Seana. 1999. "Wrongful Life, Procreative Responsibility, and the Significance of Harm." *Legal Theory* 5 (2): 127–48. http://dx.doi.org/10.1017/S1352325299052015.
Shiffrin, Seana. 2013. "Preserving the Valued or Preserving Valuing?" In *Death and the Afterlife*, by Samuel Scheffler. Edited by Nico Kolodny. New York: Oxford University Press.
Shue, Henry. 2010. "Subsistence Emissions and Luxury Emissions." In *Climate Ethics: Essential Readings*, edited by Stephen M. Gardiner, Simon Caney, Dale Jamieson, and Henry Shue, 146–62. Oxford: Oxford University Press.
Sidebottom, Harry. 2004. *Ancient Warfare: A Very Short Introduction*. Oxford: Oxford University Press.
Simmons, A. John. 1979. *Moral Principles and Political Obligation*. Princeton, NJ: Princeton University Press.
Singer, Peter. 2002. *One World*. New Haven, CT: Yale University Press.

Slack, Tim, and Leif Jensen. 2008. "Birth and Fortune Revisited: A Cohort Analysis of Underemployment, 1974–2004." *Population Research and Policy Review* 27 (6): 729–49. http://dx.doi.org/10.1007/s11113-008-9091-8.

Slaughter, Steven. 2005. "The Republican State: An Alternative Foundation for Global Environmental Governance." In *The State and the Global Ecological Crisis*, edited by John Barry and Robyn Eckersley, 207–27. Cambridge, MA: MIT Press.

Sparrow, Robert. 2005. "Defending Deaf Culture: The Case of Cochlear Implants." *Journal of Political Philosophy* 13 (2): 135–52. http://dx.doi.org/10.1111/j.1467-9760.2005.00217.x.

Spinner-Halev, Jeff. 2007. "From Historical to Enduring Injustice." *Political Theory* 35 (5): 574–97. http://dx.doi.org/10.1177/0090591707304585.

Synodinou, Katerina. 1977. *On the Concept of Slavery in Euripides.* Greece: University of Ioannina.

Taylor, Charles. 1994. "The Politics of Recognition." In *Multiculturalism*, edited by Amy Gutmann, 25–73. Princeton, NJ: Princeton University Press.

Taylor-Smith, Patrick. 2013. "The Intergenerational Storm: Dilemma or Domination." *Philosophy and Public Issues* 3 (1): 207–44.

Thomas, M. Halsey, ed. 1973. *The Diary of Samuel Sewall, 1674–1729.* 2 vols. New York: Farrar, Strauss and Giroux.

Thompson, Janna. 2002. *Taking Responsibility for the Past: Reparation and Historical Injustice.* Cambridge: Polity.

Thompson, Janna. 2008. "Apology, Justice, and Respect: A Critical Defense of Political Apology." In *The Age of Apology: Facing Up to the Past*, edited by Mark Gibney, Rhoda E. Howard-Hassmann, Jean-Marc Coicaud, and Niklaus Steiner, 31–44. Philadelphia: University of Pennsylvania Press.

Thompson, Janna. 2009. *Intergenerational Justice: Rights and Responsibilities in an Intergenerational Polity.* London: Routledge.

Tully, James. 1995. *Strange Multiplicity: Constitutionalism in an Age of Diversity.* Cambridge: Cambridge University Press. http://dx.doi.org/10.1017/CBO9781139170888.

Vallentyne, Peter, and Hillel Steiner. 2000. *Left-Libertarianism and Its Critics: The Contemporary Debate.* New York: Palgrave.

Vernon, Richard. 2001. *Political Morality: A Theory of Liberal Democracy.* London: Continuum.

Vernon, Richard. 2010. *Cosmopolitan Regard: Political Membership and Global Justice.* Cambridge: Cambridge University Press. http://dx.doi.org/10.1017/CBO9780511676369.

Vernon, Richard. 2011. "Punishing Collectives: States or Nations?" In *Accountability for Collective Wrongdoing*, edited by Tracy Isaacs and Richard Vernon, 287–306. New York: Cambridge University Press.
Vernon, Richard. 2012. *Historical Redress*. London: Continuum.
Vico, Giambattista. 1970. *The New Science of Giambattista Vico*. Ithaca, NY: Cornell University Press. First published 1744.
Wagner, Henry Raup. 1967. *The Life and Writings of Bartolomé de las Casas*. Albuquerque: University of New Mexico Press.
Waldron, Jeremy. 1992. "Superseding Historical Injustice." *Ethics* 103 (1): 4–28. http://dx.doi.org/10.1086/293468.
Walzer, Michael. 1985. *Interpretation and Social Criticism*. Cambridge, MA: Harvard University Press.
Walzer, Michael. 2000. *Just and Unjust Wars: A Moral Argument with Historical Illustrations*. 3rd ed. New York: Basic Books.
Wenar, Leif. 2006. "Reparations for the Future." *Journal of Social Philosophy* 37 (3): 396–405. http://dx.doi.org/10.1111/j.1467-9833.2006.00344.x.
Wheeler, Nicholas J. 2000. *Saving Strangers: Humanitarian Intervention in International Society*. Oxford: Oxford University Press.
Wilks, Ivor. 1975. *Asante in the 19th Century: The Structure and Evolution of a Political Order*. New York: Cambridge University Press.
Williams, Bernard. 1985. *Ethics and the Limits of Philosophy*. Cambridge, MA: Harvard University Press.
Williams, Melissa. 1998. *Voice, Trust and Memory: Marginalized Groups and the Failings of Liberal Representation*. Princeton, NJ: Princeton University Press.
Winch, Peter. 1958. *The Idea of a Social Science*. London: Routledge.
Winch, Peter. 1964. "Understanding a Primitive Society." *American Philosophical Quarterly* 1 (4): 307–24.
Winter, Stephen. 2010. "Against Posthumous Rights." *Journal of Applied Philosophy* 27 (2): 186–99. http://dx.doi.org/10.1111/j.1468-5930.2009.00477.x.
Wissenburg, M.L.J. 2011. "Parenting and Intergenerational Justice: Why Collective Obligations Towards Future Generations Take Second Place to Individual Responsibility." *Journal of Agricultural and Environmental Ethics* 24 (6): 557–73.
Witt, John Fabian. 2012. *Lincoln's Code: The Laws of War in American History*. New York: Free Press.
Wittgenstein, Ludwig. 1963. *Philosophical Investigations*. Translated by G.E.M. Anscombe. Oxford: Basil Blackwell.
Wolff, Jonathan. 1996. *Introduction to Political Philosophy*. Oxford: Oxford University Press.

Woozley, A.D. 1979. *Law and Obedience: The Argument of Plato's Crito*. London: Duckworth.

Young, Iris M. 2006. "Responsibility and Global Justice: A Social Connection Model." In *Justice and Global Politics*, edited by Ellen Frankel Paul, Fred D. Miller, Jr., and Jeffrey Paul, 102–30. Cambridge: Cambridge University Press. http://dx.doi.org/10.1017/CBO9780511550744.005.

Ypi, Lea. 2013. "What's Wrong with Colonialism?" *Philosophy & Public Affairs* 41 (2): 158–91. http://dx.doi.org/10.1111/papa.12014.

Ypi, Lea, Robert E. Goodin, and Christian Barry. 2009. "Associative Duties, Global Justice, and the Colonies." *Philosophy & Public Affairs* 37 (2): 103–35. http://dx.doi.org/10.1111/j.1088-4963.2009.01152.x.

Index

www.ingramcontent.com/pod-product-compliance
Lightning Source LLC
LaVergne TN
LVHW040151080826
844660LV00014B/915/J